PLANT BIOTECHNOLOGY AND INDUSTRIAL APPLICATIONS

ENV BOOKS SERIES

PLANT BIOTECHNOLOGY AND INDUSTRIAL APPLICATIONS

Editors

Dr. Alka Chauhan

Society for Environment, Health, Awareness of Nutrition & Toxicology (SEHAT)
1775, Sohan Ganj, Near Clock Tower
Delhi - 110 007 (India)

&

Dr. Pawan Kumar 'Bharti'

Society for Environment, Health, Awareness of Nutrition & Toxicology (SEHAT)
1775, Sohan Ganj, Near Clock Tower
Delhi - 110 007 (India)
E-mail: gurupawanbharti@rediffmail.com

DPH

DISCOVERY PUBLISHING HOUSE PVT. LTD.
INDIA

Published by:
Namit Wasan

DISCOVERY PUBLISHING HOUSE PVT. LTD.
4383/4B, Ansari Road, Darya Ganj
New Delhi-110 002 (India)
Phone : +91-11-23279245, 43596064-65
Fax : +91-11-23253475
E-mail : discoverypublishinghouse@gmail.com
namitwasan9@gmail.com
sales@discoverypublishinggroup.com
web : www.discoverypublishinggroup.com

***First Edition:* 2017**

ISBN: 978-93-5056-884-2

Plant Biotechnology and Industrial Applications

Printed at:
Infinity Imaging Systems
Delhi

ENV Books Series, India

Calls descriptive and error free chapters for upcoming volumes of books on various environmental issues. Send your manuscripts to envbooks@gmail.com

Founding Editor (Editor-in-Chief)

Dr. Pawan Kumar 'Bharti'
Society for Environment, Health, Awareness of Nutrition & Toxicology (SEHAT-India)
1775, Sohanganj, Near Clock Tower, Delhi-7, (India)
E-mail:*gurupawanbharti@rediffmail.com*

Other Important Titles by Editor-in-Chief:

1. **Advances in Biotechnology and Ecological Sciences**
   Bharti, P.K., Chauhan, A. and Ray, J. (eds.)
   (ISBN: 978-93-5056-358-8).
2. **Advances in Agriculture and Ecology**
   Bharti, P.K.; Chauhan, A. and Ezeaku Peter Ikemefuna (eds.)
   (ISBN: 978-93-5056-362-5).
3. **Agriculture and Environmental Biotechnology**
   Bharti, P.K. and Chauhan, A. (eds.)
   (ISBN: 978-93-5056-479-0).
4. **Agriculture Crops and Food Security**
   Bharti, P.K. and Chauhan, Alka (eds.)
   (ISBN: 978-93-5056-881-1).
5. **Agriculture Development and Sustainable Environment**
   Ray, J. and Bharti, P.K. (eds.)
   (ISBN: 978-93-5056-759-3).
6. **Agriculture Ecology and Environment**
   Bharti, P.K. and Olubukola O. Babalola (eds.)
   (ISBN: 978-93-5056-480-6).
7. **Agriculture Ecology, Sustainable Development and Agribusiness Management**
   Mehta Piyush; Sharma Pankaj; and 'Bharti' P.K. (eds.)
   (ISBN: 978-93-5056-851-4).
8. **Agriculture, Environment and Nano-science**
   Bharti, Pawan K. (ed.)
   (ISBN: 978-93-5056-760-5).

9. **Agricultural Practices and Crop Disease Control**
Chauhan Alka and Sharma Anubhuti (eds.)
(ISBN: 978-93-5056-859-0).

10. **Agro-biodiversity:** ***Conservation and Sustainable Development***
Sharma, Pankaj; Singh, Narayan; and Bharti, P.K. (eds.)
(ISBN: 978-93-505-782-1).

11. **Agro-forestry and Climate Change**
Bharti, Pawan K. and Singh, Narayan (eds.)
(ISBN: 978-93-5056-514-8).

12. **Agro-forestry and Sustainable Agriculture**
Sharma, Pankaj; Bharti, P.K. (eds.)
(ISBN: 978-93-5056-786-9).

13. **Air Pollution and Ecosystem Health**
Swami Abhishek and Bharti, P.K. (eds.)
(ISBN: 978-93-5056-877-4).

14. **Aquaculture and Fisheries Environment**
Gupta, S.K. and Pawan K. Bharti (eds.)
(ISBN: 978-93-5056-408-0).

15. **Aquatic Biodiversity and Pollution**
Bharti, P.K.; Chauhan, A. and Kaoud, H.A.H. (eds.)
(ISBN: 978-93-5056-359-5).

16. **Aquatic Ecology and Biotechnology**
Bharti, P.K. and Zaki, M.S.A. (eds.)
(ISBN: 978-93-5056-451-6).

17. **Aquatic Environment and Toxicology**
Bharti, Pawan K. (ed.)
(ISBN: 978-93-5056-236-9).

18. **Biodiversity, Biotechnology and Environmental Conservation**
Bharti, P.K. and Bhandari, G. (eds.)
(ISBN: 978-93-5056-750-0).

19. **Biodiversity, Biotechnology and Pollution Control**
Bharti, P.K. and Chauhan, Alka (eds.)
(ISBN: 978-93-5056-887-3).

20. **Biodiversity of Aquatic Ecosystem:** ***Significance, Threat and Conservation*** **(2013)**
Bharti, P.K. and Kaoud, H.A.H. (eds.)
(ISBN: 978-93-5056-297-0).

21. **Biological Diversity and Ecology**
Arya, M.K.; Bharti, P.K. and Ritesh Joshi (eds.)
(ISBN: 978-93-5056-785-2).

22. **Bioremediation and Microbial Biotechnology**
Gupta, Sandeep; and Bharti, P.K. (eds.)
(ISBN: 978-93-5056-783-8).
23. **Biotechnological Approaches and Water Ecosystem**
Zaki, M.S.A.; and Bharti, P.K. (eds.)
(ISBN: 978-93-5056-779-1).
24. **Biotechnology, Agro-ecology and Environment**
Chauhan, Avnish and Bharti, P.K. (eds.)
(ISBN: 978-93-5056-757-9).
25. **Biotechnology and Environmental Management**
Arya Arun; Maheswari Raaz K., & Bharti, P.K (eds.)
(ISBN: 978-93-5056-862-0).
26. **Clean Technologies and Environmental Protection**
Chauhan, A.; Sharma, S. and Bharti, P.K. (eds.)
(ISBN: 978-93-5056-731-9).
27. **Climate Change and Agriculture**
Bharti, P.K. and Chauhan, Avnish (eds.)
(ISBN: 978-93-5056-148-5).
28. **Climate Change and Biodiversity**
Bharti, P.K. and Chauhan, Avnish (eds.)
(ISBN: 978-93-5056-360-1).
29. **Climate Change, Disaster Management and Environment**
Chauhan, Alka; Bharti, P.K. (eds.)
(ISBN: 978-93-5056-784-5).
30. **Conservation and Cultivation of Medicinal Plants**
Bharti, P.K. and Singh Narayan (eds.)
(ISBN: 978-93-5056-740-1).
31. **Crop Productivity and Plant Disease Management**
Chauhan, Alka; Bharti, P.K. and Sadana, Deepti (eds.)
(ISBN: 978-93-5056-791-3).
32. **Eco-toxicology and Eco-technology**
Bharti, P.K. and Zaki, M. (eds.)
(ISBN: 978-93-5056-313-7).
33. **Environmental Biotechnology and Application**
Bharti, P.K. and Chauhan, Avnish (eds.)
(ISBN: 978-93-5056-262-8).
34. **Environmental Conservation and Biotechnology**
Chauhan, A. and P.K. Bharti (eds.)
(ISBN: 978-93-5056-512-4).
35. **Environmental Health and Problems**
Bharti, P.K. and Gajananda, Kh. (eds.)
(ISBN: 978-93-5056-263-5).

36. **Environmental Pollution and Biodiversity**
Bharti, P.K.; Chauhan, Avnish and Kumar, P. (eds.)
(ISBN: 978-93-5056-149-2).
37. **E-Waste and Environmental Issues**
Bhalla, Resham and Bharti, P.K. (eds.)
(ISBN: 978-93-5056-886-6).
38. **Farming Techniques and Crop Production**
Chauhan Alka; Sharma Anubhuti; Ray Jaswant and 'Bharti' P.K. (eds.)
(ISBN: 978-93-5056-855-2).
39. **Fisheries and Toxicology**
Zaki, M.S.A.; Bharti, P.K. and Chauhan, A. (eds.)
(ISBN: 978-93-5056-452-3).
40. **Fish Habitat and Aquaculture**
Bharti, P.K.; Gupta Kr. Sanjay (eds.)
(ISBN: 978-93-5056-744-9).
41. **Forest and Biodiversity Conservation**
Chauhan Alka; Bharti, P.K. (eds.)
(ISBN: 978-93-5056-873-6).
42. **Food Processing, Management and Nanotechnology**
Chauhan, Avnish; Bharti, P.K. (eds.)
(ISBN: 978-93-5056-796-8).
43. **Freshwater Ecosystem and Xenobiotics**
Bharti, P.K.; Zaki, M. and Chauhan, A. (eds.)
(ISBN: 978-93-5056-299-4).
44. **Geospatial Technology and Water Management**
Chauhan, Alka; Bharti, P.K. (eds.)
(ISBN: 978-93-5056-885-9).
45. **Heavy Metals and Metalloids in Biosphere:** ***Impacts & Assessment***
Chauhan, Avnish, Gupta, Sandeep; and Bharti, P.K. (eds.)
(ISBN: 978-93-5056-860-6).
46. **Land Reclamation, Soil Quality and Agriculture**
Bharti, P.K. and Chauhan, Alka (eds.)
(ISBN: 978-93-5056-882-8).
47. **Limnology and Aquatic Science**
Sharma, S., and Bharti, P.K. (eds.)
(ISBN: 978-93-5056-735-7).
48. **Medicinal and Nutritional Values of Plants**
Chauhan, Alka; Bharti, P.K. (eds.)
(ISBN: 978-93-5056-883-5).
49. **Medicinal Plants:** ***Distribution, Utilization and Significance***
Sharma, P.; Bharti, P.K. and Narayan Singh (eds.)
(ISBN: 978-93-5056-734-0).

50. **Microbial Applications and Environment**
Bharti, Pawan K. (ed.)
(ISBN: 978-93-5056-515-5).

51. **Microbial Ecology and Habitat**
Bharti, Pawan K. (ed.)
(ISBN: 978-93-5056-514-8).

52. **Microbial Environment and Bioremediation**
Chauhan Alka; K. Rathoure Ashok; and K Maheshwari Raaz (eds.)
(ISBN: 978-93-5056-856-9).

53. **Microbiological and Pharmacological Aspects of Biodiversity**
Sharma Pankaj; Sharma Gautam Neha and Sharma Pankaj (eds.)
(ISBN: 978-93-5056-878-1).

54. **Natural Ecosystem and Climate Change**
Bharti, P.K., and Kh. Gajananda (ed.)
(ISBN: 978-93-5056-745-6).

55. **Pest Management and Agro-Techniques**
Biswas, Asim; Bharti, P.K., Chauhan, Avnish (eds.)
(ISBN: 978-93-5056-794-4).

56. **Prakriti me Aushadhi (*in Hindi*)**
Singh, J.R.; Bharti, P.K. and Bharti, B.
(ISBN: 978-93-5056-200-0).

57. **Seed Technology, Plant Growth and Cropping System**
Tyagi, P.K. and Bharti, P.K. (eds.)
(ISBN: 978-93-5056-738-8).

58. **Seed Treatment, Plant Heath and Agro-technology**
Chauhan, A. and Bharti, P.K. (eds.)
(ISBN: 978-93-5056-810-1).

59. **Soil Characteristics and Agro-ecology**
Avnish Chauhan and Bharti, P.K. (eds.)
(ISBN: 978-93-5056-758-6).

60. **Soil Contamination and Conservation**
Ezeaku, P.I. and Bharti, P.K. (eds.)
(ISBN: 978-93-5056-737-1).

61. **Soil Quality and Contamination**
Bharti, P.K. and Chauhan, Avnish (eds.)
(ISBN: 978-93-5056-361-8).

62. **Sustainable Aquaculture Management**
Gupta, S.K.; Bharti, P.K (eds.)
(ISBN: 978-93-5056-797-5).

63. **Waste Disposal and Management**
Bharti, P.K.; Tabassum, B. and Bajaj, P. (eds.)
(ISBN: 978-93-5056-729-6).

64. **Waste Generation and Utilization**
Bajaj Priya; Tabassum, B., and Bharti, P.K. (eds.)
(ISBN: 978-93-5056-792-0).

65. **Waste Management and Environmental Health**
Tabassum, B., Bajaj Priya, and Bharti, P.K. (eds.)
(ISBN: 978-93-5056-777-7).

66. **Water Resources:** ***Mapping Monitoring and Management***
Tyagi, P.K., Chauhan, Avnish and Bharti, P.K. (eds.)
(ISBN: 978-93-5056-861-3).

67. **Water Resources and Agriculture**
Bharti, P.K. and Ezeaku Peter Ikemefuna (eds.)
(ISBN: 978-93-5056-481-3).

68. **Waste Resources Management:** ***Monitoring and Assessment***
Gupta, Sandeep and Bharti, P.K. (eds.)
(ISBN: 978-93-5056-799-9).

Preface

The application of Biotechnology to solve the environmental problems in the environment and in the ecosystems is called Environmental Biotechnology. It is applied and it is used to study the natural environment. According to the international Society for environmental Biotechnology the environmental Biotechnology is defined as an environment that helps to develop, efficiently use and regulate the biological systems and prevent the environment from pollution or from contamination of land, air and water have work efficiently to sustain an environment" friendly Society.

The present book updates the subject content of plant biotechnology, applications of biotechnology in industrial production and environmental pollution control.

Thanks are due to publisher and contributors from various prestigious institutions and universities. The book will be helpful for the researchers, academia working in the field of plant biotechnology, applications of biotechnology in industrial production and environmental pollution control.

Editors
(envbooks@gmail.com)

Contents

Introduction

Biotechnology has application in four major industrial areas, including health care (medical), crop production and agriculture, non food (industrial) uses of crops and other products (e.g. biodegradable plastics, vegetable oil, biofuels), and environmental uses.

Biotechnology is reducing agriculture's environmental footprint by reducing fossil fuel use, soil tillage and run-off from farmer's fields. Studies show that since commercial plantings of biotech crops began in 1996, farmers have saved 551 million gallons of fuel because of reduced field operations. In 2006, 252 million acres of biotech crops reduced carbon dioxide emissions by nearly 15 million metric tons, equivalent to removing nearly 6.56 million cars from the road for an entire year.

Farmers using biotech crops may also use pesticides less frequently because of the pestresistance traits within the plants themselves. Within the United States alone, biotech crop varieties eliminated the use of 70 million pounds of pesticide applications in 2005.

Future crops designed to tolerate environmental stresses, such as salty or toxic soils, drought, and freezing temperatures, will make agriculture more efficient and sustainable by producing more food, fuel and fiber on less land. Biotech plants being tested also use nitrogen more efficiently, leading to the potential decrease in fertilizer usage. Biotechnology can also be used to produce renewable plant-based energy and industrial products and biological agents to clean up contaminated soils.

Industrial biotechnology applies life science tools, such as microbes and enzymes, to traditional manufacturing and chemical processes to produce biobased or cleaner, more sustainable products and materials. The Industrial and Environmental Section develops policies to help drive the growth of advanced biofuels, biomass supply, specialty crops, biobased products and materials, specialty chemicals, food and nutritional ingredients and synthetic biology and genomics research. We work closely with the U.S. Congress, federal agencies, and international organizations to encourage the development of technologies that make our lives and environment cleaner, safer and healthier. This Section is also active in promoting technologies that support a growing biobased economy and meet the demand for sustainable sources of energy.

The application of Biotechnology to solve the environmental problems in the environment and in the ecosystems is called Environmental Biotechnology. It is applied and it is used to study the natural environment. According to the international Society for environmental Biotechnology the environmental Biotechnology is defined as an environment that helps to develop, efficiently use and regulate the biological systems and prevent the environment from pollution or from contamination of land, air and water have work efficiently to sustain an environment" friendly Society.

There are five major different types of Applications of Environmental Biotechnology. They are as follows:

(a) *Biomarker:* This type of Application of environmental Biotechnology gives response to a chemical that helps to measure the level of damage caused or the exposure of the toxic or the pollution effect caused. In other word, Biomarker can also be called as the Biological markers the major use of this applications helps to relate the connection between the oils and its sources.

(b) *Bioremediation:* The process of cleaning up the hazardous substances into non-toxic compounds is called the Bioremediation process. This process is majorly used for any kind of technology clean up that uses the natural microorganisms.

(c) *Bioenergy:* The collective purport of Biogas, biomass, fuels, and hydrogen are called the Bioenergy. The use of this application of Environment Biotechnology is in the industrial, domestic and space sectors. As per the recent need it is concluded that the need of clean energy out of these fuels and alternative ways of finding clean energy is the need of the hour. One of the pioneer examples of green energy are the wastes collected from the organic and biomass wastes; these wastes help use to over the pollution issues caused in the environment. The Biomass energy supply has become a prominent importance in every country.

(d) *Biotransformation:* The changes that take place in the biology of the environment which are changes of the complex compound to simple non-toxic to toxic or the other way round is called the biotransformation process. It is used in the Manufacturing sector where toxic substances are converted to Bi-products.

The major benefits of environmental biotechnology are it helps to keep our environment safe and clean for the use of the future generations. It helps the organisms and the engineers to find useful ways of getting adapted to the changes in the environment and keep the environment clean and green. The benefit of environmental biotechnology helps us to avoid the use of hazardous pollutants and wastes that affect the natural resources and the environment. The development of the society should be done in such a way that it helps to protect our environment and also helps us to development it.

The environmental biotechnology has a role to play in the removal of the pollutants. It is becoming an advantage for the scientists and the environmentalists to find ways to convert the waste to re-useable products. The applications of environmental biotechnology are becoming a benefiting factor for the environment; the applications includes genomics, proteomics, bioinformatics, sequencing and imaging processes are providing large amounts of information and new ways to improvise the environment and protect the environment.

During the Industrial Revolution of the eighteenth and nineteenth centuries, pollution became a major problem with the introduction of the steam engine and a series of technological advances that led to the production of goods shifting from homes and small factories to large industrial factories. The invention of more productive processes to manufacture cotton textiles contributed greatly to the number of mills located in England, and later in the northeastern United States. The steam engine allowed capitalists to transfer their manufacturing plants away from naturally flowing waters (outside the city) to areas inside and around cities where more abundant labor was available. Pollution increased because of the more concentrated conditions within the industrializing cities and because of the use of artificially produced power (such as coal) that replaced the natural power of fast-running rivers.

Some of the major effects of industries on environment are as follows:

Industrialization contributes major part for the economic development and prosperity of a country. On one hand it provides employment opportunities and wealth generation while on other hand it leads to following environmental deterioration:

1. It leads to the depletion of natural resources.
2. It leads to air pollution, water pollution and soil pollution.
3. Global warming, climatic changes are the major consequences of industrialization.
4. It causes acid rain.
5. It leads to the degradation of land quality.
6. It leads to the generation of hazardous waste whose safe disposal become a big problem.
7. These industries are responsible for the following adverse diseases and ill effect like silicosis and pneumoconiosis, tuberculosis, skin diseases and deafness.

Effects of Industries on environment:

1. Metallic contaminant like Cd, Zn, Hg etc., destroy bacteria and beneficial microorganisms in the soil.
2. Industrial wastes including toxins enter in the food chain causes number of undesirable effects to living beings and animals.
3. Industrial effluent damages the natural biological purification mechanism of sewage treatment causing several soil and water borne diseases.
4. Radioactive industrial pollutant cause undesirable disease when food containing radio-nuclides is taken by man.

The goal of balancing the economic and social benefits of chemicals with their health and environmental risks is easy to understand and agree to. But how to achieve this balance is a highly complex problem–or rather, it requires understanding and solving many complex problems. Managing the risks of chemicals is interconnected with many other issues, including wastes and pollution, global warming, resource depletion, agriculture, biotechnology, loss of biodiversity, poverty and women's rights. Wastes (including hazardous wastes), pollution and climate change have received increasing attention in the last two or three decades, even if much remains to be done in industrialized and developing countries.

References

http://www.pollutionissues.com/Ho-Li/Industry.html#ixzz4KtLwPsGp

http://www.yourarticlelibrary.com/environment/7-major-effects-of-industries-on-environment/12328/

http://www.inecc.gob.mx/descargas/dgipea/effects_env_tax_pesticides_mex.pdf

Plant Biotechnology and Industrial Applications
Edited by: Alka Chauhan and Pawan Kumar 'Bharti'
ISBN: 978-93-5056-884-2
Edition: 2017
Published by: Discovery Publishing House Pvt. Ltd., New Delhi (India)

1 Agro Ecology and Environmental Biotechnology

[1]Kalla Aruna Kumari, [2]T. Thomson

Environmental biotechnology in particular is the application of processes for the protection and restoration of the quality of the environment. Environmental biotechnology can be used to detect, prevent and remediate the emission of pollutants into the environment in a number of ways.

Solid, liquid and gaseous wastes can be modified, either by recycling to make new products, or by purifying so that the end product is less harmful to the environment. Replacing chemical materials and processes with biological technologies can reduce environmental damage.

In this way environmental biotechnology can make a significant contribution to sustainable development. Environmental Biotechnology is one of today's fastest growing and most practically useful scientific fields. Research into the genetics, biochemistry and physiology of exploitable microorganisms is rapidly being translated into commercially available technologies for reversing and preventing further deterioration of the earth's environment.

Objectives of Environmental Biotechnology (According to Agenda 21):

The aim of environmental biotechnology is to prevent arrest and reverse environmental degradation through the appropriate use of biotechnology in combination with other technologies, while supporting safety procedures as a primary component of the programme.

Specific Objectives are:

1. To adopt production processes that make optimal use of natural resources, by recycling biomass, recovering energy and minimizing waste generation.
2. To promote the use of biotechnological techniques with emphasis on bioremediation of land and water, waste treatment, soil conservation, reforestation, afforestation and land rehabilitation.

[1] Teaching Associate, (Assistant Professor), Department of Biotechnology, Dr. Y.S.R. Horticultural University, Venkataramannagudem, West Godavari Dist. Andhra Pradesh, INDIA-534101

[2] Ph.D. Scholar, Department of Vegetable Science, Dr. Y.S.R. Horticultural University, Venkataramannagudem, West Godavari Dist. Andhra Pradesh, INDIA-534101

3. To apply biotechnological processes and their products to protect environmental integrity with a view to long-term ecological security.

Use of biotechnology to treat pollution problems is not a new idea. Communities have depended on complex populations of naturally occurring microbes for sewage treatment for over a century. Every living organism—animals, plants, bacteria and so forth—ingests nutrients to live and produces a waste as a by-product. Different organisms need different types of nutrients.

Certain bacteria thrive on the chemical components of waste products. Some microorganisms feed on materials toxic to others. Research related environmental biotechnology is vital in developing effective solutions for mitigating, preventing and reversing environmental damage with the help of these living forms. Growing concern about public health and the deteriorating quality of the environment has prompted the development of a range of new, rapid analytical devices for the detection of hazardous compounds in air, water and land. Recombinant DNA technology has provided the possibilities for the prevention of pollution and holds a promise for a further development of bioremediation.

Applications of Environmental Biotechnology

Environmental protection is an integral component of sustainable development. The environment is threatened every day by the activities of man. With the continued increase in the use of chemicals, energy and non-renewable resources by an expanding global population, associated environmental problems are also increasing. Despite escalating efforts to prevent waste accumulation and to promote recycling, the amount of environmental damage caused by over-consumption, the quantities of waste generated and the degree of unsustainable land use appear likely to continue growing.

The remedy can be achieved, to some extent, by the application of environmental biotechnology techniques, which use living organisms in hazardous waste treatment and pollution control. Environmental biotechnology includes a broad range of applications such as bioremediation, prevention, detection and monitoring, genetic engineering for sustainable development and better quality of living.

Bioremediation

Bioremediation refers to the productive use of microorganisms to remove or detoxify pollutants, usually as contaminants of soils, water or sediments that otherwise intimidate human health. Bio treatment, bio reclamation and bio restoration are the other terminologies for bioremediation. Bioremediation is not a new practice. Microorganisms have been used for many years to remove organic matter and toxic chemicals from domestic and manufacturing waste discharge.

However, the focus in environmental biotechnology for fighting different pollution is on bioremediation. The vast majority of bioremediation applications use naturally occurring microorganisms to identify and filter toxic waste before it is introduced into the environment or to clean up existing pollution problems.

Some more advanced systems using genetically modified microorganisms are being tested in waste treatment and pollution control to remove difficult-to-degrade materials. Bioremediation can be performed in situ or in specialized reactors (ex situ). Bioremediation by microorganisms need appropriate environment for the cleanup of the polluted site.

Addition of nutrients, terminal electron acceptors (O_2/NO_2), temperature, and moisture to promote the growth of a particular organism may be required for the microbial activity in the polluted site. Bioremediation operations may be made either on-site or off-site, in situ or ex situ. Bioremediation has a vast potential to clean up water and soil contaminated by a variety of hazardous pollutants, domestic wastes, radioactive wastes etc.

Biological cleaning procedures make use of the fact that most organic chemicals are subjected to enzymatic attack of living organisms. The most common approach is the use of enzymes as substitute chemical catalysts. Significant reduction or complete elimination of harsh chemicals may be achieved as is observed in leather, textile processing and pulp and paper industry.

Only 1-2 g of hemicellulose is substituted for 10-15 kg of chlorine to treat 1 tons of pulp, thereby significantly reducing the chlorinated organic effluent. Environmental protection and remediation presently combine biotechnological, chemical, physical and engineering methods.

The relative importance of biotechnology is increasing as scientific knowledge and methods improve. Its lower requirements for energy and chemicals, combined with lower production of minor wastes, make it an increasingly desirable alternative to more traditional chemical and physical methods of remediation. Applications of bioremediation for maintenance of environment are several. In this chapter a few are dealt with as handling of waste water and industrial effluents, soil and land treatment, air and waste gases management.

Waste Water and Industrial Effluents

Water pollution is a serious problem in many countries of the world. Rapid industrialization and urbanization have generated large quantities of waste water that resulted in deterioration of surface water resources and ground water reserves. Biological, organic and inorganic pollutants contaminate the water bodies.

In many cases, these sources have been rendered unsafe for human consumption as well as for other activities such as irrigation and industrial needs. This illustrates that degraded water quality can, in effect; contribute to water scarcity as it limits its availability for both human use and the ecosystem. Treatment of the waste water before disposal is of urgent concern worldwide.

In sewage treatment plants microorganisms are used to remove the more common pollutants from waste water before it is discharged into rivers or the sea. Increasing industrial and agricultural pollution has led to a greater need for processes that remove specific pollutants such as nitrogen and phosphorus compounds, heavy metals and chlorinated compounds.

Methods include aerobic, anaerobic and physico-chemical processes in fixed-bed filters and in bioreactors in which the materials and microbes are held in suspension. Sewage and other waste waters would, if left untreated, undergo self-purification but the process requires long exposure periods. To speed up this process bioremediation measures are used.

However, Five Key Stages are Recognized in Wastewater Treatment

(*a*) Preliminary treatment–grit, heavy metals and floating debris are removed.

(*b*) Primary treatment–suspended matters are removed.

(*c*) Secondary treatment–bio oxidize organic materials by activities of aerobic and anaerobic microorganisms.

(*d*) Tertiary treatment–specific pollutants are removed (ammonia and phosphate).

(*e*) Sludge treatment–solids are removed (final stage).

Aerobic Biological Treatment

Trickling filters, rotating biological contactors or contact beds, usually consist of an inert material (rocks/ash/wood/metal) on which the microorganisms grow in the form of a complex biofilm. These have been used for more than 70 years for sewage and waste water treatment. In these processes the degradable organic matter is oxidized by the microorganisms to CO_2 that can be vented to the atmosphere.

Activated Sludge Process

This process is used for treatment and removal of dissolved and biodegradable wastes, such as organic chemicals, petroleum refining wastes textile wastes and municipal sewage. The microorganisms in activated sludge generally are composed of 70-90% organic and 10-30% inorganic matters.

The microorganisms found in this sludge are usually bacteria, fungi, protozoa and rotifers. Petroleum hydrocarbons are degraded by species of bacteria (Acinetobacter, Mycobacteria, Pseudomonas etc.), yeasts, Cladosporium and Scolecobasidium. Pesticides (aldrin, dieldrin, parathion, malathion) are detoxified by fungus Xylaria xylestrix. Pseudomonas (a predominant soil microrganism) can detoxify organic compounds like hydrocarbons, phenols, organophosphates, polychlorinated biphenyls and polycyclic aromatics.

Utilisation of immobilized cyanobacterium Phormidium laminosum in batch and continuous flow bioreactors for the removal of nitrate, nitrite and phosphate from water has been reported by Garbisu *et al.*, (2003). Blanco *et al.*, (2003) showed the biosorption of heavy metal by Phormidium laminosum immobilised in micro-porous polymeric matrices. Photo-bioreactors are currently used to grow algae and cyanobacteria under closely controlled environmental conditions, with a view to making high-value products (such as beta-carotene and gamma-linoleic acid), designing efficient effluent treatment processes, and providing new energy sources.

The costs of wastewater treatment can be reduced by the conversion of wastes into useful products. Sulphur metabolizing bacteria can remove heavy metals and sulphur compounds from waste streams of the galvanization industry and reused. Most anaerobic wastewater treatment systems produce useful biogas.

In some cases, the by-products of the pollution-fighting microorganisms are themselves useful. Methane, for example, can be derived from a form of bacteria that degrades sulphur liquor, a waste product of paper manufacturing.

Soil and Land Treatment

As the human population grows, its demand for food from crops increases, making soil conservation crucial. Deforestation, over-development, and pollution from man-made chemicals are just a few of the consequences of human activity and carelessness. The increasing amounts of fertilizers and other agricultural chemicals applied to soils and industrial and domestic waste-disposal practices, led to the increasing concern of soil pollution. Pollution in soil is caused by persistent toxic compounds, chemicals, salts, radioactive materials, or disease-causing agents, which have adverse effects on plant growth and animal health.

Many species of fungi can be used for soil bioremediation. Lipomyces sp. can degrade herbicide paraquat. Rhodotorula sp. can convert benzaldehyde to benzyl alcohol. Candida sp. degrades formaldehyde in the soil. Aspergillus niger and Chaetomium cupreum are used to degrade tannins (found in tannery effluents) in the soil thereby helping in plant growth.

Phanerochaete chrysosporium has been used in bioremediation of soils polluted with different chemical compounds, usually recalcitrant and regarded as environmental pollutants. Decrease of PCP (Pentachlorophenol) between 88-91% within six weeks was observed in presence of Phanerochaete chrysosporium.

Bioremediation of contaminated soil has been used as a safe, reliable, cost-effective and environment friendly method for degradation of various pollutants.

This can be effected in a number of ways, either in situ or by mechanically removing the soil for treatment elsewhere.

In situ treatments include adding nutrient solutions, introducing microorganisms and ventilation. Ex situ treatment involves excavating the soil and treating it above ground, either as compost, in soil banks, or in specialised slurry bioreactors. Bioremediation of land is often cheaper than physical methods and its products are largely harmless.

During biological treatment soil microorganisms convert organic pollutants to CO_2, water and biomass. Degradation can take place under aerobic as well as under anaerobic conditions. Soil bioremediation can also be accomplished with the help of bioreactors. Degradation can take place under aerobic as well as under anaerobic conditions. Soil bioremediation can also be accomplished with the help of bioreactors. Liquids, vapours, or solids in a slurry phase are treated in a reactor. Microbes can be of natural origin, cultivated or even genetically engineered.

Research in the field of environmental biotechnology has made it possible to treat soil contaminated with mineral oils. Solid-phase technologies are used for petroleum-contaminated soils that are excavated, placed in a containment system through which water and nutrients percolate. Biological degradation of oils has proved commercially viable both on large and small scales, in situ and ex situ.

In situ soil bioremediation involve the stimulation of indigenous microbial populations (e.g. by adding nutrients or aeration). In this process the environmental conditions for the biological degradation of organic pollutants are optimized as far as possible. Oxygen has to be supplied by artificial aeration or by adding electron acceptors such as nitrates or oxygen releasing compounds. Ozone dissolved in water and H_2O_2 are sometimes used which degrade the organic contaminants.

Air and Waste Gases

With the onset of human civilization, the air is one of the first and most polluted components of the atmosphere. Most air pollution comes from one human activity: burning fossil fuels—natural gas, coal, and oil—to power industrial processes and motor vehicles. When fuels are incompletely burned, various chemicals called volatile organic chemicals (VOCs) also enter the air. Pollutants also come from other sources.

For instance, decomposing garbage in landfills and solid waste disposal sites emits methane gas, and many household products give off VOCs. Expanding industrial activities have added more contaminants in the air.

The concept of biological air treatment at first seemed impossible. With the development of biological waste gas purification technology using bioreactors—which includes bio filters, bio trickling filters, bio scrubbers and membrane bioreactors—this problem is taken care of. The mode of operation of all these reactors is similar.

Air containing volatile compounds is passed through the bioreactors, where the volatile compounds are transferred from the gas phase into the liquid phase. Microbial community (mixture of different bacteria, fungi and protozoa) grow in this liquid phase and remove the compounds acquired from the air.

In the bio filters, the air is passed through a bed packed with organic materials that supplies the necessary nutrients for the growth of the microorganisms. This medium is kept damp by maintaining the humidity of the incoming air. Biological off-gas treatment is generally based on the absorption of the VOC in the waste gases into the aqueous phase followed by direct oxidation by a wide range of voracious bacteria, which include Nocardia sp. and Xanthomonas sp.

Prevention

Sustainable development and quality living depends upon the rational, eco-friendly use of natural resources with economic growth. To comply with this trend, industrial development has to change to sustainable style from degradative type and for such a purpose cleaner technologies have to be adopted.

According to United Nations Environment Programme (1996) 'the continuous application of an integrated preventive environmental strategy to processes, products and services to increase eco-efficiency and reduce risks to humans and the environment' defines the eco-friendly concept. The application of preventive and clean concept can only be achieved by the 5R policies (Olguin *et al.*, 2003).

Five Environmental Buzzwords are the 5Rs for Efficient Use of Energy and Better Control of Waste, Which Might Help in Sustainable Development and Quality Living:

1. Reduce (Reduction of waste)
2. Reuse (Efficient use of water, energy)
3. Recycle (Recycling of wastes)
4. Replace (Replacement of toxic/hazardous raw materials for more environment-friendly inputs)
5. Recover (useful non-toxic fractions from wastes)

Innovation and adoption of clean technologies is the target of research and development worldwide. Industrial companies are developing processes with reduced environmental impact responding to the international call for the development of a sustainable society. There is a pervading trend towards less harmful products and processes; away from "end-of-pipe" treatment of waste streams. Environmental biotechnology, with its appropriate technologies, is suitable to contribute to this trend.

Enzyme Application

Enzymes are widely employed in industries for many years. Enzymes, non-toxic and biodegradable, are biological catalysts that are highly competent and have numerous advantages over non-biological catalysts. The use of enzyme by man, both directly and indirectly, have been for thousands of years.

In the recent years enzymes have played important roles in the production of drugs, fine chemicals, amino acids, antibiotics and steroids. Industrial processes can be made eco-friendly by the use of enzymes. Enzyme application in the textile, leather, food, pulp and paper industries help in significant reduction or complete elimination of severe chemicals and are also more economic in energy and resource consumption.

Biotechnological methods can produce food materials with improved nutritional value, functional characteristics, shelf stability. Plant cells grown in fermenters can produce flavours such as vanilla, reducing the need for extracting the compounds from vanilla beans. Food processing has benefited from biotechnologically produced chymosin which is used in cheese manufacture; alpha-amylase, which is used in production of high-fructose corn syrup and dry beer; and lactase, which is added to milk to reduce the lactose content for persons with lactose intolerance.

Genetically engineered enzymes are easier to produce than enzymes isolated from original sources and are favoured over chemically synthesized substances because they do not create by-products or off-flavours in foods.

Environmental Detection and Monitoring

A wide range of biological methods are in use to detect pollution and for the continuous monitoring of pollutants. The techniques of biotechnology have novel methods for diagnosing environmental problems and assessing normal environmental conditions so that human beings can be better-informed of the surroundings. Applications of these methods are cheaper, faster and also portable.

Rather than gathering soil samples and sending them to a laboratory for analysis, scientists can measure the level of contamination on site and know the results immediately. Biological detection methods using biosensors and immunoassays have been developed and are now in the market. Microbes are used in biosensors contamination of metals or pollutants. Saccharomyces cerevisiae (yeast) is used to detect cyanide in river water while Selenastrum capricornatum (green alga) is used for heavy metal detection. Immunoassays use labelled antibodies (complex proteins produced in biological response to specific agents) and enzymes to measure pollutant levels. If a pollutant is present, the antibody attaches itself to it making it detectable either through colour change, fluorescence or radioactivity.

Biosensors

A biosensor is an analytical device that converts a biological response into an physical, chemical or electrical signal. The development of biosensors involves integration of a specific and sensitive biologically derived sensing elements (immobilized cells, enzymes or antibodies) are integrated with physico-chemical transducers (either electrochemical or optical). Immobilized on a substrate, their properties change in response to some environmental effect in a way that is electronically or optically detectable.

It is then possible to make quantitative measurements of pollutants with extreme precision or to very high sensitivities. The biological response of the biosensor is determined by the bio catalytic membrane, which accomplishes the conversion of reactant to product. Immobilised enzymes possess a number of advantageous features which makes them particularly applicable for use in such systems.

They may be re-used, which ensures that the same catalytic activity is present for a series of analyses. Biosensors are powerful tools, which rely on biochemical reactions to detect specific substances, which have brought benefits to a wide range of sectors, including the manufacturing, engineering, chemical, water, food and beverage industries. They are able to detect even small amounts of their particular target chemicals, quickly, easily and accurately.

For this character of biosensors they have been ardently adopted for a variety of process monitoring applications, principally in respect to pollution assessment and control. Biosensors for detection of carbohydrates, organic acids, glucosinolates, aromatic hydrocarbons, pesticides, pathogenic bacteria and others have already been developed.

The biosensors can be designed to be very selective, or sensitive to a broad range of compounds. For example, a wide range of herbicides can be detected in river water using algal-based biosensors; the stresses inflicted on the organisms being measured as changes in the optical properties of the plant's chlorophyll. Biosensors are of different types such as calorimetric biosensors, immunosensors, optical biosensors, BOD biosensors, gas biosensors.

The remarkable ability of microbes to break down chemicals is proving useful, not only in pollution remediation but also in pollutant detection. A group of scientists at Los Alamos National Laboratory work with bacteria that degrade a class of organic chemicals called phenols. When the bacteria ingest phenolic compounds, the phenols attach to a receptor.

The phenol-receptor complex then binds to DNA, activating the genes involved in degrading phenol. The Los Alamos scientists added a reporter gene that, when triggered by a phenol-receptor complex, produces an easily detectable protein, thus indicating the presence of phenolic compounds in the environment. Biosensors employing acetylcholine esterase can be used for the detection of organophosphorus compounds in water.

Feed the World: Agro Ecology and/or Biotechnology?

Transgenic crops (GMCs: genetically modified crops), main products of agricultural biotechnology, are increasingly becoming a dominant feature of the agricultural landscapes of the USA and other countries such as China, Argentina, Mexico and Canada.

Nearly half of American farms grow GMCs (genetically modified crops)

- Worldwide, the areas planted to transgenic crops jumped more than twenty-fold in the past six years, from (Donegan, 1995) million hectares in 1996 to nearly 44.2 million hectares in 2000 (Kendall *et al.*, 1997).
- In the USA, Argentina and Canada, over half of the average for major crops such as soybean, corn and canola are planted in transgenic varieties.
- Herbicide resistant crops (HRCs) and insect resistant crops (Bt crops) accounted respectively for 59 and 15 percent of the total global area of all transgenic crops in 2000.

Big business claims GMCs will reduce the use of chemical pesticides

Transnational corporations (TNCs) such as Monsanto, DuPont, and Novartis, the main proponents of biotechnology, argue that carefully planned introduction of these crops should reduce or even eliminate the enormous crop losses due to weeds, insect pests, and pathogens. In fact, they argue that the use of such crops will have added beneficial effects on the environment by significantly reducing the use of agrochemicals. However, ecological theory predicts that as long as transgenic crops follow closely the pesticide paradigm prevalent in modern agriculture, such biotechnological products will do nothing but reinforce the pesticide treadmill in agro ecosystems, thus legitimizing the concerns that many environmentalists and some scientists have expressed regarding the possible environmental risks of genetically engineered organisms. In fact, there are several widely accepted environmental drawbacks associated with the rapid deployment and widespread commercialization of such crops in large monocultures, including (Robinson, 1996; Steinbrecher, 1996).

Pests show rapid evolution in resisting the pesticide properties of GMCs
Toxic buildup in GMCs harms useful insects

- the spread of transgenes to related weeds or conspecifics via crop-weed hybridization.
- reduction of the fitness of non-target organisms through the acquisition of transgenic traits via hybridization.

- the rapid evolution of resistance of insect pests such as Lepidoptera to Bt.
- accumulation of the insecticidal Bt toxin, which remains active in the soil after the crop is ploughed under and binds tightly to clays and humic acids.
- disruption of natural control of insect pests through intertrophic-level effects of the Bt toxin on predators.
- unanticipated effects on non-target herbivorous insects (i.e., monarch butterflies) through deposition of transgenic pollen on foliage of surrounding wild vegetation (Mellon and Rissler, 1998).
- vector-mediated horizontal gene transfer and recombination to create new pathogenic organisms.

Biotechnology, Agrodiversity and Farmers' Options

Monoculture, or farming only one crop, can lead to economic disaster and hunger

The spread of transgenic crops threatens crop diversity by promoting monocultures which leads to environmental simplification and genetic erosion. History has repeatedly shown that uniformity characterizing agricultural areas sown to a smaller number of varieties is a source of increased risk for farmers, as the genetically homogeneous fields may be more vulnerable to disease and pest attack (Saxena *et al.*, 1999).

Farmers have many choices, other than biotechnology, that work

Several people think that HRCs and Bt crops have been a poor choice of traits to feature the technology, given predicted environmental problems and the issue of resistance evolution. In fact, there is enough evidence to suggest that both these types of crops are not really needed to address the problems they were designed to solve. On the contrary, they tend to reduce the pest management options available to farmers. There are many alternative approaches, (e.g., rotations, polycultures, cover crops, biological control, etc.) that farmers can use to effectively regulate the insect and weed populations that are being targeted by the biotechnology industry. To the extent that transgenic crops further entrench the current monocultural system, they impede farmers from using a plethora of alternative methods (Altieri, 2000).

Ecological Wffects of HRCs

Gene Flow

Are we altering the genetic structure of living things in the name of utility and profit?

Just as it occurs between traditionally improved crops and wild relatives, pollen mediates gene flow between GMCs and wild relatives or conspecifics despite all possible efforts to reduce it. Little is known about the long-term persistence of crop genes in wild populations or about the impact of fitness-related crop genes on the population dynamics of weedy relatives. The main concern with transgenes that confer significant biological advantages is that they may transform wild/weed plants into new or worse weeds.

Hybridization of HRCs with populations of free living relatives will make these plants increasingly difficult to control, especially if they are already recognized as agricultural weeds and if they acquire resistance to widely used herbicides. For example:

- Transgenic resistance to glufosinate can be passed on from Brassica napus to populations of weedy Brassica napa, and persist under natural conditions (Steinbrecher, 1996).
- In Europe there is a major concern about the possibility of pollen transfer of herbicide tolerant genes from *Brassica*oilseeds to *Brassica nigra* and *Sinapis arvensis* (Hilbeck, 1998).

Economic and Agronomic Implications

The majority of GMCs have been engineered to repel unwanted plants or weeds. World-wide in 2000, transgenic herbicide resistant crops were planted on 74% of the 44.2 million hectares devoted to transgenic crops. (Kendall, 1997). In North America, transgenic glufosinate resistant cultivars of canola and corn, and transgenic glyphosate resistant cultivars of soybean, corn, cotton, and canola are now commercially available. Bromoxynil resistant transgenic cotton has also been developed. The so-called Round-up ready soybeans are the most prevalent GMCs.

Transgenic herbicide resistance in crop plants simplifies chemically based weed management because it typically involves compounds that are active on a very broad spectrum of weed species. Post-emergence application timing for these materials fits well with reduced or zero-tillage production methods, which can conserve soil and reduce fuel and tillage costs (Gill, 1995)

However, HRCs also have significant problems.

Editor's note: Sales of biotechnology products are reaching $60 billion/year

- Reliance on HRCs perpetuates the weed resistance problems and species shifts that are common to conventional herbicide based approaches.
- Herbicide resistance becomes more of a problem as the number of herbicide modes of action to which weeds are exposed becomes fewer and fewer, a trend that HRCs may exacerbate due to market forces.
- Given industry pressures to increase herbicide sales, acreage treated with broad-spectrum herbicides will expand, exacerbating the resistance problem. For example, it has been projected that the acreage treated with glyphosate will increase to nearly 150 million acres. Although glyphosate is considered less prone to weed resistance, the increased use of the herbicide will result in weed resistance, even if more slowly, as it

has been already documented with Australian populations of annual ryegrass, quackgrass, birdsfoot trefoil and *Cirsium arvense* (Goldberg, 1992).

- Perhaps the greatest problem of using HRCs to solve weed problems is that they steer efforts away from crop diversification and help to maintain cropping systems dominated by one or two annual species. Crop diversification can:
  - ➢ reduce the need for herbicides.
  - ➢ improve soil and water quality.
  - ➢ minimize requirements for synthetic nitrogen fertilizer.
  - ➢ regulate insect pest and pathogen populations.
  - ➢ increase crop yields and reduce yield variance.

Thus, to the extent that transgenic HRCs inhibit the adoption of diversified cropping systems that include rotational crops, cover crops and green manure, they hinder the development of sustainable agriculture.

Ecological Risks of Bt Crops

The number of crops engineered for insect resistance is on the rise

Based on the fact that more than 500 species of pests have already evolved resistance to conventional insecticides, pests can also evolve resistance to Bt toxins present in transgenic crops. No one questions if Bt resistance will develop, the question is now how fast it will develop. Susceptibility to Bt toxins can therefore be viewed as a natural resource that could be quickly depleted by inappropriate use of Bt crops.[15] However, cautiously restricted use of these crops should substantially delay the evolution of resistance. But is cautious use of Bt crops possible given commercial pressures that have resulted in a rapid rollout of Bt crops reaching 8.2 million hectares worldwide in 2000?

Organic farmers can produce a significant yield without insecticides

The refuge strategy of setting aside 20-30% of land to non-Bt crops to delay resistance is very difficult to implement regionally. Data from the Midwest shows that Bt corn saves on some insecticide use and yields are 2.4 Bu/acre higher than conventional corn but only under high European corn borer infestations (USDA 1999). On the other hand organic corn growers use no insecticides and obtain yields (4.8-9 t/ha) similar or slightly higher than conventional farmers (5.0-7.1 t/ha).

GMCs may have unintended victims, such as the monarch butterfly or lacewing

BT Crops and Beneficial Insects

Bacillus thuringiensis proteins are becoming ubiquitous, highly bioactive substances in agroecosystems. Most non-target herbivores colonizing Bt crops in the field ingest plant tissue containing Bt protein which they can pass on to their natural enemies in a more or less processed form. Polyphagous natural enemies (polyphagous: subsisting on many kinds of foods) that move between crop cultures are found to frequently encounter Bt-containing non-target herbivorous prey in more than one crop. This is a major ecological concern given previous studies that documented that Cry1 Ab adversely affected the predaceous lacewing *Chrysoperla carnea* reared on Bt corn-fed prey larvae.

These findings are problematic for small farmers in developing countries who rely on insect pest control, which involves a complexity of predators in their mixed cropping systems. Research shows that natural enemies can be affected directly through inter-trophic level effects of the toxin present in Bt crops. This raises serious concerns about the potential disruption of natural pest control, as polyphagous predators will encounter Bt-containing, non-target prey that move within and between crop cultivars throughout the crop season. Disrupted biocontrol mechanisms will likely result in increased crop losses due to pests or to the increased use of pesticides by farmers with consequent health and environmental hazards.

Effects on the Soil Ecosystem

The possibilities for soil biota to be exposed to transgenic products are very high. The little research conducted in this area has already demonstrated:

Toxins from GMCs remain active in the soil, decreasing soil fertility

- There is long term persistence of insecticidal products (Bt and proteinase inhibitors) in soil.
- The insecticidal toxin produced by Bacillus thuringiensis subsp. kurskatki remain active in the soil, where it binds rapidly and tightly to clays and humic acids.
- The bound toxin retains its insecticidal properties and is protected against microbial degradation by being bound to soil particles, persisting in various soils for at least 234 days.
- The presence of the toxin in exudates from Bt corn and verified that it was active in an insecticidal bioassay using larvae of the tobacco hornworm.

Given the persistence and the possible presence of exudates, there is potential for prolonged exposure of the microbial and invertebrate community to such toxins, and therefore studies should evaluate the effects of transgenic plants on both microbial and invertebrate communities and the ecological processes they mediate.

If transgenic crops substantially alter soil biota and affect processes such as soil organic matter decomposition and mineralization, this would be of serious concern to organic farmers and most poor farmers in the developing world. These farmers cannot purchase or don't want to use expensive chemical fertilizers. They rely instead on local residues, organic matter and especially soil organisms for soil fertility (e.g., key invertebrate, fungal or bacterial species) which can be affected by the soil bound toxin. Soil fertility could be dramatically reduced if crop leachates inhibit the activity of the soil biota and slow down natural rates of decomposition and nutrient release.

The long-term impacts of GMCs are not yet known

- the massive use of transgenic crops poses substantial potential risks from an ecological point of view the ecological effects are not limited to pest resistance and creation of new weeds or virus strains.
- transgenic crops can produce environmental toxins that move through the food chain and also may end up in the soil and water affecting invertebrates and probably ecological processes such as nutrient cycling
- No one can really predict the long-term impacts that will result from such massive deployment of such crops.

Not enough research has been done to evaluate the environmental and health risks of transgenic crops, an unfortunate trend. Most scientists feel that such knowledge is crucial to have before biotechnological innovations are implemented. There is a clear need to further assess the severity, magnitude and scope of risks associated with the massive field deployment of transgenic crops. Much of the evaluation of risks must move beyond comparing GMC fields and conventionally managed systems to include alternative cropping systems featuring crop diversity and low-external input approaches. This will allow real risk/benefit analysis of transgenic crops in relation to known and effective alternatives.

The loss of agricultural diversity may lead to disaster in developing countries

Moreover, the large-scale landscape homogenization with transgenic crops will exacerbate the ecological problems already associated with monoculture agriculture. Unquestioned expansion of this technology into developing countries may not be wise or desirable. There is strength in the agricultural diversity of many of these countries, and it should not be inhibited or reduced by extensive monoculture, especially when consequences of doing so results in serious social and environmental problems.

The repeated use of transgenic crops in an area may result in cumulative effects such as those resulting from the buildup of toxins in soils. For this reason, risk assessment studies not only have to be of an ecological nature in order to capture effects on ecosystem processes, but also of sufficient duration so that probable accumulative effects can be detected. The application of multiple diagnostic methods will provide the most sensitive and comprehensive assessment of the potential ecological impact of transgenic crops.

Biotechnology companies often claim that genetically modified organisms (GMOs)—specifically genetically altered seeds—are essential scientific breakthroughs needed to feed the world, protect the environment, and reduce poverty in developing countries. The Consultative Group on International Agricultural Research (CGIAR) and its constellation of international centers around the world charged with research to enhance food security in the developing world echo this view, which rests on two critical assumptions. The first is that hunger is due to a gap between food production and human population density or growth rate. The second is that genetic engineering is the only or best way to increase agricultural production and, thus, meet futurefoodneeds. Our objective is to challenge the notion of biotechnology as a magic bullet solution to all of agriculture's ills, by clarifying misconceptions concerning these underlying assumptions.

1. There is no relationship between the prevalence of hunger in a given country and its population. For every densely populated and hungry nation like Bangladesh or Haiti, there is a sparsely populated and hungry nation like Brazil and Indonesia. The world today produces more food per inhabitant than ever before. Enough food is available to provide 4.3 pounds for every person everyday: 2.5 pounds of grain, beans and nuts, about a pound of meat, milk and eggs and another of fruits and vegetables. The real causes of hunger are poverty, inequality and lack of access to food and land. Too many people are too poor to buy the food that is available (but often poorly distributed) or lack the land and resources to grow it themselves (Lappe, Collins & Rosset 1998).
2. Most innovations in agricultural biotechnology have been profit-driven rather than need-driven. The real thrust of the genetic engineering industry is not to make third world agriculture more productive, but rather to generate profits (Busch *et al.,* 1990). This is illustrated by reviewing the principle technologies on the market today: (1) herbicide resistant crops, such as Monsanto's "Roundup Ready" soybeans, seeds that are tolerant to Monsanto's herbicide Roundup, and (2) "Bt" (*Bacillus thuringiensis*) crops which are engineered to produce their own insecticide. In the first instance, the goal is to win a greater herbicide market-share for a proprietary product and, in the second, to boost seed sales at the cost of damaging the usefulness of a key pest management product (the *Bacillus thuringiensis* based microbial insecticide) relied upon by many farmers, including most organic farmers, as a powerful alternative to insecticides. These technologies respond to the need of biotechnology companies to intensify farmers' dependence upon seeds protected by so-called "intellectual property rights" which conflict directly with the age-old rights of farmers to reproduce, share or store seeds (Hobbelink, 1991). Whenever possible corporations will require farmers to buy a company's brand of inputs and will forbid farmers from keeping or selling seed. By controlling germplasm from seed to

sale, and by forcing farmers to pay inflated prices for seed-chemical packages, companies are determined to extract the most profit from their investment (Krimsky & Wrubel, 1996).

3. The integration of the seed and chemical industries appears destined to accelerate increases in per acre expenditures for seeds plus chemicals, delivering significantly lower returns to growers. Companies developing herbicide tolerant crops are trying to shift as much per acre cost as possible from the herbicide onto the seed via seed costs and technology charges. Increasingly price reductions for herbicides will be limited to growers purchasing technology packages. In Illinois, the adoption of herbicide resistant crops makes for the most expensive soybean seed-plus-weed management system in modern history—between $40.00 and $60.00 per acre depending on fee rates, weed pressure, and so on. Three years ago, the average seed-plus-weed control costs on Illinois farms was $26 per acre, and represented 23% of variable costs; today they represent 35-40% (Benbrook, 1999). Many farmers are willing to pay for the simplicity and robustness of the new weed management system, but such advantages may be short-lived as ecological problems arise.

4. Recent experimental trials have shown that genetically engineered seeds do not increase the yield of crops. A recent study by the United States Department of Agriculture (USDA) Economic Research Service shows that in 1998 yields were not significantly different in engineered versus non-engineered crops in 12 of 18 crop/region combinations. In the six crop/region combinations where Bt crops or herbicide tolerant crops (HTCs) fared better, they exhibited increased yields between 5-30%. Glyphosphate tolerant cotton showed no significant yield increase in either region where it was surveyed. This was confirmed in another study examining more than 8,000 field trials, where it was found that Roundup Ready soybean seeds produced fewer bushels of soybeans than similar conventionally bred varieties (USDA, 1999).

5. Many scientists claim that the ingestion of genetically engineered food is harmless. Recent evidence, however, shows that there are potential risks of eating such foods as the new proteins produced in such foods could: (1) act themselves as allergens or toxins; (2) alter the metabolism of the food producing plant or animal, causing it to produce new allergens or toxins; or (3) reduce its nutritional quality or value. In the case of (3), herbicide resistant soybeans can contain less isoflavones, an important phytoestrogen present in soybeans, believed to protect women from a number of cancers. At present, developing countries are importing soybean and corn from the United States, Argentina, and Brazil. Genetically engineered foods are beginning to flood the markets

in the importing countries, yet no one can predict all their health effects on consumers, who are unaware that they are eating such food. Because genetically engineered food remains unlabeled, consumers cannot discriminate between genetically engineered (GE) and non-GE food, and should serious health problems arise, it will be extremely difficult to trace them to their source. Lack of labeling also helps to shield the corporations that could be potentially responsible from liability (Lappe & Bailey, 1998).

6. Transgenic plants which produce their own insecticides, closely follow the pesticide paradigm, which is itself rapidly failing due to pest resistance to insecticides. Instead of the failed "one pest-one chemical" model, genetic engineering emphasizes a "one pest-one gene" approach, shown over and over again in laboratory trials to fail, as pest species rapidly adapt and develop resistance to the insecticide present in the plant (Alstad & Andow, 1995). Not only will the new varieties fail over the short-to-medium term, despite so-called voluntary resistance management schemes (Mallet & Porter, 1992), but in the process may render useless the natural Bt-pesticide which is relied upon by organic farmers and others desiring to reduce chemical dependence. Bt crops violate the basic and widely accepted principle of integrated pest management (IPM), which is that reliance on any single pest management technology tends to trigger shifts in pest species or the evolution of resistance through one or more mechanisms (NRC, 1996). In general, the greater the selection pressure across time and space, the quicker and more profound the pests evolutionary response. An obvious reason for adopting this principle is that it reduces pest exposure to pesticides, retarding the evolution of resistance. But when the product is engineered into the plant itself, pest exposure leaps from minimal and occasional to massive and continuous exposure, dramatically accelerating resistance (Gould, 1994). *Bacillus thuringiensis* will rapidly become useless, both as a feature of the new seeds and as an old standby sprayed when needed by farmers that want out of the pesticide treadmill (Pimentel *et al.*, 1989).

7. The global fight for market share is leading companies to massively deploy transgenic crops around the world (more than 30 million hectares in 1998) without proper advance testing of short- or long-term impacts on human health and ecosystems. In the United States, private sector pressure led the White House to decree "no substantial difference" between altered and normal seeds, thus evading normal Food and Drug Administration (FDA) and Environmental Protection Agency (EPA) testing. Confidential documents made public in an on-going class action lawsuit have revealed that the FDAâs own scientists do not agree with

this determination. One reason is that many scientists are concerned that the large scale use of transgenic crops poses a series of environmental risks that threaten the sustainability of agriculture (Goldberg, 1992; Paoletti & Pimentel, 1996; Snow & Moran, 1997; Rissler & Mellon, 1996; Kendall *et al.*, 1997; Royal Society, 1998).

These risk areas are as follows:

- The trend to create broad international markets for single products, is simplifying cropping systems and creating genetic uniformity in rural landscapes. History has shown that a huge area planted to a single crop variety is very vulnerable to new matching strains of pathogens or insect pests. Furthermore, the widespread use of homogeneous transgenic varieties will unavoidably lead to "genetic erosion," as the local varieties used by thousands of farmers in the developing world are replaced by the new seeds (Robinson, 1996).
- The use of herbicide resistant crops undermines the possibilities of crop diversification, thus, reducing agrobiodiversity in time and space (Altieri, 1994).
- The potential transfer through gene flow of genes from herbicide resistant crops to wild or semidomesticated relatives can lead to the creation of superweeds (Lutman, 1999).
- There is potential for herbicide resistant varieties to become serious weeds in other crops (Duke 1996; Holt & Le Baron, 1990).
- Massive use of Bt crops affects non-target organisms and ecological processes. Recent evidence shows that the Bt toxin can affect beneficial insect predators that feed on insect pests present on Bt crops (Hilbeck *et al.*, 1998). In addition, windblown pollen from Bt crops, found on natural vegetation surrounding transgenic fields, can kill non-target insects such as the monarch butterfly (Losey *et al.*, 1999). Moreover, Bt toxin present in crop foliage plowed under after harvest can adhere to soil colloids for up to 3 months, negatively affecting the soil invertebrate populations that break down organic matter and play other ecological roles (Donnegan *et al.*, 1995; Palm *et al.*, 1996).
- There is potential for vector recombination to generate new virulent strains of viruses, especially in transgenic plants engineered for viral resistance with viral genes. In plants containing coat protein genes, there is a possibility that such genes will be taken up by unrelated viruses infecting the plant. In such situations, the foreign gene changes the coat structure of the viruses and may confer properties, such as changed method of transmission between plants. The second potential risk is that recombination between RNA virus and a viral

RNA inside the transgenic crop could produce a new pathogen leading to more severe disease problems. Some researchers have shown that recombination occurs in transgenic plants and that under certain conditions it produces a new viral strain with altered host range (Steinbrecher, 1996).

Ecological theory predicts that the large-scale landscape homogenization with transgenic crops will exacerbate the ecological problems already associated with monoculture agriculture. Unquestioned expansion of this technology into developing countries may not be wise or desirable. There is strength in the agricultural diversity of many of these countries, and it should not be inhibited or reduced by extensive monoculture, especially when consequences of doing so results in serious social and environmentalproblems (Altieri, 1996). Although the ecological risks issue has received some discussion in government, international, and scientific circles, discussions have often been pursued from a narrow perspective that has downplayed the seriousness of the risks (Kend all *et al.*, 1997; Royal Society, 1998). In fact, methods for risk assessment of transgenic crops are not well developed (Kjellsson & Simmsen, 1994) and there is justifiable concern that current field biosafety tests tell little about potential environmental risks associated with commercial-scale production of transgenic crops. A main concern is that international pressures to gain markets and profits is resulting in companies releasing transgenic crops too fast, without proper consideration for the long-term impacts on people or the ecosystem.

8. There are many unanswered ecological questions regarding the impact of transgenic crops. Many environmental groups have argued for the creation of suitable regulation to mediate the testing and release of transgenic crops to offset environmental risks and demand a much better assessment and understanding of ecological issues associated with genetic engineering. This is crucial, as many results emerging from the environmental performance of released transgenic crops suggest that in the development of resistant crops not only is there a need to test direct effects on the target insect or weed, but the indirect effects on the plant. Plant growth, nutrient content, metabolic changes, and effects on the soil and non-target organisms should all be examined. Unfortunately, funds for research on environmental risk assessment are very limited. For example, the USDA spends only 1% of the funds allocated to biotechnology research on risk assessment, about \$1-2 million per year. Given the current level of deployment of genetically engineered plants, such resources are not enough to even discover the "tip of the iceberg". It is a tragedy-in-the-making that so many millions of hectares have been planted without proper biosafety standards.

Worldwide such acreage expanded considerably in 1998 with transgenic cotton reaching 6.3 million acres, transgenic corn reaching 20.8 million acres, and transgenic soybean 36.3 million acres. This expansion has been helped along by marketing and distribution agreements entered into by corporations and marketers (i.e., Ciba Seeds with Growmark and Mycogen Plant Sciences with Cargill), and in the absence of regulations in many developing countries. Genetic pollution, unlike oil spills, cannot be controlled by throwing a boom around it.

9. As the private sector has exerted more and more dominance in advancing new biotechnologies, the public sector has had to invest a growing share of its scarce resources in enhancing biotechnological capacities in public institutions, including the CGIAR, and in evaluating and responding to the challenges posed by incorporating private sector technologies into existing farming systems. Such funds would be much better used to expand support for ecologically based agricultural research, as all the biological problems that biotechnology aims at can be solved using agroecological approaches. The dramatic effects of rotations and intercropping on crop health and productivity, as well as of the use of biological control agents on pest regulation have been confirmed repeatedly by scientific research. The problem is that research at public institutions increasingly reflects the interests of private funders at the expense of public good research, such as biological control, organic production systems and general agroecological techniques. Civil society must request for more research on alternatives to biotechnology by universities and other public organizations (Krimsky & Wrubel, 1996). There is also an urgent need to challenge the patent system and intellectual property rights intrinsic to the World Trade Organization (WTO) which not only provide multinational corporations with the right to seize and patent genetic resources, but will also accelerate the rate at which market forces already encourage monocultural cropping with genetically uniform transgenic varieties. Based on history and ecological theory, it is not difficult to predict the negative impacts of such environmental simplification on the health of modern agriculture (Altieri, 1996).
10. Much of the needed food can be produced by small farmers located throughout the world using agroecological technologies (Uphoff & Altieri, 1999). In fact, new rural development approaches and low-input technologies spearheaded by farmers and non-governmental organizations (NGOs) around the world are already making a significant contribution to food security at the household, national, and regional levels in Africa, Asia and Latin America (Pretty, 1995). Yield increases are being achieved by using technological approaches, based on

agroecological principles that emphasize diversity, synergy, recycling and integration; and social processes that emphasize community participation and empowerment (Rosset, 1999). When such features are optimized, yield enhancement and stability of production are achieved, as well as a series of ecological services such conservation of biodiversity, soil and water restoration and conservation, improved natural pest regulation mechanisms, and so on (Altieri *et al.*, 1998). These results are a breakthrough for achieving food security and environmental preservation in the developing world, but their potential and further spread depends on investments, policies, institutional support, and attitude changes on the part of policy makers and the scientific community; especially the CGIAR who should devote much of its efforts to the 320 million poor farmers living in marginal environments. Failure to promote such people-centered agricultural research and development due to the diversion of funds and expertise towards biotechnology will forego an historical opportunity to raise agricultural productivity in economically viable, environmentally benign, and socially uplifting ways.

CONCLUSION

Agricultural biotechnology is driven by profit, not by scientific research

Although biotechnology is an important tool, at this point alternative solutions exist to address the problems that current GMCs, developed mostly by profit motives, are designed to solve. The dramatic positive effects of rotations, multiple cropping, and biological control on crop health, environmental quality and agricultural productivity have been confirmed repeatedly by scientific research. Biotechnology should be considered as one more tools that can be used, provided the ecological risks are investigated and deemed acceptable, in conjunction with a host of other approaches to move agriculture towards sustainability.

REFERENCES

Altieri, M.A. (1994). Biodiversity and Pest Management in Agroecosystems. New York: Haworth Press.

Altieri, M.A. (1996). The Science of Sustainable Agriculture. *Agroecology:* Westview Press, Boulder.

Alstad, D.N. and Andow, D.A. (1995). Managing the Evolution of Insect Resistance to Transgenic Plants. *Science*, 268, 1894-1896.

Altieri, M.A., Rosset, P., and Thrupp, L.A. (1998). The Potential of Agroecology to Combat Hunger in the Developing World (2020 Brief No. 55). International Food Policy Research Institute, Washington, DC.

Altieri M.A. (2000). "The Ecological Impacts of Transgenic Crops on Agroecosystem Health." *Ecosystem Health* 6: 13-23.

Benbrook, C. (1999). World Food System Challenges and Opportunities: GMOs, Biodiversity and Lessons from America's Heartland. Unpublished Manuscript.

Busch, L., Lacey, W.B., Burkhardt, J., and Lacey, L. (1990). Plants, Power and Profit. Oxford, England: Basil Blackwell.

Donegan, K.K., C.J. Palm, V.J. Fieland, L.A. Porteous, L.M. Ganis, D.L. Scheller and R.J. Seidler (1995). "Changes in Levels, Species, and DNA Fingerprints of Soil Microorganisms Associated with Cotton Expressing the *Bacillus thuringiensis* var. *Kurstaki* Endotoxin." *Applied Soil Ecology* 2, 111-124.

Donegan, K.K. and R.J. Seidler (1999). "Effects of Transgenic Plants on Soil and Plant Microorganisms." Recent Res. Devel. *Microbiology* 3: 415-424.

Duke, S.O. (1996). Herbicide Resistant Crops: Agricultural, Environmental, Economic, Regulatory, and Technical Aspects. Boca Raton: Lewis Publishers.

Gill, D.S. (1995). "Development of Herbicide Resistance in Annual Ryegrass Populations in the Cropping Belt of Western Australia." *Australian Journal of Exp.* Agriculture 3, 67-72.

Goldberg, R.J. (1992). "Environmental Concerns with the Development of Herbicide-tolerant Plants." *Weed Technology* 6, 647-652.

Gould, F. (1994). Potential and Problems with High-dose Strategies for Pesticidal Engineered Crops. *Biocontrol Science and Technology*, 4, 451-461.

Hilbeck, A., Baumgartner, M., Fried, P.M., and Bigler, F. (1998). Effects of Transgenic Bacillus Thuringiensis Corn Fed Prey on Mortality and Development Time of Immature Chrysoperla Carnea Neuroptera: Chrysopidae. *Environmental Entomology*, 27: 460-487.

Hobbelink, H. (1991). Biotechnology and the Future of World Agriculture. London: Zed Books, Ltd.

Holt, J.S. and Le Baron, H.M. (1990). Significance and Distribution of Herbicide Resistance. *Weed Technology*, 4: 141-149.

Kendall, H.W., Beachy, R., Eismer, T., Gould, F., Herdt, R., Ravon, P.H., Schell, J. and Swaminathan, M.S. (1997). Bioengineering of Crops (Report of the World Bank Panel on Transgenic Crops, pp.1-30). Washington DC: World Bank.

Kjellsson, G. and Simonsen, V. (1994). Methods for Risk Assessment of Transgenic Plants. Basil, Germany: Birkhauser Verlag.

Krimsky, S. and R.P. Wrubel (1996). Agricultural Biotechnology and the Environment: Science, Policy and Social Issues. University of Illinois Press, Urbana.

Lappe, F.M., Collins, J., and Rosset, P. (1998). World Hunger: Twelve Myths. New York: Grove Press.

Lappe, M and Bailey, B. (1998). Against the Grain: Biotechnology and the Corporate Takeover of Food. Monroe, Maine: Common Courage Press.

Losey, J.E., L.S. Rayor and M.E. Cater (1999). "Transgenic Pollen Harms Monarch Larvae." *Nature* 399: 241.

Lutman, P.J.W. (1999). (Ed.). Gene Flow and Agriculture: Relevance for Transgenic Crops. British Crop Protection Council Symposium Proceedings, 72: 43-64.

Mallet, J. and Porter, P. (1992). Preventing Insect Adaptations to Insect Resistant Crops: are Seed Mixtures or Refugia the Best Strategy? Proceedings of the Royal Society of London Series B Biology Science, 250: 165-169.

Mellon, M and J. Rissler (1998). "Now or Never: Serious Plans to Save a Natural Pest Control." Union of Concerned Scientists. Washington DC.

National Research Council (1984) *Alternative Agriculture*. National Academy Press. Washington DC.

National Research Council (1996). "Ecologically Based Pest Management." *National Academy of Sciences*, Washington, DC.

National Research Council (NRC). (1996). Ecologically Based Pest Management. Washington DC: National Academy of Sciences.

Palm, C.J., D.L. Schaller, K.K. Donegan and R.J. Seidler (1996). "Persistence in Soil of Transgenic Plant Produced *Bacillus thurigiensis var. Kustaki* Endotoxin." *Canadian Journal of Microbiology* (in press).

Paoletti, M.G. and D. Pimentel (1996). "Genetic Engineering in Agriculture and the Environment: Assessing Risks and Benefits." *BioScience* 46, 665-671.

Pimentel, D., Hunter, M.S., LaGro, J.A., Efroymson, R.A., Landers, J.C., Mervis, F.T. McCarthy, C.A. and Boyd, A.E. (1989). Benefits and Risks of Genetic Engineering in Agriculture. BioScience, 39: 606-614.

Pretty, J. (1995). Regenerating Agriculture: Policies and Practices for Sustainability and Self-relieance. London: Earthscan.

Rissler, J. and M. Mellon (1996). *The Ecological Risks of Engineered Crops*. MIT Press, Cambridge.

Robinson, R.A. (1996). "Return to Resistance: Breeding Crops to Reduce Pesticide Resistance." *AgAccess*, Davis.

Rosset, P. (1999). The Multiple Functions and Benefits of Small farm Agriculture in the Context of Global Trade Negotiations, (IFDP Food First Policy Brief No. 4). Washington DC: Institute for Food and Development Policy.

Royal Society. (1998, February). Genetically Modified Plants for Food Use. Statement 2/98. London: Royal Society.

Saxena, D., S. Flores and G. Stotzky (1999). "Insecticidal Toxin in Root Exudates from Bt Corn." *Nature* 401,480.

Snow, A.A. and P. Moran (1997). "Commercialization of Transgenic Plants: Potential Ecological Risks." *BioScience* 47: 86-96.

Steinbrecher, R.A. (1996). "From Green to Gene Revolution: The Environmental Risks of Genetically Engineered Crops." *The Ecologist* 26: 273-282.

United States Department of Agriculture (1999). "Genetically Engineered Crops for Pest Management." *USDA Economic Research Service*, Washington DC.

Uphoff, N and Altieri, M.A. (1999). Alternatives to Conventional Modern Agriculture for Meeting World Food Needs in the Next Century (Report of a Bellagio Conference). Ithaca, NY: Cornell International Institute for Food, Agriculture and Development.

Plant Biotechnology and Industrial Applications
Edited by: Alka Chauhan and Pawan Kumar 'Bharti'
ISBN: 978-93-5056-884-2
Edition: 2017
Published by: Discovery Publishing House Pvt. Ltd., New Delhi (India)

2

Colletotrichum Leaf Spot Disease of Turmeric and Its Management

[1]R.S. Mishra, [2]A.N. Chaube and [3]V.P. Pandey

ABSTRACT

Genus *Colletotrichum* is one of the main infectious agent of turmeric, causing alterations during developmental stages of plants. Pathogent controlled by synthetic fungicides; however, the use of these is progressively restricted due to both, the harmful effects of pesticides on the environment and human health and development of highly resistant fungal strains. Therefore, there is a great demond for novel natural fungiceides. Higher plants and cow products are rich source of bioactive compounds, that have antifungal activity represent an alternative for achieving a sustainable control of pathogenic fungi and to reduce the heavy yield loss and use of synthetic fungicides. The five plant extract namely; neem (*Azadirachta indica*), onion (*Allium cepa*); garlic (*Allium sativum*), madar (*Calotropis procera*) and datura (*Datura stramonium*) were used with Cow urine, acetone and distilled water separately and all extract mixed with botanical formulations against *Colletotrichum capsici*. All the nineteen treatments showed significant reduction of mycelial growth of the test fungus. The maximum reduction was found in cow urine based botanical formulation 50.83-56.05 per cent followed by acetone based botanical formulation 49.92-54.31 per cent, distilled water based botanical formulation 44.51-52.35 per cent. Cow urine based botanical formulation was found most effective in comparison to acetone based botanical formulation and distilled water based botanical formulation at 60, 75 and 90 days after planting. Foliar application of Propiconazole (0.1%) at 45 and 90 days after planting were significantly superior to minimize the percent disease intensity (27.61 PDI) of leaf spot in comparison to foliar spray + rhizome treatment of Hexaconazole (28.50 PDI) and Tricyclazole (33.73 PDI) with increasing the fresh rhizome yield 33.96 to 34.33 t ha^{-1} in Propiconazole and 31.15 to 33.22t ha^{-1} in Hexaconazole as compared to the control (28.17t ha^{-1}).

Key words: *C. capsici*, cow urine, plant extracts, fungicides,inhibition per cent, percent disease control,

[1-3]Department of Vegetable Science, N.D.University of Agril. & Technology, Kumarganj, Faizabad UP, India

Introduction

Turmeric (*Curcuma longa* L.) is third important spice's crop of India and grown for its underground rhizomes, which is known as "Haridra" in Sanskrit and "Haldi" in Hindi. It is an herbaceous perennial crop and is native of the genus *Curcuma longa* L., considered to be a triploid with a somatic chromosome number 63 ($2n = 3x = 63$) belonging to family Zingiberaceae, originated in the Indo-Malayan region (Purse glove, 1968). It comprises 40 genera with 400 tropical species in World. It has versatile used in flavoring, dye making, drug preparation, cosmetics and medicine (Kallupurachkal and Ravindran, 2002; Dixit *et al.*, 2002). Besides, it has around hundred active constituents (Ross, 1999). The annual production of turmeric in India is about 59.86 lakh tonnes from an area of 892,213 ha. In Uttar Pradesh, the area under turmeric cultivation is 1828 ha, with the production of 5149 metric tonnes and productivity 2.817 tonnes/ha. (Anonymous, 2012).

1. Disease

Turmeric is highly prone to several fungal diseases (Naidu, 1988; Rangaswami and Mahadevan, 2001: Pruthi, 1998). The major diseases and causal organisms of turmeric plant are: Leaf blotch: *Taphrina maculans*, Leaf spot: *Colletotrichum capsici*, Leaf blight: *Rhizoctonia solani*, Root rot: *Pythium graminicolum*, Basal rot: *Sclerotium rolfsii*, Storage rot: *Macrophomina phoseolina.* One of them is turmeric leaf spot disease caused by *Colletotrichum capsici* (Syd.) Butler & Bisby. This disease was first reported in Coimbatore district, India by Mc Rae in 1917 (Ramakrishnan, 1954) and yield loss was reported between 15-60% (Joshi and Sharma, 1980; Pruthi, 1998; Narasimhudu and Balasubramanian, 2001b). The dry weight of the rhizome is also reduced 62% approximately. The disease is found throughout India, but more severe in southern state (Gomathi, 2001). There are nearly 1000 species of *Colletotrichum,* which have been described on the basis of disease caused on various hosts. *Colletotrichum capsici* was also reported as unspecialized parasite from more than 100 crops in a wide range of angiosperm families. Sydow (1913) first described *Colletotrichum capsici* as *Vermicularia capsici* from pepper fruit collected by W. Mc Rae in India. Dickson (1925) made a comprehensive review regarding the *Colletotrichum* spp. He examined the specimens of various species of *Vermicularia* from potato. Several other workers have been carried out research on the pathogen's morphology, physiology, nutrition requirements, enzyme activity, production and the role of chemical and biological fungicides in controlling the disease. A study made by Pring *et al.*, (1995) on the infection process and host range of *C. capsici* from different hosts (cowpea, bean and beetle vine) revealed that the pathogen infection process might be used to predict whether the pathogen has a narrow or wide host range. The susceptible host tissues get completely rotten in 8-10 days with covering acervuli on entire surface of hypocotyls. The infecting hyphae penetrate the cuticle and spread beneath the cuticle and epidermal cells, which is causing extreme wall degradation. Subsequently the hyphae grew in and destroyed the cuticle cells. This is associated with extensive death of adjacent cells causing the production of water soaked lesions.

Symptoms of leaf spot of turmeric

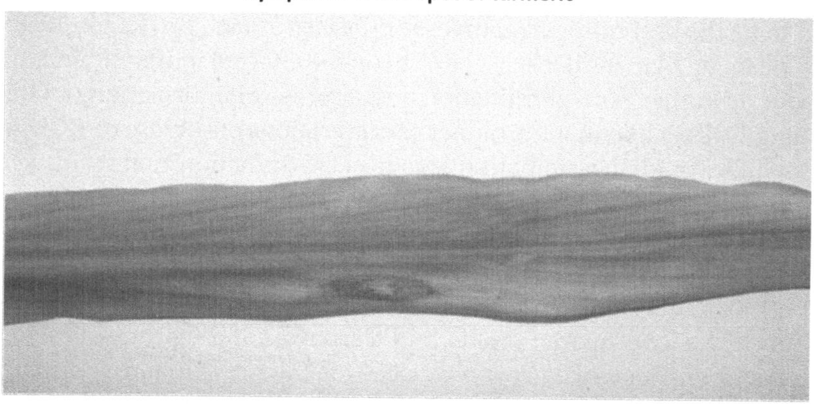

2. Pathogen

The occurrence of different species of *Colletotrichum* on the leaves of turmeric plant was reported in West Bengal (Kar and Mahapatra, 1981). Palarpawar and Ghrude (1989) reported the saprophytic colonization of *C. capsici* on turmeric leaf. *C. capsici* and *C. curcumae* competed with each other and established their colony in the susceptible dead leaf sheath of turmeric. Hence the colonies of *C. capsici* in the buried dead leaf tissue acted as primary source of inoculums for initiation of the leaf spot disease. Turmeric is seriously affected with leaf spot disease caused by *Colletotrichum capsici.* It produces elliptical to oblong spots with grayish white center and concentrically arranged black acervuli in the center. The acervuli of *C. capsici* are hemispherical in shape and conidia are single celled hyaline, smooth walled, falcate or sickle shaped with blunt ends measuring 16-24 × 2.5-3.5 micro meter. (Gorawar *et al.*, 2006).

Misra and Mahmood (1960 a) investigated the effects of different temperature, light intensities, pH, atmospheric humidity and different media on spore germination of *C. capsici*. The conidia germinate readily within 4 h in tap water and percentage of spore germination increased with the increasing temperature up to 30°C. Light has no effect on spore germination. Maximum spore germination took place in neutral solution i.e. pH 7 and 1% sucrose solution. Maximum sporulations were found in the Czapek's media, whereas the Richard's media was found to be the next best for mycelia growth of *C. capsici*. Good mycelia growth and sporulations were also recorded in Potato dextrose agar media. C: N ratio of 1:1/4 was most suitable for the growth and sporulations of *C. capsici* (Misra and Mahmood 1960b). Misra and Dutta (1963) observed differences in morphological characters, carbon and nitrogen requirement, growth rate, sporulations and virulence of two isolates of *Colletorrichum capsici* collected from two different locations of Orissa. The optimum temperature for *C. dematium* growth was 25°C and the growth was highly inhibited at higher temperature (40°C). He also reported that xylose, glucose, maltose were found to be the best carbon sources and urea, glycine, D-I-alanine and L-lucine have been found to be the best nitrogen sources for *Colletotrichum* spp (Rajak, 1983). The report made by Manandhar *et al.*, (1995a) on the effect of inorganic and organic compounds in the spore germination and appressorial formation of *C. capsici* in pepper fruits stated that the higher concentrations of sucrose or KCL greatly increased the conidial germination and mycelial formation along with reduced appressorial formation. Appressorial formation in *C. capsici* was found to be higher at 10 mm sucrose. *C. capsici* conidial germination was stimulated by Fe-resorcilic acid. Tricyclazole compound inhibited the appressorial formation of *C. capsici*, whereas the isoprothiolane compound stimulated the appressorial formation. The investigation made by Palarpawar and Ghrude (1997) on the requirement of different nitrogen sources for the growth and sporulation of *Colletotrichum* spp. He was reported that peptone acted as a good source for *C. capsici* mycelial growth. Ammonium oxalate, sodium nitrite, urea and thiourea were reported to inhibit the mycelial growth of *C. capsici*. All the nitrogen sources especially sodium nitrite and ammonium oxalate were reported to inhibit the sporulation of *C. capsici*. On the other hand, Dura raj (1956) observed that the urea and ammonium oxalate belonging to the nitrogen sources acted as very best sources for mycelial growth of *C. capsici*. Growth and sporulation of *C. capsici* was found to be lesser in different solid and liquid media containing extracts of tobacco mosaic virus-infected leaves than in media containing extract of healthy leaves (Bansal *et al.*, 1985). Hence it was reported that the essential metabolites required for the growth and spore germination of *C. capsici* were either lacking or present in very low quantity in the leaf extract of the virus-infected plants. Bansal *et al.,* (1978) reported that the Tobacco mosaic virus-infected pepper plant showed increased resistance to *Colletotrichum capsici* in the field condition prior to fungus infection. Muruganandam *et al.,* (1987) reported to influence of some nitrogen sources on the growth of anthracnose fungi. Asparagines induced maximum appressoria formation in the *Colletotrichum* spp.

The morphological and pathological study of four isolates of *C. capsici* and *C. indicum* were done from pepper and cotton plants by Roberts and Snow (1990) and brought out the fact that all the isolates regardless the host was pathogenic on unwounded cotton bolls. They suggested that the conidial dimension was nearly identical for both the species; hence *C. indicum* was considered as a synonym for *C. capsici.* Narain and Das (1970) confirmed the production of colletotin by *C. capsici,* which killed the host tissues. Grewal and Grover (1974) have reported that *C. capsici* inhibited the photosynthetic process thereby altering the physiology of the host plant. Sahni *et al.,* (1974) recorded the toxin production from *Colletotrichum gossypii, C. capsici, C. gloeosporioides* and *C. falcatum* isolated from cotton, chilies, citrus and sugarcane. The toxic metabolites produced by above species were not host specific. Jeumkya and Byungkook (1998) brought out the influence of inoculums density, wetness duration, plant age, and inoculation method and cultivar resistance on infection of pepper by *Colletotrichum* spp. They stated that the symptom development in host plant was positively correlated with inoculums density of the pathogen and leaf wetness periods of the host plant.

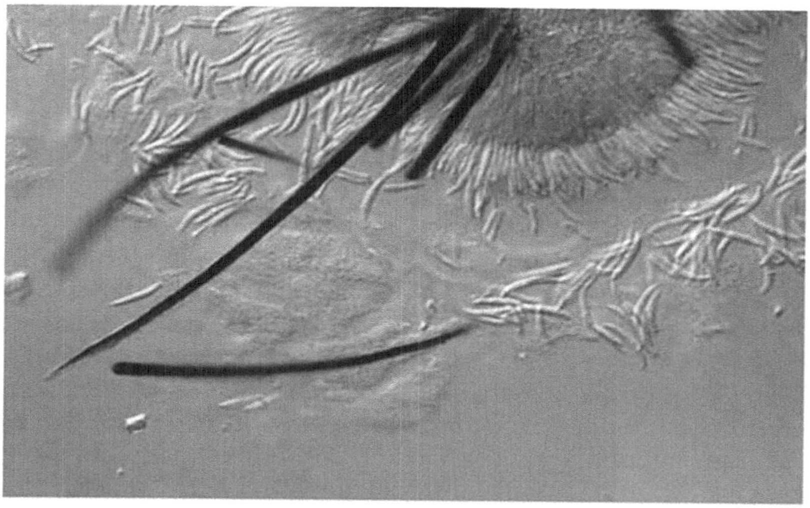

Colletotrichum capcisi

3. Chemical Control

Efficacy of four fungicides were evaluated and found best carbendazim + Mancozeb (0.1%) for managing the leaf spot disease and rhizome germination of turmeric (91.13%) followed by Propiconazole (88.40%) and Hexaconazole

(87.30%) (Mishra and Pandey, 2014) Foliar application of Propiconazole (0.1%) at 45 and 90 days after planting were significantly superior to minimize the percent disease intensity (27.61 PDI) of leaf spot disease of turmeric in comparison to hexaconazole and tricyclazole. The rhizome treatment and foliar application of propiconazole (0.1%) at 45 and 90 days after planting were significantly superior in reducing the disease index (28.8%) of leaf spot disease of turmeric and increasing the fresh rhizome yield 17.13 t ha^{-1} as compared to other fungicides (Narasimha *et al.*, 2012). Three to four sprays of perinox, Bordeaux mixture, Dithane Z-78 and yellow copper oxide at 15-21 days intervals have been found to control the infection of *C. capsici* in chilli (Chandler, 1958; Chandler and Dempsey, 1963; Crover and Bansal, 1970;). Application of ziram was found to inhibit the conidial germination of *C. capsici* and inhibit its infection on the fruits of *C. annum*. The effects of different fungicides on the control of leaf spot disease and yield of turmeric was carried out with the used of Dithane Z-78, Dithane M-45, Blitox-50, Bavistin. Dithane Z-78 was found to most effective for controlling the leaf spot disease and obtaining maximum yield, which was followed by Dithane M-45, Biltox-50, Bavistin and Cuman. They also suggested for the spray of Benlate @ 0.1% or Ziram @ 0.2% or bavistin @0.1% to effective control of the disease (Narain and Panigrahi, 1971).

Foliar spray of carbandzim (0.1%) or copper oxychloride (0.25%) at disease initiation and 15 days intervals has proved to effective control method against leaf spot disease caused by *Colletolrichum capsici*. He also reported that the foliar spray of bavistin (0.1%) was found superior for controlling the leaf spot disease with appreciable increase in the yield of turmeric (Thamburaj, 1991). Pruthi (1998) reported that rhizomes treated with Dithane M-45 @ 3 g/liter of water or bavistin @ 1 g/liter of water was found to be very effective against the leaf spot disease of turmeric. Besides, the foliar spray of Dithane M-45 @ 2.5 g/liter of water or bavistin @1 g/liter of water in two to three sprays at fortnightly intervals gave best results against leaf spot disease caused by *C. capsici*. Narasimhudu and Balasubramanian (2001a) studied the effects of eight chemical fungicides and neem oil against *Collefolrichum capsici* causing leaf spot of turmeric. Evaluation of different fungicides against *C. capsici* causing leaf spot in turmeric under *in-vitro* condition made by Narasimhudu and Balasubramanian (2001b). Among the different fungicides viz. mancozeb, copper oxychloride, ediphenphos, chlorothaionil, carbendazim, thiophanate methyl, trldermorph, kitazin and neem oil. They found thiophanate methyl (0.1%) was superior for controlling the growth of *C. capsici*. The effective growth control of *C. capsici* has reported in thiophanate methyl (0.1%) followed by mancozeb (0.25%) and carbendazim (0.1%) Rangaswami and Mahadevan (2001) reported that the leaf spot disease of turmeric was effectively controlled by spraying @1% bordeaux mixture, curpravit or dithane Z-78 at least 3 times during the season, six weeks after plantation and repeated at 2-3 week intervals. Pre-treatment of rhizomes with benlate before plantation was very effective in seed protection against the pathogen incidence. Rao *et al.,* (2012), tested the efficacy of four fungicides *viz.* Propiconazole (0.1%), Hexaconazole (0.1%), Tricyclazole (0.1%) and carbendazim + mancozeb (0.1%) against leaf spot disease of turmeric. The rhizome treatment with two foliar spray of propiconazole at 45 and 90 days after planting were significantly superior in reducing the disease index (20.01%) of leaf spot disease and increase the fresh rhizome yield (17.13 t ha^{-1}). Jagtap *et al.,* (2013) found the high efficacy of Propiconazole for inhibiting the mycelia growth of *C. capsici and it* was higher than Hexaconazole, Chlorothalonil and azoxystrobin at 100, 500 and 1500 ppm, respectively.

Table 2.1: Effect of Fungicides on Management of Leaf Spot Disease of Turmeric (Pooled Analysis of 2010-12)

Treatments	Percent germina-tion	Leaf spot disease		Yield (tha^{-1})	%Yield increase over control	Cost benefit ratio
		PDI	PEDC			
T1 Rhizome treatment +foliar spray of Hexaconazole (0.1%) on 45 and 90 DAP	87.33 (69.14)	29.84 (33.09)	35.28 (35.97)	33.22	17.92	1:2.45
T2 Rhizome treatment +foliar spray of Propiconazole (0.1%) on 45 and 90 DAP	88.43 (70.49)	28.50 (32.19)	42.00 (40.16)	33.96	20.55	1:2.51
T3 Rhizome treatment +foliar spray of Tricyclazole (0.1%) on 45 and 90 DAP	86.43 (68.42)	33.72 (35.43)	32.95 (34.62)	30.65	8.83	1:2.14
T4 Rhizome treatment +foliar spray of Carbendazim + Mancozeb (0.1%) on 45 and 90 DAP	91.13 (73.05)	35.90 (36.79)	27.72 (31.60)	30.99	10.06	1:2.22
T5Foliar spray of Hexaconazole (0.1%) on 45 and 90 DAP	84.53 (67.09)	30.23 (33.21)	37.73 (37.29)	31.15	10.56	1:2.32
T6Foliar spray of Propiconazole (0.1%) on 45 and 90 DAP	87.80 (69.32)	27.61 (31.60)	42.35 (40.24)	34.33	21.86	1:2.65
T7Foliar spray of Tricyclazole (0.1%) on 45 and 90 DAP	86.10 (68.16)	36.97 (37.42)	23.42 (28.55)	30.33	7.66	1:2.21
T8Foliar spray of Carbendazim + Mancozeb (0.1%) on 45 and 90 DAP	87.00 (68.52)	38.72 (38.43)	21.08 (27.17)	30.99	10.06	1:2.28
T9 Control	81.53 (64.62)	49.94 (44.96)	—	28.17	—	1:2.09
SEMCD (P<0.05)	1.353.97	2.2146. 612	4.59413. 722	2.186.48	—	—

*Figures in the paranthesis are arc sine transformed values: **DAP** = Days after planting; **PDI** = Percent disease intensity, **PEDC** = Percent efficacy of disease control

4. Botanical Control

Some plant contains components that are toxic to pathogens. When extracted from the plant and applied on infested crops, these components are called botanical pesticides. It is sustainable solution in agriculture, reduce crop losses, eco-friendly, easily bio-degradable, organic forming, cheaper and integrated disease management. Plants have ability to synthesize aromatic secondary metabolites, like phenols, phenolic acides, quinines, flavones, flavonoides, tannins and coumarins. The components with phenolic structures, like carvacrol, eugenol and thymol were highly active against the pathogen. These groups of compounds show antimicrobial effect and serve as plant defense mechanisms against pathogenic microorganisms (Das *et al.*, 2010). The volatile antimicrobial substance allicin is synthesized in garlic when the tissues are damaged and substrate alliin mixed with the enzyme alliin-lyase. These allicin effectively control the pathogens caused seed and foliar diseases of plants. Besides it's, the thousands of phyto chemicals which have inhibitory effects on all types of microorganisms. Bio-efficacy of 10% Phyto-extracts *viz.* garlic, tulsi, cinnamon, piper, lemon grass, neem and aloevera were tested and found all phyto-extracts significantly inhibiting the mycelial growth of *F. pallidoroseum* over control. Garlic and cinnamon extracts completely inhibited the mycelial growth (100%). The next best treatment in order to merit was tulsi and piper. Vikas and Ratnoo (2011) tested phyto-extract of Azadirachtin and neem oil against *Erysiphae polygoni* causing powdery mildew of fenugreek. The azadirachtin and neem oil were sprayed on fenugreek plants and found 66.0 and 60.13 percent disease control efficiency, respectively. *In vitro* effect of plant extracts have showed maximum inhibition in neem leaf extract (78.15%) followed by garlic (58.89%), Sadafuli (57.04%) and tulsi (55.93%). The least reduction in the colony diameter of *Colletotrichum gloesporoides* was in glyricidia (25.93%) (Watve *et al.*, 2009). The leaf extract of *Azardirachta indica, Allium sativum, Ocimum centum, Datura stramonium, Polyalthia longifolia, Vinca rocea* and *Withania sominifera* were effective in controlling *C. capsici*. Plant extract of *Adenocalyma alleceum* and *Bougainvillea spectabilis* were found most effective for inhibiting the mycelia growth of *C. gloesporioides followed* by *Ahutilon indicum, Acalypha indica, Agiratum coninjoides, Allium cepa, Ocimum centum and Terminalia cepula.*(Prabhakar *et al.*, 2003). The antifungal properties of eleven species of botanicals *viz.* Ashoka, Babul, Bael, Parthenium, Neem, Besharam, Mehandi, Tulsi, Garlic, Onion and Lantana *in vitro* against *C. capsici* at 5, 10 and 15% concentrations using PDA as basal medium by Poisoned food Technique (Jagtap *et al.*, 2013; Nene and Thapliyal, 1993). All eleven leaf extract tested were found significantly effective in checking the mycelia growth of *C. capsici* as compared with control. *Polyalthia longifolia recorded maximum* inhibition 76.16% at 15 % concentration followed by Allium sativum bulb extract (68.88%) and *Allium cepa* (63.96%). The nine aqueous leaf extracts were tested against *Colletotrichum trancatum,* significantly highest mycelia growth inhibition (81.82%) was recorded in garlic extracts followed by Tulsi (65.17%) and Onion (60.31%) (Jagtap, 2012).

5. Cow Urine

Panchgavya is being sought to improve crop establishment and health (Shakuntala *et al.*, 2012). It is an organic formulation, which in Sanskrit means the blend of five products obtained from cow i.e. milk, ghee, curd, dung and urine. All these products are individually called as "Gavy" and collectively named as Panchgavya. Panchgavya has got reference in the scripts of Vedas and Vrikshayurveda (Natarajan, 2002). In India use of Panchgavya in organic forming is gaining popularity in recent years especially in state like Tamil Nadu and Kerala (Shailaja *et al.*, 2014). It is also called cowpathy treatment based on products obtained from cows used in ayurvedic medicine and of religious significance for Hindu (Srimathi *et al.*, 2013). Panchagavya is an organic product recommended for crop improvement in organic agriculture (Sangeetha and Thevanathan, 2010). It is used as a foliar spray, soil application along with irrigation, as well as seed treatment (Natarajan, 2002). Panchgavya has played a significant role in providing resistance to pests and diseases, which is resulting increase of yields (Tharmaraj *et al.*, 2011). Panchgavya possess the properties of fertilizers and bio pesticides and have gave the positive effect on growth and yield of crops as reported by Somasundaram *et al.*, (2007). Effective microorganisms in panchgavya are a mixed culture of naturally occurring beneficial microbes mostly lactic acid bacteria (*Lactobacillus*), yeast (*Saccharomyces*), actinomycetes (*Streptomyces*), photosynthetic bacteria (*Rhodopsuedomonas*) and certain fungi (*Aspergillus, Penicillium* etc.) (Xu, 2001, Swaminathan, *et al.*, 2007). Chemolethotrops and autotrophic nitrifiers (Ammonifers and nitrifiers) are present in panchagavya, which colonize on the leaves and increased the ammonia uptake and enhance the total N supply (Papen *et al.*, 2002). The P^H of panchgavya was lowered to 4.5 at 30 days of fermentation and this might due to *Lactobacillus* bacteria in panchgavya, which produced more organic acid during fermentation (Mathivanan *et al.*, 2006).

The beneficial microorganisms of panchgavya and their establishment in the soil hove improved the sustainability of agriculture as the microorganisms present in the rhizospheric environment i.e. around the roots, which influence the plant growth and crop yield was might due to presence of growth accelerating enzyme in panchgavya which favored rapid cell division and multiplication (Vasumathi 2001, Sanjutha *et al.*, 2008). Naik and Sreenivasa (2009) reported that panchgavya contains bacteria producing plant growth promoting substances. The microbes viz. *Rhizobium, Azotobactor, Azospirillum, Trichoderma* and *Pseudomonas* present in panchgavya act as liquid bio fertilizers and bio pesticides (Ali 2011). Sometimes seed germination and seedling quality have reduced with increasing concentration of organic fortification which might be due to optimal dose of the organic product that is normally specific for crops to crop (Henig-Severa *et al.*, 2000). Panchgavya enhance the growth and vigor of crops, including resistance to pest and diseases with increasing the keeping quality of vegetables and fruits (Natarajan 2002). Mishra *et al.*, (2015) reported that the maximum reduction of mycelium growth was found in cow urine based botanical formulation 50.83 to 56.05% followed by acetone based botanical formulation 49.92 to 54.31%, and distilled water based botanical formulation 44.51 to 52.35%. The effectiveness of cow urine based onion extract was 51.58% at 20% concentration after 72 h incubation periods. Sugha (2005) evaluated the antifungal potentiality of panchgavya against *R. solani, S. rolfsii, F. solani, S. sclerotiorum* and *Phytophthora colocasiae,* which resulted complete suppression of mycelial growth of *R. solani* and other pathogens, the growth inhibition range was 88.1-92.3%.

Out of twelve organic inputs tested, eight inputs *viz.* biosol, matka khad, agnihotra ash + cow urine, panchgavya, Vermicompost, cow pat pit compost, NADEP compost and biodynamic compost showed 60.2-100 per cent mycelial growth inhibition of *S. sclerotiorum* without autoclaving (Shalika 2009). Sreenivasa and Naik (2011) observed 92.1 and 57.3 per cent mycelial growth inhibition of *Fusarium* sp. at 15 and 20 per cent concentrations of cow urine *in vitro.* Czaczyk *et al.,* (2000) isolated four strains of *Bacillus* from cow dung compost, all the strains possessed strong inhibition properties 56.2-71.0 per cent against the mycelial growth of *R. solani, Bipolaris sorokiniaria, S. sclerotiorum, Trichothecium roseum, F. solani* and *F. oxysporum.* Chung *et al.,* (2000) isolated *Paenibacillus koreensis* from compost that have antifungal activity against *Fusarium oxysporum, Colletotrichum lagenarium, Sclerotinia sclerotiorum, Botrytis cinerea* and *Rhizoctonia solani. Aspergillus niger, Trichoderma harzianum, Bacillus cereus* and *Bacillus subtilis* were found major microbes in cow dung compost. The microbes *Bacillus subtilis* and *B. cereus* were cultured with the seedling blight inducing pathogens such as *Sclerotium rolfsii, F. oxysporum, Pythium aphanidermatum, H. maydis* and *R. solani,* the mycelial growth of all tested pathogenic fungi were inhibited to the tune of 40.0-57.8 and 35.5-53.3 per cent, respectively (Muhammad and Amusa 2003). Charest *et al.,* (2005) observed the presence of two bacteria *Pseudomonas aeruginosa* and *Rhizobium radiobacter* in cow dung manure. Both bacterial isolates were evaluated against *Pythium ultimum* and was resulted 2-3 per cent mycelia growth inhibition by *R. radiobacter.* Khaing *et al.,* (2008) reported the presence of ten species of beneficial microbes such as *Serratia marcescens, Bacillus megatarium, Azotobacter chroococcum, Pseudomonas medocina* and *Flavobacterium* spp. Invermiwash. Species of *Bacillus, Serratia, Pseudomonas* and Actinomycetes were obtained from panchgavya and evaluated for their antifungal potentiality against soil borne pathogens *viz. S. rolfsii, F. oxysporum, F. solani* and *R. solani.* The maximum inhibition was possessed by *Serratia* (99.0%) followed by *Bacillus* (72.7-99.0%) and Actinomycetes (48.6-99.0%) against all the test pathogens (Ashlesha and Sugha 2008). Actinomycetes present in cow dung compost possessed antimicrobial activity against fifty three pathogens (Pinto *et al.,* 2010). Sinha *et al.,* (2010) documented the presence of nitrogen fixing bacteria, phosphate solubilizing bacteria, Actinomycetes and mycorrhizal fungi in vermicompost and vermiwash, which showed antifungal activity against soil borne pathogens.

Sreenivasa and Naik (2011) exhibited the presence of beneficial micro-organisms in panchgavya and beejamrutha, which has been reported to improve seed germination, seedling length and vigour in wheat and soybean. There are numerous reports on the effectiveness of cow milk, cow urine and cow dung in the management of viral diseases of ornamental and other plants (Joseph and Sankarganesh 2011). Nakasone *et al.*, (1999) advocated the use of cow dung paint for the control of smoky blight canker of apple and obtained 86.7 per cent healing of wounds Raja and Kurucheve (1999) studied the fungi toxicity of animal dung and urine against *Fusarium oxysporum* f.sp. *lycopersici*, the causal agent of tomato wilt. Sharma and Deshpande (2006) soaked pigeon pea seeds in 10 per cent cow urine, vermiwash, neem leaf extract, biogas slurry, cow dung slurry, homa farming ash and cow dung slurry (10%) + homa farming ash (10%) for 6 h. All the treatments significantly enhanced seed germination, shoot length, root length and vigour index. Fruit yield of guava was found maximum (38.8 kg/tree) in homa atmosphere followed by 29.2 kg with homa + Rishi Krishi and homa + panchgavya (Mohan 2008). Amendment of cow dung compost in soil minimized more than 50 per cent growth of *Fusarium, Sclerotinia* and *Phytophthora* and 26 per cent growth reduction was observed in *Rhizoctonia solani* (Rakesh *et al.*, 2013). Cow's urine is an important constituent of Panchgavya and is used in several Panchgavya formulations (Okigbo and Nameka, 2005). Cow's Urine based Nigerian herbal formulation were prepared with the use of several herbs like tobacco, garlic, lemon juice, basic and bulbs of onion. These herbal formulations have been described for the use in medicinal and agricultural applications. (Fulzele *et al.*, 2001). The cow is a mobile medical dispensary and capable for treating many curable as well as incurable diseases. It has been used extensible in ayurvedic preparation since time in memorial as cited in ancient holy texts like Charaksainhita, sushruta, Atharva Veda and Bhava Prakash (Pathak *et al.*, 2003). The biochemical estimation of cow urine has shown that it contains sodium, nitrogen, sulphur, vitamin A, B, C, D, E, minerals and salts (Jain *et al.*, 2010). Cow urine contains all these substances having a balance proximate composition. Cow urine boosted the annual rye grass yield due to increase of nitrogen component in soil and marked depression in N fixation by 10% annually particularly in winter (Saunders, 1982). The inhibitory effect of cow urine extract with four plants namely *Anacardium occidentale* L., *Pimenta dioice, Alpinia galansii* and *Anisomels indica were tested* against *C. capsici* isolated from anthracnose of chilli by Poison food technique. All the extracts have inhibitory properties against the test fungus but in a varied extent (Prashith Kekuda, 2014). Cow urine has been possesses antimicrobial activity against *C. capsici* (Kambar *et al.*, 2013). Prabhu (2009) prepared panchgavya by using the

Table 2.2a: Effect of Plant Extracts with Cow Urine, Acetone and Distilled Water on Percent Disease Control of *Colletotrichum leaf spot of turmeric* at 45, 60, 90 and 120 Days After Planting

Treat-ments	Neem extract conc.				Onion extract conc.				Garlic extract conc.			
	60 DAS	75 DAS	90 DAS	120 DAS	60 DAS	75 DAS	90 DAS	120 DAS	60 DAS	75 DAS	90 DAS	120 DAS
Cow urine	37.84 (37.96)	38.87 (36.82)	24.06 (29.20)	36.95 (37.34)	42.27 (40.67)	31.82 (35.81)	18.96 (26.68)	32.61 (35.04)	35.01 (36.24)	33.97 (35.64)	22.62 (28.39)	33.20 (35.13)
Acetone	33.79 (40.74)	33.76 (38.63)	21.17 (27.25)	35.19 (36.15)	40.77 (39.55)	29.67 (32.85)	20.17 (26.45)	32.33 (34.53)	45.09 (42.12)	36.50 (37.00)	14.67 (22.45)	28.79 (32.45)
Distilled water	42.44 (35.50)	35.88 (35.31)	23.08 (28.49)	34.20 (35.73)	33.90 (35.69)	34.19 (34.30)	20.22 (25.61)	33.14 (29.97)	33.01 (34.76)	26.43 (30.97)	13.60 (21.46)	23.04 (28.64)
Control	0.00 (0.00)	0.00 (0.00)	0.00 (0.00)	0.00 (0.00)	0.00 (0.00)	0.00 (0.00)	0.00 (0.00)	0.00 (0.00)	0.00 (0.00)	0.00 (0.00)	0.00 (0.00)	0.00 (0.00)
SEm±	1.657	2.163	2.188	1.820	2.432	2.175	1.948	1.265	1.972	3.040	1.268	0.847
CD (p=0.05)	5.733	7.487	7.572	6.299	8.416	7.526	6.740	4.377	6.824	10.519	4.387	2.931

Table 2.2b: Effect of Plant Extracts with Cow Urine, Acetone and Distilled Water for Percent Disease Control of *Colletotrichum leaf spot of turmeric* at 45, 60, 90 and 120 Days After Planting

Treatments	Madar extract conc.				Datura extract conc.				Botanical-formulation			
	60 DAS	75 DAS	90 DAS	120 DAS	60 DAS	75 DAS	90 DAS	120 DAS	60 DAS	75 DAS	90 DAS	120 DAS
Cow urine	46.09 (38.84)	27.79 (34.31)	15.90 (23.48)	22.27 (28.70)	46.26 (42.91)	30.90 (36.96)	17.67 (24.82)	26.53 (33.35)	57.45 (48.79)	62.96 (52.40)	44.04 (42.44)	36.63 (38.25)
Acetone	38.17 (42.60)	29.36 (32.76)	22.58 (27.75)	30.10 (33.28)	44.43 (41.75)	28.99 (32.58)	14.95 (22.36)	19.35 (25.71)	56.62 (47.23)	58.94 (50.150	37.22 (41.54)	36.55 (37.19)
Distilled water	39.72 (38.26)	31.73 (31.83)	16.65 (24.05)	23.49 (27.94)	41.21 (39.65)	36.16 (33.81)	16.68 (24.01)	30.41 (30.91)	54.18 (49.27)	58.04 (49.60)	45.61 (37.63)	38.35 (37.16)
Control	0.00 (0.00)	0.00 (0.00)	0.00 (0.00)	0.00 (0.00)	0.00 (0.00)	0.00 (0.00)	0.00 (0.00)	0.00 (0.00)	0.00 (0.00)	0.00 (0.00)	0.00 (0.00)	0.00 (0.00)
SEm±	3.199	1.222	2.531	1.760	2.209	1.469	1.703	1.873	1.641	0.849	2.384	1.735
CD (p=0.05)	11.071	4.230	8.760	6.092	7.644	5.085	5.895	6.480	5.680	2.939	8.250	6.005

ingredients viz. cow dung (5 kg), cow urine (3 liter), cow milk (2 liter), cow curd (2 liter), cow ghee (1 liter), sugarcane juice (3 liter), tender coconut water (3 liter) and ripened banana (12 NO_3). All the above substrates were added to a wide mouthed mud pot and kept open under shade. The content was stirred twice a day for about 20 minutes both in morning and evening to facilitate aerobic microbial activity.

REFERENCES

Ali M.N (2011) Sustainable Agriculture with Low Cost Technologies (SALoCT). School of Agriculture and Rural Development, Ramakrishna Mission Vivekananda University, Belur Math, West Bengal pp. 47.

Anonymous (2012). All India Co-ordinate Research Project on Spices, Annual Report. 2012.

Ashlesha and Sugha S.K. (2008) *In vitro* Antifungal Bio-efficacy of Microbes Present in Panchgavya against Major Soil Borne Pathogens. *Plant Disease Research,* 23(1):68-74.

Bansal, R.D., Khatri, H.L. and Sharma, O.P. (1985). Growth, Sporulation and Spore Mermination of *Colletotrichum capsici* as Influenced by Tobacco Mosaic Virus in *Capsicum annuum* L. *Phytopath.* 113: 36-42.

Bansal, RD., Khatri, H.L. and Sharma, O.P. (1978). Interaction between Tobacco Mosaic Virus and *Collerotrichun capsici* in *Capsicum annuum* L. *Phytopathol.* 17: 210-21.

Chandler, W.A. (1958). Control of Bacterial Spot and Ripe Rot of Pimineto Pepper PI Dis Reptr. 42: 652455.

Chandler, W.A. and Dempsey, A.N. (1963). Disinfectant Treatments for Freshly Harvested Pepper Seed. *PI Dis. Report.* 47: 325-327.

Charest M.H, Beauchamp C.J and Antoun H(2005) Effects of the Humic Substances of Deinking Paper Sludge on the Antagonism between Two Compost Bacteria and *Pythiumultimum. FEMS Microbiology Ecology* 52(3):219-227.

Chung Y.R., Kim C.H., Hwang I and Chun J (2000) *Paenibacilluskoreensis* sp. *nov.*, A New Species that Produces an Iturin like Antifungal Compound. *International Journal of Systematic and Evolutionary Microbiology,* 50(3): 1495-1500.

Crover, R.K. and Bansal, R.D. (1970). Seed-borne Nature of Colletotrichum Capsici in Chilli Seeds and Its Control by Seed Dressing Fungicides. *Indian Phytopath.* 23: 664-668.

Czaczyk K., Trojanowska K and Stachowiak B(2011) Antifungal Activity of *Bacillus* sp. Isolated from Compost. *Folia Microbiology,* 45(3):552.

Das, K; Tiwari,R.K.S. and Srivastava, D.K. (2010) Techniques of Evaluation of Medicinal Plant Products as Anti-microbial Agent: Current Methods and Future Trends. J. Medicinal Pl. Res. 4,104-111.

Dickson, B.T. (1925). Colletotrichum v Vrrmicularia. Mycologia. 17: 213-21 7.

Dixit D, Srivastava NK, Kumar R, Sharma S (2002). Cultivar Variation in Yield, Metabolism Translocation and Partitioning of 14 CO_2 Assimilated Photosynthate into Essential Oil and Curcurmin of Turmeric (*Curcuma longa* L.). *J Plant Biol* 29: 65-70. 4.

Durairaj, V. (1956). Growth of *Colletotrichum capsici* in pure culture. *J Indian Bio. Sci.* 35: 409413.

Fulzele, S.V., Satturwar, P.M. and Dorle, A.K. (2001). Immunostimulant Activity of Cow's Urine. *Journal of Immunology* and *Pathology.* 3(2): 87-88.

Gomathi, V. (2001). Studies on the Antifungal Effects of Plant Extracts on *Collerotrichum* spp. Infecting *Capsicum annum* L. Ph.D. Thesis, Department of Biological Sciences, Pondicherry University, Pondicheny, India, 158.

Gorawar, M.M., Hedge, Y.R. and Kulkarni, S. (2006) Biology and Management of Spot of Turmeric Caused by *Colletotrichum capsici, Journal of Plant Disease Science;* 1(2): 156-158.

Grewal, A.S., and Grover, R.K. (1974). Changes in the Amino Acids, Carbohydrates and Capsaicin Content of Red Fruits of Chilies Infected with *Colletotrichum piperanum. Indian Phytopath.* 27: 603404.

Henig-Severa N, Eshelb A, and Neemana G (2000) Regulation of The Germination of Aleppo Pine (*Pinushalepensis*) by Nitrate, Ammonium and Gibberellin, and Its Role in Post-fire Forest Regeneration. *Physiologiaplantarum.* 108:390-397.

Jagtap, G.P. (2012). Control of *Colletotrichum trancatum* Causing Anthracnose/pod Blight of Soybean by Aqueous Leaf Extracts, Bio-control Agents and Fungicides. *Scientific Journal of Agriculture.* 1(2) 39-52.

Jagtap, G.P., Mali, A.K. and Utpal D. (2013). Bio Efficacy of Fungicides, Bio-control Agents and Botanicals against Leaf Spot of Turmeric Incited by *Colletotrichum capsici. African Journal of Microbiology Research;* Vol. 7(18): 1865-1873.

Jain, N.K., Gupta V.B., Garg R. and Silawat (2010) N. Efficacy of Cow Urine Therapy on Various Cancer Patients in Mandsaur District, India—A survey. *Int J Green Pharm;* 4: 29-35.

Jeumkya, H. and Byungkook, H. (1998). Influence of Inoculum Density, Wetness Duration, Plant Age and Inoculation Method and Cultivar Resistance on Infection of Pepper Plants by *Colletotrichum capsici. Plant Dis.* 82: 1079-1083. 012.

Joseph B and Sankarganesh P (2011) Antifungal Efficacy of Panchagavya. *International Journal of Pharm Tech Research,* 3:585-588.

Joshi, L.K. and Sharma, N.D. (1980). Diseases of Ginger and Turmeric, Proceedings of the National Seminar on Ginger and Turmeric held at Calicut. April 8-9, pp 104-109.

Kallupurackal, J.A. and Ravindran, P.N. (2002). Turmeric: Hints for Cultivation. *Spice India* 15: 6-1 1.

Kambar, Y., Vivek, M. N., Manas, M., Kekuda, P.T.R., Nawaz, N.A.S. (2013). Inhibitory Effect of Cow Urine against *Colletotrichum capsici* Isolated from Anthracnose of Chili (*Capsicum annum* L.). *Science Technology and Arts Research Journal.* 2(4): Article in Press.

Kar, A.K. and Mahapatra, H.S. (1981). New Host Records of Colierotrichum Species from India. *Indian Phytopath.* 34: 219-221.

Karnataka J. Agric. Sci., 22(1):231-232.

Khaing N.S., Khai A.A., Aye K.S. and Khaing O.Z. (2008) Maintenance of Beneficial Microbes in Vermiwash Carrier System and Its Application in Crop. *GMSARN International,* 14(3):12-16.

Manandhar, J.B., Hadman, C.L. and Wang, T.C. (1995a). Conidial Germination and Appressorial Formation of *Colletorrichum capsici* and *Colletotrichum gloeosporioides* Isolates from Pepper. *Plant Dis.* 79: 361-366.

Manandhar, J.B., Hadman, C.L. and Wang, T.C. (1995b). Semiselective Medium for Colletotrichum Gloeosporioides and Occurrence of Three Colletotrichum spp. on Pepper Plants. *Plant Dis.* 79: 376-379.

Mathivanan R., Edwin, S.C.,Viswanathan K., and Chandrasekaran D. (2006) Chemical Microbial Composition and Anti-bacterial Activity of Modified Panchagavya. *International Journal of Cow Science,* 2(2): (retrieved 12.02.10 from *Indian Journals.com*).

Mishra R.S., Ramveer and Pandey V.P. (2015) Antifungal Effect of Cow Urine Extracts against *Colletptrichumcapsici* Causing Leaf Spot Disease of Turmeric, *African Journal of Biotechnology,* 14(20):XXX.

Mishra, R.S. and Pandey, V.P. (2014). Management of Leaf Spot of Turmeric caused by *Colletotrichum capsici* through Fungicides. "National Symposium on Plant Pathology in Genomic Era and 66th Annual Meeting of IPS". 26th to 28th May 2014 Raipur pp. 22.

Misra, A.P. and Dutta, K.K. (1963). Studies in Anthracnose Fungi, 111. A Comparative Study of Two Isolates of *Colletotrichum capsici* (Syd.) Butler and Risby. *J Indian Bio Sci.* 42: 74-84.

Misra, A.P. and Mahmood, M. (1960a). Factors Affecting the Growth of *Collerotrichum capsici. Indian Phytopath.* 13: 12-1 7.

Misra, A.P. and Mahmood, M. (1960b). Effects of Carbon and Nitrogen Nutrition on Growth and Sporulation of *Colletorrichum capsici* (Syd.) Butler and Bisby. *J Indian Bio Sci* 39: 314-321.

Muhammad S. and Amusa N.A. (2003) *In vitro* Inhibition of Growth of Some Seedling Blight Inducing Pathogens by Compost Inhibiting Microbes. *African Journal of Biotechnology,* 2(6):161-164.

Muruganandam, V., Suryanarayanan, R.S. and Venkataehalam, S. (1987). Formation of Infection Structure of *Colletotrichum capsici* as Influenced by Nitrogen Sources. *Curr Sci.* 13: 674475.

Naidu, P.H. (1988). Spices Newsl. Spices Board, Cochin, June pp. 10-13.

Naik N, and Sreenivasa M.N (2009) Influence of Bacteria Isolated from Nakasone A.K., Bettiole W, and Souze R.M.D. (1999) The Effect of Water Extracts of Organic Matter on Plant Pathogens. *Summa Phytopathologica,* 25:330-35.

Narain, A. and Das, D.C. (1970). Toxin Production during Pathogenesis of *Colletotrichum capsici* Causing Anthracnose of Chili. *Indian Phytopath.* 23: 484-490.

Narain, A. and Panigrahi, C. (1971). Efficacy of Some Fungicidal Compounds to Control *Colletotrichum capsici in vitro* and *in vivo. Indian Phytopath* 24: 593- 596.

Narasimha Rao, S., Ravindra, K.K. and Anandraj, M. (2012). Management of Leaf Spot of Turmeric (*Curcuma longa* L.) Incited by *Colletotrichum capsici* Through Fungicides. *Journal of Spices and Aromatic Crops.* Vol. 21(2):151-154.

Narasimhudu, Y., and Balasubramanian, K.A. (2001b). Laboratory Evaluation of Fungicides against *Colletotrichum capsici* causing Leaf Spot of Turmeric. *Pesrology.* 25: 31-32.

Narasimhudu, Y. and Balasubramanian, K.A. (2001a). Effect of Fungicides on Growth and Vigour of Turmeric. *Pesrology.* 25: 20-21.

Natarajan K. (2002). Panchagavya : A manual, Other India Press, Mapusa, Goa, India, pp. 33.

Nene, Y.L. and Thaplial, P.N. (1993). Evaluation of Fungicides in ; Fungicides in Plant Disease Control (2011 new ed.) *Oxford, IBM Publishing Co.,* New Delhi, 331 pp.

Okigbo, R.N. and Nameka, I.A. (2005). Control of Yam Tuber with Leaf Extracts of *Xylopia aethiopica* and *Zingiber officinale. Afr. J. Biotechnol.* 4(8): 804-807.

Palarpawar, M.Y. and Ghrude, V.R. (1989). Saprophytic Colonization of Leaf Sheath of Turmeric by *Colletotrichum capsici* and *Colletotrichum curcumae. Indian J of Mycol. PI Patho* 19: 202-203.

Palarpawar, M.Y. and Ghrude, V.R. (1997). Influence of Different Nitrogen Sources on Growth and Sporulation of *Colletotrichum capsici* and (*Colletotrichum curcumae*) *J. of Mycol. and PI. Pathol.* 27: 227-228.

Panchagavya on Seed Germination and Seed Vigour in Wheat.

Papen H., Gabler A., Zumbusch E. and Rennenberg, H. (2002). Chemo Litho Autotrophic Nitrifiers in the Phyllosphere of a Spruce Ecosystem Receiving High Nitrogen Input. *Curr. Microbiol,* 44:56-60.

Pathak, M.I. and Kumar, A. (2003). Go-mutra Destructive Study. *Sachitra Ayurveda*. 7: 81-84.

Pinto S.S., Mann M.B., Campos F.S., Franco A.C., Germani J.C. and Van Der SST (2010). Preliminary Characterization of Some *Streptomyces* Species Isolated from a Composting Process and their Anti-microbial Potential. *World Journal of Microbiology and Biotechnology*, 26(10):1847-1856.

Prashith Kekuda, T.R., Vivek, M.N., Manasa, N., Kambar, Y., Noornawaz, A.S. and Raghvendra, H.L. (2014). Antifungal Effect of Cow Urine Extracts of Selected Plants against *Collrtotrichum capsici* Isolated from Anthracnose of chili. *International Journal of Scinces*. 7 (3):142-143.

Pring, R.J., Nash, C., Zakaria, M. and Bailey, J.A. (1995). Infection Process and Host Range of *Colletotrichum capsici*. *Physiol. Mol PI Parhol*. 46: 137-152.

Pruthi, J.S. (1998). Major Spices of India Crop Management, Post-harvest Technology. Publ. Publication and Information Div., ICAR, New Delhi.

Raja J. and Kurucheve V. (1999) Fungicidal Activity of Buffalo (*Babulusbubalis*) Urine: A New Record. *Madras Agricultural Journal* 86(10/12):614-616.

Rakesh K.N., Dileep N., Syed Junaid, Prashith Kekuda T.R., Vinayaka K.S. and Noor Nawaz A.S. (2013) Inhibitory Effect of Cow Urine Extracts of Selected Plants against Pathogens Causing Rhizome Rot of Ginger. *Science, Technology and Arts Research Journal*, 2(2): 92-96.

Ramakrishnan, T.S. (1954). Leaf Spot Disease of Turmeric (Curcumu ir~ngu L) caused by *Colletotrichum capsici* (Syd.) Butler and Bisby. *Indran Phytopath*. 7: 111-117.

Rangaswami, G. and Mahadevan, A (2001). Diseases of Crop Plants of India. IV Edition, (Eds.) Prentice Hall of India (P.) Ltd., New Delhi, pp. 453-455.

Roberts, R.G. and Snow, J.P. (1990). Morphological and Pathological Studies of *Colletotrichum capsici* and *C. indicum*. *Mycologia*. 82: 82-90.

Ross, I.A. (1999). Medicinal Plants of the World. Chemical Constituents, Traditional and Modern Medicinal Uses. Humana Press.

Sahni, S.S., Chabal, D.S. and Nirmaljit Singh. (1974). *In-vitro* Production of Toxic Metabolite by Different Species of Colletotrichum. *Indian J Mycol. PI Parhol*. 4: 222-223.

Sangeetha V., Thevanathan R. (2010a) Effect of TMV Strains in a Local Lesion Host. Journal of Panchagavya on Nitrate Assimilation by Experimental Ecobiol, 31:28-131. Plants, *The Journal of American Science*, 6: 80-86.

Sanjutha S., Subramanian S., Rani I. and Maheswari (2008) Integrated Nutrient Management in *Andrographispaniculata*. *Research Journal of Agriculture and Biological Sciences*, 4(2):141-145.

Saunders, W.H.M. (1982). Effect of Cow Urine and Its Major Constituents on Pasture Properties. *NZ J. Agricul. Res*. 25 (1): 61-68.

Shailaja B, Mishra Ipsita, Gampala Srihima, Singh Vikram Jeet and Swathi K. (2014) Panchagavya—An Eco-friendly Insecticide and Organic Growth Promoter of Plants. *International Journal of Advanced Research*, 2:(11) 22-26.

Shalika (2009) Non-Chemical Management of Stalk Rot of Cauliflower caused by *Sclerotiniasclerotiorum* (Lib.) de Bary. M Sc Thesis, Department of Plant Pathology, CSK Himachal Pradesh Krishi Vishvavidyalaya, Palampur, India, p. 48.

Sharma A. and Deshpande V.K. (2006). Effect of Pre-soaking of Pigeon Pea Seeds with Organics on Seed Quality. *Karnataka Journal of Agricultural Sciences*, 19:396-399.

Sinha R.K., Valani D., Chauhan K. and Agarwal S. (2010). Embarking on a Second Green Revolution for Sustainable Agriculture by Vermin Culture Biotechnology using

Earthworms: Reviving the Dreams of Sir Charles Darwin. *Journal of Agricultural Biotechnology and Sustainable Development*, 2:113-128.

Somasundaram, E and Amanullah M.M. (2007) Panchagavya on Growth and Productivity of Crops: *A review. Green Farming*, 1:22-26.

Sreenivasa M.N. and Naik N. (2011). Impact of Bacteria Isolated from Organic Liquidmanures on Seed Germination and Seedling Vigour Index of Wheat and Soybean. *Organic Farming Newsletter*, 7:3-5.

Srimathi P., Mariappan N., Sundaramoorthy, L. and Paramathma, M. (2013).

Swaminathan C., Swaminathan V. and Vijay Lakshmi K. (2007). Panchgavya Boon Toorganic Farming. *International Book Distributing Co. Lucknow*, P. 332.

Sydow, H. (1913). Beitrage Zur Kenntnis der Pilzflora des sudlichen Osrindiens I *Ann Mycol.* 11: 329-330.

Thamburaj, S. (1991). Research on Spice Crops at TNGDNAU. *Spice India*. 4: 17-21.

Tharmaraj K., Ganesh P., Suresh Kumar R., Anandan A. and Kolanjinathan K. (2011)"A Critical Review on Panchagavya—A Boon Plant Growth," *International Journal of Pharmaceutical and Biological Archive*, 2(6):1611–1614.

Vasumathi, R. (2001). Influence of Organic Manures, Bio-fertilizers and Plant Density on Growth, Yield and Alkaloid Content of Bhumyamalaki (*Phyllanthusamarus* Schum and Thonn.) M.Sc., (Hort.) Thesis TNAU, Coimbatore-3. India.

Vikas and Ratnoo, R.S. (2011). Evalution of Fungicides and Phytoextract against Powdery Mildew (*Erysiphe polygoni* de.) of Fenugreek. Journal of Plant Disease Scinces. Vol. 6 Issue 1, pp. 71-73.

Watve, Y.G., Diwakar, M.P., Sawant, U.K. and Kadam, J.J. (2009). Studies on Effect of Different Fungicides and Phyto-extract on *Colletotrichum gloesporiodes* Penz. Causing Leaf Spot of Jatropha. *J. Pt. Dis. Sci.* 4(1): 95-98.

Xu H.L. (2001) Effects of a Microbial Inoculants and Organic Fertilizers on the Growth, Photosynthesis and Yield Attributes and Economics of Rice (*Oryzasativa*). *Crop Res.*, 31:1-5.

Plant Biotechnology and Industrial Applications
Edited by: Alka Chauhan and Pawan Kumar 'Bharti'
ISBN: 978-93-5056-884-2
Edition: 2017
Published by: Discovery Publishing House Pvt. Ltd., New Delhi (India)

3

Microbial Aspects of Fungal Volatile Organic Compounds
A Brief Account

[1]Pooja Pathania

ABSTRACT

Volatile organic compounds (VOCs), are carbon based compounds that easily diffuse in atmosphere due to its small size. Along with carbon, they have oxygen, hydrogen, chlorine, sulfur, nitrogen etc. Fungi produces approximately 300 volatile organic compounds, several of which have distinctive odor. Both primary and secondary metabolic pathways are involved in production of these volatiles. VOCs potential is recognized as biofuel, mycofumigation, biocontrol agents and in food industry particularity in fermentation products. One of the unsafeattribute of these volatiles are referred as 'sick building syndrome' in soggy moldy construction. Various sources of volatiles are filamentous fungus, mushrooms, truffles and by fungal endophytes. These all symbolize the huge diversity in these molecules in fungal world and opened a new area of study and new edge in bioprospecting of these molecules and assured the findings, which will be offered for exploitation in various segments.

Key words: Volatile organic compounds; Fungal endophytes; Biofumigation; Biodiesel.

INTRODUCTION

The fungi are distinctive among the living organisms and have become nearly omnipresent in the biosphere. They are important organisms in the world due to their influence on humans and human-related activities as they play important roles in ecosystem functions (Muller and Bills, 2004) like symbiont, decomposer and pathogens.The total numbers of fungi from earth havebeen estimated as 1.5 million species (Hawksworth, 1991), only a fraction of total fungal bio-diversity has been subjected to scientific scrutiny and mycologists continue to unravel the unexplored, hidden and fascinating fungal biodiversity as many macro-fungi are becoming extinct or facing threat of extinction because of habitat destruction and global climate change. (Crous *et al.*, 2006).

[1] ICAR-National Bureau of Plant Genetic Resources, PUSA Campus, New Delhi-110012, India

Most of the fungal species differ considerably in habitat, morphologies, ecologies and life history strategies. Fungi live in close proximity with plants, animals, and bacteria in their ecosystem where inter-organism communication and signaling is crucial. In terrestrial habitats, volatiles provide a way for microbes to communicate with one another, both within and between species. Beneficial behavior of fungi contributing to human welfare is well known. Fermented foods like Miso, Tempeh, cheeses, alcoholic beverages have been known for long and practiced since centuries. Now screening of fungal diversity for bioactive metabolites increased with reliable assay for identification and purification. Fungal Volatiles are produced in low amount and the technology to explore such new compounds increased intensively and industrial application of such novel blends has gained powerful foot hold globally. Brief account of fungal Volatile Organic Compounds (VOCs), have been provided in this chapter. Purpose here is to document biological diversity displayed by VOCs and their role in fungal associations, which have opened a new dimension to fungal world.

VOLATILE ORGANIC COMPOUNDS (VOCs)

Volatile Organic Compounds (VOCs) are a large group of low molecular weight, carbon containing compounds that dissipate effortlessly at normal temperature and pressure in environment (Bennent and Inamdar, 2015). Industrial VOCs are best acknowledged because they are important part of our daily life include air fresheners, paint thinners, dry cleaning fluids, petroleum fuels, adhesives, photographic materialsand automotive products etc. Some VOCs produced by human activities are coupled with contamination of ground water and air pollution (Hodgeson and Levi, 1997), while the exposure to longer duration of elevated concentration of volatiles like xylene, form aldehyde, benzene etc., have detrimental effects on human fitness (McFeeand Zavon, 1988). VOCs are released by plants and microbes are known as biogenic volatiles. The biogenic VOCs include numerous diverse chemicals classes like aromatics,amines, aldehydes, ketones, terpenes, halogenated and sulfur based compounds, oxygenated compounds such as methanol, hexane derivatives, 2-methyl-3-buten-2-ol, isoprene, monoterpenes and sesquiterpenes etc. Plants produced volatile for example, monoterpenes like menthanol, limonene and pinene, etc. are well acknowledged (Atkinson *et al.*, 2000).

FUNGAL VOLATILE ORGANIC COMPOUNDS (VOCs): A BRIEF ACCOUNT

Fungi produce a variety of VOCs, roughly estimate of identified VOCs from fungi was 300, they come about as mixture of simple hydrocarbons, heterocycles, alcohols, aliphatic alcohols thioesters, phenols, ketones, aldehydes and their derivatives and others like cyclohexane, benzene derivatives, nitrogen containing compounds and volatile sulfur compounds (Chiron and Michelot, 2005; Korpi *et al.*, 2009; Ortiz-Castro *et al.*, 2009). Primary and secondary both metabolic pathways produce VOCs in fungus (Korpi *et al.*, 2009) and majority of fungal allied volatiles compounds are unique to fungal metabolism (Chiron and Michelot, 2005; Korpi *et al.*, 2009; Lemfack *et al.*, 2014). Fungi release unusual volatile mixture in laboratory depending upon various physiological conditions like media, nutrients, temperature, moisture, hydrogen ion concentration (pH) and different stages of fungus culturei.e. incubation period (Wilkins and Larsen, 1995; Morath *et al.*, 2012; Bennett *et al.*, 2013). Fungal VOCs attracts the interest of peoples because of their distinctive odors, and associated properties (table 3.1), and indicate the chemical diversity of natural occurring molecules.

Table 3.1: Fungal Volatiles with their Distinctive Odors and Properties

Compounds	Characterstic odor	Properties
1-Octen-3-ol	Earthy, mushroom odor	Semiochemical
1-Butanol-3-, methyl-, acetate	banana odor	Antifungal
Sabinene (Bicyclic monoterpenes)	peppery odor	Antifungal
6-Pentyl-a-pyrone	coconut odor	Antibiotic
b-Caryophyllene	woody-spicy odor	Plant-growth promoting
Isobutyric acid	rancid cheese-like odor	Antifungal
Benzyl aldehyde	almond odor	Anti-microbial
1,8-Cineole	camphor-like odor	Antifungal
2-Methyl-1-propanol	mild alcohol odor	Fungivore attractant
2-Heptanone	cheese odor	Flavoring agent
3-Methyl-butanol	component of truffle odor	Flavoring agent

VOCs from Macroscopic and Microscopic Fungi

Several macro fungi such as mushrooms and truffles have characteristic odor profiles.The appetizing odor of truffles, valued in the cooking andbelieved to have aphrodisiacal properties, consist of over 100 unusual VOCs, of which aromatics, alcohols, aldehydes, and thiols dominate (Splivallo *et al.*, 2007). The most widespread volatile reported from both macroscopic and microscopic fungi, is 1-octen-3-ol, which is also called "mushroom alcohol," or "matsutake alcohol" and first identified from *Tricholomamatsutake* (Wood and Fesler, 1986). Some of the reported characteristic odor of different mushrooms (table 3.2).

Breheret *et al.*, (1997), investigated the odorous volatile organic compounds from fruiting bodies of 82 wild mushrooms. Wide variety of molecules are extracted from them, 37 mushroom show monoterpenes as dominant molecules and 27 different monoterpenes are reported like, camhene, limonene, pinene and linalool etc. Some of the identified monoterpene compounds (table 3.3).

Table 3.2: Different Reported Characteristic Odors/ VOCs from Different Macro Fungus

Characteristic odors/ VOCs	Mushroom/truffle	References
Anise-like odors	*Clitocybeodora, Lentinelluscochleatus,* and *Agaricusessettie*	Rapior *et al.*, 2002
Boiled potato or farm feed odor	*Suillus spp.*	de Pinho *et al.*, 2008
stench of stinkhorns (high concentrations of dimethyl oligosulphides)	*Phallus spp.*	Borg-Karlson *et al.*, 1994
organosulfur "alliaceous" compounds	*Lentinula edodes, Tricholoma spp.* and *Marasmius spp.*	Bloch and Deorazio, 1994; Sneeden *et al.*, 2004
Sulfur-containing volatiles	Truffles	Mauriello *et al.*, 2004
1-octen-3-ol (mushroom alcohol, or matsutake alcohol)	*Tricholomamatsutake*	Wood and Fesler, 1986
1-octen-3-ol(mushroom alcohol)	*Volvariellavolvacea*	Mau *et al.*, 1997
Indole and 1-octen-3-ol (Coal tar odor)	*Tricholomainamoenum*	Wood *et al.*, 2004
Almondy odor (Benzaldehyde and benzyl alcohol)		Wood and Largent, 1999

Table 3.3: Monoterpene Profile of Various Mushrooms

Monoterpene Molecules	Sensory assessment	Mushroom spp.
α- pinene	Resinous, piney	*G.glutinosus, A. citrina, A. phalliodes, T. caligatum, A. ovoidea, B. aestivalis, M. rosea, C.cibarius, S. lutenus, T. portentosum, M. pura, H. agathosmus, T. sulfureum, C. cinnamomeus, C. amianthinum, C. carcharias*
β- pinene	Resinous, piney	*G. glutinosus, A. ovoidea, T. caligatum, S. lutenus, M. pura*
Sabinene	Woody, herbaceous	*G. glutinosus, A. ovoidea*
Trans-sabinene hydrate	Citrusy-lemon	*A. avoidea, C. carcharias, C.odora*
Cis- sabinene hydrate	Citrusy-lemon	*A. avoidea*
Myrcene	Sweet, balsamic, resinous	*G. glutinosus, A. ovoidea, C. carcharias, M. rosea*
p-cymene	Gassy, kerosene like	*B. lupinus, M. rosea, A. avoidea, T. caligatum*
Limonene	Sweet citrusy	*G. glutinosus, A. citrina, A. phalliodes, B. erythropus, A. spissa, P. betulinus, A. proxima, H. aurantiaca, C. odora, S. grevillei*

Linalool	Refreshing, floral	*G. glutinosus, A. aegerita, C. odora, L. nuda, L. salmonicolor, T. sulfureum*
Cis-linalool oxide (furanoid)	Sweet, woody	*L. nuda, C. nebularis, T. saponaceum*
Trans-linalool oxide furanoid)	Sweet, woody	*L. nuda, C.odora, C. nebularis*
Piperitol	Fresh, pungent	*A. ovoidea*
α-phellandrene	Fresh , Citrusy	*A. ovoidea*
β-phellandrene	Peppery, minty	*A. ovoidea, T.caligatum, C.cinnamomeus G. glutinosus, H. agathosmus, S. luteus, M. pura, T. portentosum*
γ-terpinene	Herbaceous, citrusy	*A. ovoidea*

Similarly, microscopic fungi release composite mixture of VOC. Nearly everyone are aware of musty smell in damp buildings and other closed indoor places particularly during rainy season. "Sick building syndrome" is regarded as the harmful affect these VOCs on human health and is a major concern for peoples leaving in these buildings. The odor profile of strains depend on area and various environmental factors, and even how a discrepancy among species (Pasanen *et al.*, 1997; Nilsson *et al.*, 2004; Fiedler *et al.*, 2005). *Penicillium*and *Aspergillus*species, release higher the concentration of VOCs after sporulation (Borjesson *et al.*, 1993).

VOCs from Endophytic Fungi

Ability of fungal endophytes to synthesize valuable plant metabolites is well recognized (Tan and Zou, 2001) but their potential as a source of VOCs is quite recent and gained the attention of scientific world. VOCs help to arbitrate interaction between fungi and other organisms like plants in the case of endophytes.Fungal endophytes produce a mixture of VOCs which include various esters, ketones , acids, alcohols and lipids with synergetic activities against pathogenic fungi and bacteria (Mitchell *et al.*, 2010) and potential ranging as biocontrol agents, commodity chemical and biofuels (Strobel and Daisy, 2003; Griffin *et al.*, 2010; Spakowicz and Strobel, 2015). Rundell *et al.*, (2015) reported less than 3% of endophytes are described for their potential of production VOCs, but still they are approximately 140 out of which 126 are well identified up to molecular formula. These VOCs covered about 70 promising mono- and sesquiterpenoids, along with alkenes, alcohols, and acids. Monoterpenoids are exclusively produced by the *Phomopsis/ Diaporthe*genus (Singh *et al.*, 2011). Endophytic fungi produce compounds like monoterpenoids has fascinated picky interest because of the prospective utility as biofuel additives (Morath *et al.*, 2012; Rude and Schirmer, 2009).

*Muscodoralbus*is an endophyte have remarkable ability to produce VOCs exhibiting broad spectrum of bio-activity bacteria and pathofenic fungi (Strobel *et al.*, 2001), are extensively used in agriculture and allied sectors. *Gliocladium*, an endophytic sp. isolated from *Eucryphila*produce one interesting unstable and flammable compound 1,3,5,7 cyclooctatetraene or annulene, used as rocket propellant in World War II (Stinson *et al.*, 2003). Some of the volatile producinf endophytic fungi are as follows:

Table 3.4: Some of the Volatile Producing Endophytic Fungi and their Host

Filamentous fungi	Host	References
Muscodoralbus	*Cinnamomumzeylanicum*	Worapong *et al.*, 2001
M. kashayum	*Aegle marmelos*	Meshram *et al.*, 2013
M. crispans	*Ananasananassoides*	Mitchell *et al.*, 2008
M. roseus	*Grevillea pteridifolia*	Lee *et al.*, 2009
M. oryzae	*Oryzarufipogon*	Ezra and Strobel, 2003
M. musae	*Musa acuminata*	Ezra and Strobel, 2003
M. strobelii	*C. zeylanicum*	Meshram *et al.*, 2013
M. darjeelingensis	*C. camphora*	Saxena *et al.*, 2014a
M. tigerii	*C. camphora*	Saxena *et al.*, 2014b
M. suthepensis	*C. bejolghota*	Ezra and Strobel, 2003
M. yucatanensis	*Burserasimaruba*	Gonzalez *et al.*, 2009
M. vitigenus	*Paulliniapaullinioides*	Daisy *et al.*, 2002
M. equiseti	*Equisetum debile*	Ezra and Strobel, 2003
M. sutura	*Prestoniatrifidi*	Kudalkar *et al.*, 2012
M. fengyangensis	*Actinidiachinensis*	Zhang *et al.*, 2010
Hypoxylon sp.	*Perseaindica*	Tomsheck *et al.*, 2010
Myrothecium inunduatum	*Acalyphaindica*	Banerjee *et al.*, 2010
Gliocladium sp.	*Eucryphiacordifolia*	Stinson *et al.*, 2003
Bionectriaochroleuca	*Nothapodytesfoetida*	Samaga *et al.*, 2014
Phomopsis sp.	*Odontoglossum sp.*	Singh *et al.*, 2011
Phoma sp.	*Larrea tridentate*	Strobel *et al.*, 2011
Gloeosporium sp.	*Tsugaheterophylla*	Schaible *et al.*, 2015
Oxyporuslatemarginatus	*Capsicum annum*	Mercier *et al.*, 2010

FUNCTIONAL ROLES

Fungal Volatile Organic Compounds (VOCs) perform wide range of functional roles having both practical and scientific significance. They have been well known for their flavor properties, role in bio-signaling, as bio-control agents and semiochemicals, my cofumigation and as biodiesel potential source. Plethora of endophytic fungi also produces VOCs having complex and dynamic profile with promising application in agriculture and industrial sector. This has opened a new frontier of bioprospecting of volatileorganic compound from various fungal sources.

Flavors in Food Industry

Fungi are exploited to produce a variety of "natural aromas" by commercial bioconversion of substrate for making flavor products (Berger *et al.*, 1992; Schreier 1992). Food fermentation involving filamentous fungi are best known in cheese industry. White cheeses like Camembert, Brie and Blue cheeses such as Roquefort, Stilon and Gorgonzloa gain their typical flavor and aroma from various alcohols released by fungi like *Penicillium* (Karahadian *et al.*, 1985; Gallois and Langlois 1990). Yeast fermentation associated volatiles associated with flavor of alcoholic beverages (wines, beers etc.) have unique aroma (Meilgaard, 1975a,b; Robinson, 2006).

Biocontrol Agents and Semiochemicals

Fungal volatiles are used in agriculture sector, as a part of biological control tool against plant pathogens. Fungal VOCs give benefit to host plant to hammer the growth of neighboring flora like the VOCs emitted by *M. yucatanensis* are repressed the seed of tomato, amaranth and barnyard grass from germination (Macias-Rubalcava *et al.*, 2010). Volatiles released by *Trichoderma atroviride*, amplify the gene expression of *Pseudomonas fluorescens*, required for its biocontrol potential (Lutz *et al.*, 2004). Fungal VOCs released by soil inhibiting fungi benefit plant by activating the defense mechanism against pathogen attacks (Ryu *et al.*, 2003). Kishimoto *et al.*, (2007) reported the up regulation of defense genes in Arabidopsis thaliana when subjected to 1-octen-3-ol, a fungal VOC. *Muscodoralbus* and *M. roseus* were used in controlling plant pathogenic fungi, nematodes and poatao tuber moth (*Phthorimaeaoperculalla*), a serious pest of stored potatoes. Insecticidal activity is also reported by fungal VOCs, *Muscodor sp.*, have been revealed lethal potential against insects (Strobel *et al.*, 2010). Similarly naphthalene like compounds from *Muscodorvitigenus* has been reported as effective insect repellent (Daisy *et al.*, 2002). Mixture of VOCs produced by *Muscodorcrispans* inhibit the growth of fungus *Mycosphaerellafijiensis* causal organisms of black sigatoka of banana and *Xanthomonasaxonopodis* pv. *citri*the severe bacterial pathogen of citrus (Mitchell *et al.*, 2010).

Chemicals engaged in chemical communication between organisms are Semiochemicals or infochemicals (Nordlund and Lewis, 1976). Different studies have elucidated the role of fungal VOCs as semiochemicals that utilized as attractants and deterrents to insects and other invertebrates. Fungal VOCs are used as signaling molecules by organisms within species, between different species and transversely across kingdoms, Entomologist also recognize the potential of fungal VOCs as allomones, kariomones and pheromones etc.

(Rohlfs *et al.*, 2005; Mburu *et al.*, 2011). Fungal volatiles also provide the location related cues to in fungivorous arthropods regarding host assortment (Hedlund *et al.*, 1995). Wood rotting white fungus, *Trametesgibbosa* release 1-octen-3-ol attractant for fungus-eating beetles (Coleoptera) (Thakeow *et al.*, 2008). In behavioral studies, white rot fungi, *Trametes versicolor* released sesquiterpenes like b-guaiene, isoledene, d-cadinene and g-patchoulene, attract fungivorous beetles (Drilling and Dettner, 2009). Fungi also attract pollinators for example, by fabricating pseudoflower that imitate actual flowers by releasing volatiles (Ngugi and Scherm, 2006).

Mycofumigation or Biofumigation

Mycofumigation is characterize as the "selective antimicrobial effect against undesirable pathogen". Food industy, mycofumigation is used to check fungal growth after post harvest. Biofumigation of stored seeds is helpful in reducing the disease incidents to a significant level caused by various devastating pathogens. The biofumigation by *Muscodoralbus* (an endophyte) has been reported to control grey and blue molds (*Botryiscinerea*) of apple, brown rot of peaches (*Moniliniafructicola*) green mold (*Penicilliumdigitstum*) and sour rot of lemons (*Geotrichumcandidum*) (Mercier and Smilanick, 2005). In a experiment conducted by Strobel *et al.*, (2001) biofumigation of volatiles of *Muscodoralbus*on barley seeds contaminated with *Ustilagohordei* controlled 100% smut attack. An endophyte, *Oxyporuslatemarginatus* obtained from pepper plants reveled effective mycofumigationabilitiy at postharvest level aginst decay organisms (Lee *et al.*, 2009). Singh *et al.*, (2011) repoted a endophtic*Phomopsissp.* from *Odontoglossumsp.* release a mixture of VOCs (incudingsabinene, monoterpene with peppery odor) inhibit wide range of plant pathogens, like *Pythium, Sclerotinia, Rhizoctonia, Fusarium, Collectotrichum and Botrytis.*VOCs of *Oxyporuslatemarginatus* EF069, an endophyte released by red peppers inhibited the growth of plant pathogen those spoil the fruit after harvest (Mercier and Jimenez, 2007). *Oxyporuslatemarginatus* EF069 also used as fumigant against *B. cinerea* and *Rhizoctonia* root rot of moth orchid cause the decay of apples (Lee *et al.*, 2009). *M. albus* volatiles are also used to manage the growth of building molds and fungi (Mercier and Jimenez, 2007).

Mycodiesel

In recent times, fungal VOCs have been considered for their probable role as fuel resource,commonly referred to as "mycodiesel". Strobel *et al.*, (2008) coined the term "mycodiesel" when he establish that the endophyte *Gliocladiumroseum* formed VOCs are associated with diesel fuel. Fungal endophytes of the genus Phoma (Strobel *et al.*, 2011) and Ascocoryne (Griffin *et al.*, 2010) also produce VOCs having potential as fuel. Bicyclic monoterpenes sabinene, is a monoterpene having peppery odor produced by *Phomopsis* sp. (endophytic fungus) from an orchid in Ecuador is also reported for its fuel potential (Singh *et al.*, 2011). Rude and Shirmer (2009), also investigated numerous interrelated monoterpenes as feasible component of aircraft propellants.

Plant Health Management

Plant-microbes interaction play important role at individual and community level of plant bionetwork (Bever *et al.*, 2010; Inderjit and van der Putten 2010; Porras-Alfaro and Bayman 2011). Microorganisms are closely linked with plants and influence the health of plants by increasing the stress and enhancing the defense mechanisms and modulate nutrient recycling and utilization in their rhizosphere (Buée *et al.*, 2009; Khan *et al.*, 2009; Saunders *et al.*, 2010). Volatile compounds released by microbes are one of the ways to boost the growth and confer health to plants. Numerous plant processes are influenced by fungi associated with them (Porras-Alfaro and Bayman 2011; Saunders *et al.*, 2010). Hung *et al.*, (2013) reported that when *A. thaliana* subjected to VOCs of *T. viride* become taller, had additional lateral roots, have early-flowering and possess more chlorophyll. Several genes under the control of jasmonic acid and ethylene reliant on pathogen or wound defense signaling pathway are enhanced in *A. thaliana* when exposed to fungal VOC 1-octen-3-ol (Kishimoto *et al.*, 2007). Growth and accumulation of starch in leaves of many plants are enhanced when influenced byVOCs from *Alternariaalternata, P. aurantiogriseum*, and *Penicilliumcharlesii* (Ezquer *et al.*, 2010).

Vast diversity of fungi in and around plants plays significant role in plant health management. However, the deep studies are needed to understand the volatiles and pathway involved in enhancement of plant performance. So, these compounds could be utilized commercially to modulate the plant defense system against various pathogens.

SUMMARY

Volatiles symbolize most recent frontier in bioprospecting, and these compounds guarantee the breakthrough of novel products for human utilization (Morath *et al.*, 2012). Fungi VOCs are excellent unexplored hidden chemicals compounds having unlimited potential concealed in them. Available literature just presents the diminutive part of volatiles and their roles in ecological services. Small amount of fungal VOCs make complicated to quantify and identify the compound and pathways involved in their synthesis. So, it is necessary to conduct the multi-disciplinary investigation to reach out the prospective compounds.

Volatiles from bacteria and plants are best studied as compared to fungal VOCs. Due to declining biodiversity, there is likelihood to lose the of unraveled potential of benificial natural products to humans before their effectiveness is realized (Smith *et al.*, 2008). Research on fungal VOCs has paying attention as their role in food and flavor industry, their use in agriculture and role as bioagents against pathogens and semiochemicals for insects. In addition to these; research into fungal volatiles have been conducted to monitor spoilage, for rationale of chemotaxonomy, for make useinbiofilters and for biodiesel, to become aware of plant and animal disease, for "mycofumigation," and with high opinion to plant health. Study of fungal volatiles benefit various scientific disciplines, as the separation, quantification and identification of these volatile compounds improves by "electronic nose" technology and mapping of individual volatile become possible (Schnurer *et al.*, 1999). VOCs from fungal endophytes have many biotechnological potential. Growing fungi in the presence of *M. albus* has been used as a selection tool to isolate other fungi that produce bioactive volatiles. Species resistant to the VOCs produced by *M. albus* are then screened for the activity of their own VOC profile.

REFERENCES

Atkinson, R.; Tuazon, E.D.; Aschmann, S.M. (2000). Atmospheric Chemistry of 2-pentanone and 2-heptanone. *Environ. Sci. Technol.* 34, 623–631.

Banerjee, D.; Strobel, G.A.; Booth, E.; Geary, B.; Sears, J.; Spakowicz, D. (2010). An Endophytic Myrothecium Inundatum Producing Volatile Organic Compounds. *Mycosphere*. 1, 229-240.

Bennet, J.W.; Inamdar, A.A. (2015). Are Some Fungal Volatile Organic Compounds (VOCs) Mycotoxins? *Toxins*.7, 3785-3804.

Bennett, J.W.; Hung, R.; Lee, S.; Padhi, S. (2013). Fungal and Bacterial Volatile Organic Compounds; An Overview and their Role as Ecological Signaling Agents. In *The Mycota IX Fungal Interactions*; Hock, B., Ed.; Springer-Verlag: Berlin/Heidelberg, Germany, 373–393.

Berger R.G.; Drawert, F., Tiefel, P. (1992). Naturally Occurring Flavours from Fungi, Yeasts, and Bacteria. In: Patterson RLS, Charlwood BV, MacLeod G, Williams AA (eds) Bioinformation of Flavours. Royal Chemistry Society, Cambridge, 1–20.

Bever, J. D.; Dickie, I. A.; Facelli, E.; Facelli, J. M.; Klironomos, J.; Moora, M.; Rillig, M. C.; Stock, W. D.; Tibbett, M.; Zobel, M. (2010). Rooting Theories of Plant Community Ecology in Microbial Interactions.*Trends EcolEvol*. 25, 468-478.

Bloch, E.; Deorazio, R. (1994). Chemistry in a Salad Bowl: Comparative Organosulfur Chemistry of Garlic, Onion, and Shitake Mushrooms. *Pure ApplChem*. 66, 2205–2206.

Borg-Karlson, A.; Englund F.; Unelius, C.R. (1994) Dimethyl Oligosulphides, Major Volatiles Released from *Sauromatumguttatum* and *Phallus impudicus*. *Phytochemistry*, 35,321–323.

Borjesson, T.; Stollman, U.M.; Schnurer, J. (1993). Off Odorous Compounds Produced by Molds on Oatmeal Agar: Identification and Relation to Other Growth Characteristics. *J Agric Food Chem*. 41, 2104–2111.

Buée, M.; De Boer, W.; Martin, F.; van Overbeek, L.; Jurkevitch, E. (2009). The Rhizosphere Zoo: An Overview of Plant-associated Communities of Microorganisms, Including Phages, Bacteria, Archaea, and Fungi, and of Some of their Structuring Factors. *Plant Soil*. 321,189-212.

Chiron, N.; Michelot, D. (2005). Mushrooms Odors, Chemistry and Role in the Biotic Interactions—A Review. *Cryptogam Mycol*. 26, 299–364.

Crous, P.W.; Rong, I.H.; Wood, A.; Lee, S.; Glen, H.; Botha, W.; Slippers, B.; de Beer, W.Z.; Wingfield M.J.; Hawksworth D.L. (2006). How Many Species of Fungi are there at the Tip of Africa? *Studies in Mycology*. 55,13–33.

Daisy B.H.; Strobel, G.A.; Castillo, U.; Ezra, D.; Sears, J.; Weaver, D.K.; Runyon, J.B. (2002). Naphthalene, an Repellent, is Produced by *Muscodorvitigenus,* Anoval Endophytic Fungus. *Microbiology.* 148, 3737-3741.

de Pinho, P.G.; Ribeiro, B.; Goncalves, R.F.; Baptista, P.; Valentao, P.; Seabra, R.M.; Andrade, P.B. (2008). Correlation between the Pattern Volatiles and the Overall Aroma of Wild Edible Mushrooms. J *Agric Food Chem.* 56,1704–1712.

Ezra, D.; Strobel, G.A. (2003). Effect of Substrate on the Bioactivity of Volatile Anti-microbials Produced by *Muscodoralbus. Plant Sci.* 165, 1229-1238.

Ezquer, I.; Li, J.; Ovecka, M.; Baroja-Fernandez, E.; Munoz, F. J.; Montero, M.; de Cerio, J. D.; Hidalgo, M.; Sesma, M. T.; Bahaji, A.; Etxeberria, E.; Pozueta-Romero, J. (2010). Microbial Vlatile Emissions Promote Accumulation of Exceptionally High Levels of Starch in Leaves in Monoanddicotyledonous Plants. *Plant Cell Physiol.* 51,1674-1693.

Fiedler, N.; Laumbach, R.; Kelly-McNeil, K.; Lioy, P.; Fan, Z.H.; Zhang, J.; Ottenweller, J.; Ohman-Strickland, P.; Kipen, H. (2005). Health Effects of a Mixture of Indoor Air Volatile Organics, their Ozone Oxidation Products, and Stress. *Environ Health Perspect.* 113, 1542–1548.

Gallois, A.; Langlois, D. (1990). New Results in the Volatile Odorous Compounds of French Cheeses. 70,89–106.

Gonzalez MC, Anaya AL, Glenn AE, Macías-Rubalcava ML, Hernandez- Bautista BE, Hanlin RT. *Muscodoryucatanensis,* A New Endophytic Ascomycete from Mexican Chakah, Burserasimaruba. Mycotaxon. 2009; 110: 363-372.

Griffin, M.A.; Spakowicz, D.J.; Gianoulis, T.A.; Strobel, S.A. (2010). Volatile Organic Compound Production by Organisms in the Genus *Ascocoryne* and a Re-evaluation of Myco-diesel Production by NRRL 50072. *Microbiology.* 156, 3814–3829.

Hawksworth, D. L. (1991). The Fungal Dimension of Biodiversity: Magnitude, Significance, and Conservation. *Mycological Research.* 95, 641—655.

Karahadian, C.; Josephson, D.B.; Lindsay, R.C. (1985). Contribution of *Penicillium sp.* to the Flavourof Brie and Camembert Cheese. J *Dairy Sci.* 68, 1865–1877.

Kishimoto, K.; Matsui, K., Ozawa, R.; Takabayashi, J., (2007). Volatile 1-octen-3-ol Induces a Defensive Response in *Arabidopsis thaliana. J Gen PlantPathol.* 73, 35-37.

Khan, M. S.; Zaidi, A.; Wani, P. A.; Ahemad, M.; Oves, M. (2009). Functional Diversity Among Plant Growth-promoting Rhizobacteria: Currentstatus Microbial Strategies for Crop Improvement. In: Microbial Strategies for Crop Improvement. M. S. Khan, A. Zaidi, and J. Musarrat, eds. Springer, Berlin, 105-132.

Hung, R.; Lee, S.; Bennett, J. W. (2013). *Arabidopsis thaliana* as a Model System for Testing the Effect of *Trichoderma* Volatile Organic Compounds. *Fungal Ecol.* 6,19-26.

Korpi, A.; Jarnberg, J.; Pasanen, A.L. (2009). Microbial Volatile Organic Compounds. *Crit. Rev. Toxicol, 39,* 139–193.

Inderjit; van der Putten, W. H. (2010). Impacts of Soil Microbial Communitieson Exotic Plant Invasions. *Trends EcolEvol.* 25,512-519.

Kudalkar, P.; Strobel, G.; Riyaz-Ul-Hassan, S.; Geary, B.; Sears, J. (2012). *Muscodorsutura,* a Novel Endophytic Fungus with Volatile Anti-biotic Activities. *Mycoscience.* 53,319-325.

Lee, S.O.; Kim, H.Y.; Choi, G.J.; Lee, H.B.; Jang, K.S.; Choi, Y.H.; Kim, J.C. (2009). Mycofumigation with *Oxyporuslatemarginatus* EF069 for Control of Post Harvest Apple Decay and *Rhizoctonia* Root Rot on Moth Orchid. *J Appl Microbiol.* 106, 1213-1219.

Lemfack, M.C.; Nickel, J.; Dunkel, M.; Preissner, R.; Piechulla, B. (2014) .VOC: A database of microbial volatiles. *Nucleic Acids Res.*42, 744–748.

Meshram, V.; Kapoor, N.; Saxena, S. (2013). *Muscodorkashayum* sp. Nov. - A New Volatile Anti-microbial Producing Endophytic Fungus. *Mycology*. 4,196-204.

Mau, J.L.; Chyau, C.C.; Li, J.Y.; Tseng, Y.H. (1997.) Flavor Compounds in Straw Mushrooms *Volvariellavolvacea* Harvested at Different Stages of Maturity. *J Agric Food Chem.* 45, 4726–4729.

Mauriello, G.; Marino, R.; D'Auria, M.; Cerone,G.; Rana, G.L. (2004). Determination of Volatile Organic Compounds from Truffles via SPME-GC-MS. *J Chromatogr Sci.* 42,299–305.

Mburu, D.M.; Ndungu, M.W.; Maniania, N.K.; Hassanali, A. (2011). Comparison of Volatile Blends and Gene Sequences of Two Isolates of *Metarhiziumanisopliae* of Different Virulence and Repellency Toward the Termite *Macrotermesmichaelseni. J Exp Biol.* 214, 956-962.

McFee, D.R.; Zavon, P. (1988). Solvents. In: Plog BA (ed.) Fundamentals of Industrial Hygiene, 3rd edn. National Safety Council, Chicago, 95-121.

Meilgaard, M.C. (1975a). Flavor Chemistry of Beer. I. Flavor Interaction between Principal Volatiles. *Tech Q Master Brewers Assoc Am.* 12:107–117.

Meilgaard, M.C (1975b). Flavor Chemistry of Beer. II. Flavor and Threshold of 239 Aroma Volatiles. *Tech Q Master Brewers Assoc Am.*12:151–168.

Mercier, J.; Lego, S.F.; Smilanick, J.L. (2010). In-package Use of *Muscodoralbus* Volatile-Generating Sachets and Modified Atmosphere Liners for Decay Control in Organic Table Grapes under Commercial Conditions. *Fruits.* 65, 31-38.

Mercier, J.; Smilanick, J.L. (2005). Control of Green Mold and Sour Rot of Stored Lemon by Fumigation with *Muscodoralbus. Bological Control.* 32, 401-407.

Meshram V., Kapoor N., Saxena S. *Muscodorkashayum sp*. Nov. - A New Volatile Anti-microbial Producing Endophytic Fungus. Mycology. 2013; 4: 196-204.

Mitchell, A.M.; Strobel, G.A.; Hess, W.M.; Vargas, P.N,; Ezra, D. (2008). *Muscodorcrispans*, A Novel Endophyte from *Ananasananassoides* in the Bolivian Amazon. Fungal Divers. 31, 37-43.

Mitchell, A.M.; Strobel, G.A.; Moore, E.; Robison, R.; Sears, J.(2010). Volatile Anti-microbials from *Muscodorcrispans*, A Novel Endophytic Fungus. *Microbiology*. 156, 270-277.

Morath, S.; Hung, R.; Bennett, J.W. (2012). Fungal Volatile Organic Compounds: A Review with Emphasis on their Bio-technological Potential. *Fungal Biol. Rev.* 30, 1–11.

Mueller, G.M, Bills, G.F. (2004). Introduction. In: Mueller GM, Bills GF. Foster MS (eds). Biodiversity of Fungi Inventory and Monitoring Method. Elsevier Academic Press, San Diego.

Nilsson, A.; Kihlstrom, E.; Lagesson, V.; Wessen, B.; Szponar, B.; Larsson, L.; Tagesson, C. (2004). Microorganisms and Volatile Organic Compounds in Airborne Dust from Damp Residences. *Indoor Air*. 14,74–82.

Nordlund, D.A.; Lewis, W.J. (1976). Terminology of Chemical Releasing Stimuli in Intraspecific and Interspecific Interactions. *J Chem Ecol.* 2,211–220.

Ortiz-Castro, R.; Contreras-Cornejo, H.; Macias-Rodriguez, L.; Lopez- Bucio, J. (2009). The Role of Microbial Signals in Plant Growth and Development. *Plant Signaling Behav.* 4, 701-712.

Pasanen, P.; Korpi, A.; Kalliokosi, P.; Pasanen, A.L. (1997). Growth and Volatile Metabolite Production of *Aspergillus versicolor* in House Dust. *Environ Int.* 23, 425–432.

Porras-Alfaro, A.; Bayman, P. (2011). Hidden Fungi, Emergent Properties: Endophytes and Microbiomes. *Annu RevPhytopathol.* 49,291-315.

Rapior, S.; Breheret, S.; Talou, T.; Pelissier, Y.; Bessiere, J.M. (2002). The Anise-like Odor of *Clitocybeodora, Lentinelluscochleatus,* and *Agaricusessettie. Mycologia.* 94,373-376.

Robinson, J. (2006). The Oxford Companion to Wine, 3rd edn. Oxford, Oxford University Press.

Rohlfs, M.; Obmann, B.R.; Petersen, R. (2005). Competition with Filamentous Fungi and Its Implication for a Gregarious Lifestyle in Insects Living on Ephemeral Resources. *Ecol Entomol.* 30,556-563.

Rude, M., Schirmer, A., (2009). New Microbial Fuels: A Biotech Perspective. *Curr Opin Microbiol.* 12, 274-281.

Rundell, S.M.; Spakowicz , D.J.; Trujillo, A.N.; Strobel, S.A. (2015). The Biological Diversity and Production of Volatile Organic Compounds by Stem-Inhabiting Endophytic Fungi of Ecuador*J Fungi.* 1, 384-396.

Ryu, C.M.; Farag, M.A., Hu, C.H.; Reddy, M.S.; Wei, H.X.; Pare, P.W.; Kloepper, J.W. (2003). Bacterial Volatiles Promote Growth in *Arabidopsis. Proc Natl AcadSci* USA. 100, 4927–4932.

Samaga, P.V.; Rai, V.R.; Rai, K.M.L. (2014). *Bionectriaochroleuca* NOTL33—An Endophytic Fungus from *Nothapodytesfoetida* Producing Anti-microbial and Free Radical Scavenging Metabolites. *Ann Microbiol.* 64,275-285.

Schaible, G. A.; Strobel, G.A.; Mends, M.T.; Geary, B.; Sears, J. (2015). Characterization of an Endophytic *Gloeosporium sp.* and Its Novel Bioactivity with "Synergistans". *Microb Ecol.* 70,41-50.

Saunders, M.; Glenn, A. E.; Kohn, L. M. (2010). Exploring the Evolutionary Ecology of Fungal Endophytes in Agricultural Systems: Using Functional Traits to Reveal Mechanisms in Community Processes. *Evol Appl.* 3,525-537.

Saxena, S.; Meshram, V.; Kapoor, N. (2014b). *Muscodortigerii* sp. Nov.-Volatile Anti-biotic Producing Endophytic Fungus from the Northeastern Himalayas. *Ann Microbiol.* 65,47-57.

Saxena, S.; Meshram, V.; Kapoor, N. (2014a). *Muscodordarjeelingensis,* A New Endophytic Fungus of *Cinnamomumcamphora* Collected from Northeastern Himalayas. *Sydowia.* 66, 55-67.

Schnurer, J.; Olsson, J.; Borjesson. T. (1999). Fungal Volatiles as Indicators of Food and Feeds Spoilage. *Fungal Genet Biol.* 27,209–217.

Splivallo, R.; Bossi, S.; Maffei, M.; Bonfante, P. (2007). Discrimination of Truffle Fruiting Body versus Mycelia Aromas by Stir Absorptive Extraction. *Phytochemistry.* 68,2584-2598.

Singh, S.K.; Strobel, G.A., Kinghton, B., Geary, B.; Sears, J. ; Ezra, D.(2011). An Endophtyic *Phomopsissp.* Possessing Bioactivity and Fuel Potential with Its Volatile Organic Compounds. *Micobial Ecology.* 61, 729-739.

Stinson, M.; Ezra, D.; Hess, W.M; Sears, J.; Strobel, G. (2003). An Endophytic *Gliocladium sp.* of *Eucryphiacordifolia* Producing Selective Volatile Anti-microbial Compounds. *Plant Sci.* 165.

Strobel, G.A.; Knighton, B.; Kluck, K.; Ren, Y.; Livinghouse, T.; Griffin, M.; Spakowicz, D.; Sears, J. (2008). The Production of Myco-diesel Hydrocarbons and their Derivatives by the Endophytic Fungus *Gliocladiumroseum* (NRRL 50072). *Microbiology.* 154,3319–3328

Strobel G.A.; Singh, S.K.; Riyaz-Ul-Hassan. S.; Mitchell, A.M.; Geary, B.; Sears, J. (2011.) An Endophytic/pathogenic *Phoma sp.* from Creosote Bush Producing Biologically Active Volatile Compounds having Fuel Potential. *FEMS Microbiol Lett.* 320, 87–94.

Strobel, G.A.; Dirkse, E.; Sears, J.; Markworth C. (2001). Volatile Anti-microbials from *Muscodoralbus,* A Noval Endophytic Fungus. *Micobiology.* 147, 2943-2950.

Tomsheck, A.R.; Strobel, G.A.; Booth, E.; Geary, B.; Spakowicz, D.; Knighton, B. (2010). *Hypoxylon*sp, An Endophyte of *Perseaindica,* Producing 1,8-cineole and Other Bioactive Volatiles with Fuel Potential. *Microb Ecol.* 60, 903-914.

Wilkins, K.; Larsen, K. (1995). Identification of Volatile (Micro) Biological Compounds from Household Waste and Building Materials by Thermal Desorption-Capillary Gas Chromatography-Mass Spectroscopy. *J High Res Chrom.* 18, 373–377.

Wood, W.F., Fesler, M. (1986). Mushroom Odors: Student Synthesis of the Odoriferous Compounds of the Matsutake Mushroom. *J Chem Educ.* 63, 92.

Wood, F. W.; Largent , L. D.; Henkel, T. W. (2004). Headspace Analysis Identifies Indole and 1-octen-3-ol as the "coal tar" odor of *Tricholomainamoenum.* Mycological Progress. 3, 325-328.

Wood, W.F; Largent, D.L. (1999). Benzaldehyde and Benzyl Alcohol, the Odour Compounds from *Agaricussmithii.* Biochemical Systematics and Ecology 27:521-522.

Worapong, J.; Strobel, G.A.; Ford, E.J.; Li, J.Y.; Baird, G.; HESS, W.M. (2001). *Muscodoralbus* an Endophyte from *Cinnamomumzeylanicum. Mycotaxon.* 79,67-79.

Zhang, C.L.; Wang, G.P.; Mao, L. J.; Komon-Zelazowska, M.; Yuan, Z.L.; Lin, F.C. (2010). *Muscodorfengyangensis sp.* nov. from Southeast China: Morphology, Physiology and Production of Volatile Compounds. *Fungal Biol.* 114, 797-808.

Plant Biotechnology and Industrial Applications
Edited by: Alka Chauhan and Pawan Kumar 'Bharti'
ISBN: 978-93-5056-884-2
Edition: 2017
Published by: Discovery Publishing House Pvt. Ltd., New Delhi (India)

4 Molecular Tools in Biological Control of Crop Pests

[1]D. Sudha Rani, [2]Ch. Chiranjeevi, [2]P.V. Krishnayya and [3]D. V. Sairam Kumar

Biological control is broadly defined as the use of natural or modified organisms, genes, or gene products to reduce the effects of pest and diseases. Since, the beginning of evolutionary process of crop plants, natural pest control by bio agents *viz.*, predators, parasites and pathogens exists. The classical biological control offers potential nonchemical control of crop pests but limited due to several constraints. The natural bio control of crop pests is not always possible as the presence of these bio control agents number vary depending on host specificity and environmental factors and also by chemical interventions (indiscriminate use of pesticides) which suppress their population buildup.

The Molecular biology is a branch of biology that deals with the nature of biological phenomena at molecular level through the study of DNA and RNA, proteins and other macromolecules involved in genetic information and cell function, characteristically making use of advanced tools and techniques of separation, manipulation, imaging and analysis.

Molecular Tools Employed in Biological Control Programmes Aids In

1. Detection and differentiation of host and parasitoid species
2. Development of transgenic plants (resistant to insects)
3. Development of transgenic insects
4. Genetic improvement of natural enemies
5. Increasing virulence of entomopathogens

Detection and Differentiation of Host and Parasitoid Species

The main goals of classical biological control are introduction and establishment of natural enemies which effectively controls the pest populations and safer

[1] Corresponding Author, Scientist (Entomology) & Head, Agricultural Research Station, Garikapadu, Krishna, Andhra Pradesh, India

[2] Professor, Department of Entomology, Agricultural College, Bapatla, Guntur, Andhra Pradesh, India

[3] Associate Professor, Department of Entomology, Agricultural College, Bapatla, Guntur, Andhra Pradesh, India

to non target species. But in general, only about 60% of introductions have resulted in establishments and about 30% result in successful pest suppression. Inadequate taxonomic knowledge of the target pest and candidate natural enemies will led to failure of biological control programme (Rosen, 1986). The success or failure of a biological control project could depend on the correct identification of the pest or the natural enemy. The most successful natural enemies are highly host-specific. Therefore, the correct identification is especially important when either the pest or the natural enemy has closely related species that are morphologically indistinguishable (cryptic species) (Jenkins, 2002).

Accurate identification of natural enemies is critical to the success of classical biological control programs, not only in the initial phases when candidate natural enemies are chosen and released, but also during subsequent manipulation and evaluation phases (Zhu and Greenstone, 1999). In more recent years, molecular techniques have become important tools in insect pest management, complementing and in some cases superseding morphological methods for accurate identification of these organisms [Greenstone, 2006]. Indeed, one advantage of molecular techniques over phenotypic methods is that they bypass the need for the specialist entomological knowledge required for morphological species differentiation and can be performed in a variety of laboratory settings [Stouthaner *et al.*, 1999]. Furthermore, molecular methods can overcome difficulties in differentiating morphologically similar species, larval forms or members of cryptic species complexes [Mills *et al.*, 2010].

Molecular Tools for Detection and Differentiation of Host and Parasitoid Species

Implementation of strong molecular diagnostic techniques will lead to increased success of biological control programs through enhanced understanding of host and parasitoid population genetics and improved matching of parasitoid species to their preferred host and some of the molecular tools employed for identification include:

1. DNA-Barcoding
2. PCR based approaches

PCR	PCR-RFLP
Size differential PCR	Quantitative PCR
RAPD, AFLP	Multiple PCR
Quantitative PCR	DNA shuffling

DNA Barcoding

- DNA barcoding involves the PCR amplification and sequencing of a key genetic marker from a given specimen and is one of the most widely used molecular techniques employed in the study and management of arthropod pests and their parasitoids.

- DNA barcoding can be used as a species-specific diagnostic and has been applied relatively successfully to species identification, differentiation, and the study of geographical variation in host-parasitoid interactions.
- DNA barcodes are also widely used for taxonomic analyses. Indeed, it is prudent to conduct a phylogenetic analysis of key genetic markers within a species to determine intra-species relationships, as well as evolutionary relationships with other taxa, prior to attempting DNA barcoding as a species-specific diagnostic.
- DNA barcoding involves the PCR amplification and sequencing of a key genetic marker from a given specimen.
- DNA barcoding typically refers to the amplification and sequencing of the 5′ portion of mitochondrial cytochrome oxidase I (COI) gene.
- The COI barcode region can be considered as 'goldilocks zone' for taxonomic utility (Janzen *et al.*, 2005).
- Hebert *et al.*, (2003) cited that COI can serve as the core of a global bio identification system as the universal primers for this gene are very robust, enabling recovery of its 5′ end from representatives and COI appears to possess a greater range of phylogenetic signal than any other mitochondrial gene. The evolution of this gene is rapid enough to allow the discrimination of not only closely allied species, but also phylogeographic groups within a single species.

Some case studies of molecular barcoding and PCR approaches to identify the phylogeny and evolutionary relationships of natural enemies are mentioned hereunder.

Molecular Barcoding and Phylogeny Analysis of *Goniozus nephantidis* *(Rukshana and Sebastiana, 2015)*

- The Bethylidae family consists of nearly 2200 species of parasitic nature on larvae of many Coleoptera and Lepidoptera insects.
- *Goniozus nephanditis* is one among the bethylidans which acts as potential bioagent against larvae Coconut black headed caterpillar (*Opisinia arenosella*).
- The genus Goniozus consists of approximately 170 species worldwide.
- Phylogentic analysis using mitochondrial cytochrome oxidase subumit I (COI) gene sequence were made from thoracic leg of the experiment insect *G.nephantidis* (KM216267)-(Tirurangadi, Kerala).
- The nucleotide sequence and peptide sequence was searched for its similarity using BLAST programme of NCBI (www.ncbi.nl.nih.gov/) and inter and intra specific genetic diversity was calculated.
- The BLAST search inferred that the sequence obtained for *G.nephantidis* (KM216267) is novel and the average divergence in intragenic comparisons is 11.44 per cent.

- Partial COI DNA sequence of *G. nephantidis* (KM216267) is different to that of *G. jacintae* (KF027190) by 11.44%, G. Jacinate (KF027188) BY 13.47% and in Laelius Spp. (KF02719) by 40.85% as shown in table 4.1.
- The average nucleotide composition obtained across the species was T = 47.4%; A = 33.3%; C = 12.3% and G = 7.0%. The percent A + T is higher than that of G + C.
- The estimated transition bias (R) is 0.64
- The nucleotide frequencies are 25.00%
- The maximum log likelihood for 18 nucleotide sequence is 556.694
- The evolutionary history was inferred using the neighbor joining method
- The tree is drawn to scale with branch lengths in the same units as those of the evolutionary distances used to infer the phylogenetic tree (figure 4.1).

Table 4.1: The Evolutionary Divergence of *G. nephanditis* with various *Bethylid* spp.

S.No.	Species name with Accaession No.	% of diversity
1.	*Goniozus jacintae* (KF027190)	11.44%
2.	*Goniozus jacintae* (KF027188)	13.47%
3.	*Blattidae*_gen. (JQ574571)	13.73%
4.	*Goniozus*_sp. (KF 027184)	17.79%
5.	*Goniozus*_sp. (KF 027186)	17.79%
6.	*Rhabdepyris*_sp. (KF 027194)	20.45%
7.	*Apenesia*_sp. (KF 027181)	20.45%
8.	*Sierola*_sp. (KF 027199)	23.01%
9.	*Eupsenella*_sp. (KF 027183)	23.30%
10.	*Odontomachus meinerti* (KC 418719)	23.92%
11.	*Sclerodermus_niveifemur* (KF 027195)	28.52%
12.	*Camptothlipsis*_sp. (JF 271239)	28.52%
13.	*Neoapenesia*_sp. (AB 795312)	31.06%
14.	*Rhabdepyris*_sp. (AJ 514364)	32.09%
15.	*Cephalonomia*_sp. (KF 027182)	35.15%
16.	*Sclerodermus harmandi* (AB 795306)	40.22%
17.	*Laelius*_sp. (KF 027191)	40.85%

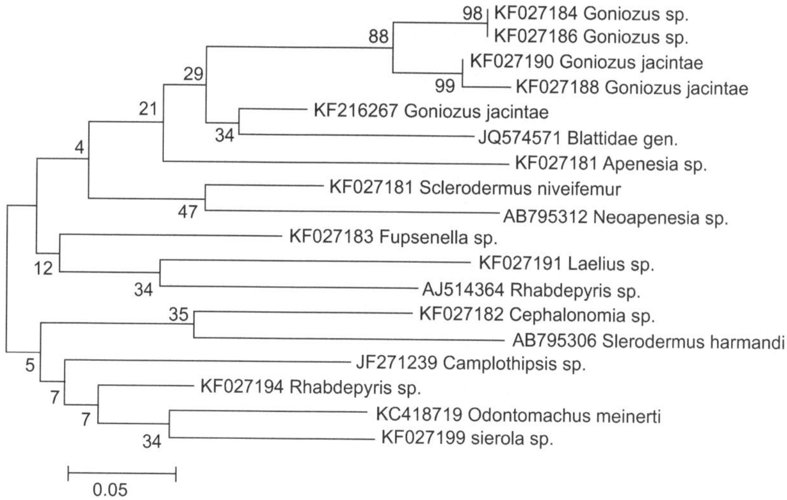

Fig. 4.1: Evolutionary divergence represented by phylogenetic tree

DNA Barcode for Identification of *Chelonus blackburni,* A Biocontrol Agent in Cotton Crop (Trang *et al.,* 2013)

- The family Braconidae species are parasitoids of key pest of agriculture playing a major role as important biocontrol agents in cotton crop for many Lepidopteran pests.
- Proper identification of some species of parasitoids is further complicated by physiological and morphological differences that are induced by the host in which they develop.
- DNA based approaches aided to generate genetic fingerprinting of numerous organism.
- Polymerase chain reaction based method was used to characterize C. blackburni at molecular level suggesting that sequence of 898bp region of the mitochondrial gene, cytochrome c oxidase I (COI), may serve as a DNA barcode for the identification of parasitoid species.
- Mitochondrial DNA (mtDNA) is a valuable marker to indicate maternal gene flow and mtDNA is more numerous than nuclear DNA. Partial CO1 sequence of *C. blackburni* was 898 bp. The sequence are analyzed by Blast (GenBank Accession No. FJ441075) (figure 4.2)
- The sequence of CO1 of mtDNA of *C. blackburni* showed 83-89% sequence identity with different species of Chelonus.
- The region which completely aligns with that of *Chelonus* sp. has nucleotide coordinate from 90 to 898 with 89% sequence identity. *Cotesia* in which the coverage region was from nucleotide 225 to 898, with 84% sequence identity (table 4.2).

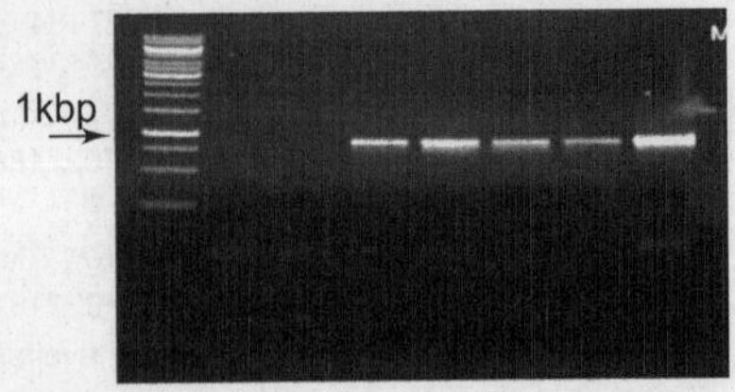

Fig. 4.2: PCR amplified COI gene of mt DNA from *C. balckburni*
Lane 1 : MarkerLane 4,5,6,7 and 8: PCR ITS products

Table 4.2: Comparison of Nucleotide Sequence of Cytochrome Oxidase Subunit 1 (CO1) of C. blackburni

No.	Name of Insects	Query coverage (%)	Max. Identity (%)	Source/ voucher
1.	*Chelonus sp*	90	89	—
2.	*Cotesia koebelei*	74	85	USA
3.	*C. acuminate*	76	84	Sweden
4.	*C. acuminate*	75	84	China
5.	*C. biquellii*	84	82	Finland
6.	*C. melitaearum*	78	83	Spain
7.	*C. acuminate*	79	83	France
8.	*C. melitaearum*	76	84	Hungary
9.	*C. acuminate*	75	83	Spain
10.	*C. acuminate*	79	83	Russia
11.	*C. melitaearum*	75	83	Sweden
12.	*C. marquiniventris*	75	83	France
13.	*C. marquiniventris*	75	83	Russia
14.	*C. marginiventris*	79	83	—

Other Such Findings

Tilmon *et al.*, (2000) developed molecular markers based on the cytochrome oxidase 1 (CO1) gene for *Peristenus pallipes, P. digoneutis, and P. conradi* to assess parasitism rates in *Lygus lineolaris* in the field.

PCR Based Approaches

- The PCR-based methodologies for species detection and discrimination differing from barcoding procedures in that they often employ primer sets specific for the species or genus under investigation.
- PCR primers with a high degree of specificity make downstream sequencing of the amplicon unnecessary because the presence/absence of an amplicon, as confirmed by electrophoresis, indicates whether an insect belongs to the target genus or species.

- In some cases, species can be differentiated based on electrophoretic analysis of amplicon size where primers are designed to target sites adjacent to genome regions that vary in length between species. The ITS regions have been used for this purpose as they tend to be quite variable in length as well as sequence, while the highly conserved ribosomal RNA genes flanking the ITS regions can be exploited as primer target sites to ensure successful amplification.

Molecular Identification and Detection of *Lysiphlebus fabarum*, Parasitoid of Aphids, by Using Polymerase Chain Reaction (Kaledeh *et al.*, 2012)

- Many species in the genus *Lysiphlebus* (Hymenoptera: Braconidae, Aphidiinae) are solitary endoparasitoids of aphids. A pair of species-specific primers as a molecular marker was designed to identify the most abundant and important aphid parasitoid wasp, *L. fabarum*, collected from Guilan province (Iran). (table 4.3)
- This primer pair, which produces a 148 bp fragment length, was developed for *L. fabarum* by using the ATPase 6 gene region of mitochondrial DNA.
- The lower detection limit to amplify DNA of *L. fabarum* in a singleplex PCR was determined to be 72 pg of parasitoid DNA/μl PCR which was enough to detect this parasitoid in early life stages within its host.
- Species specificity test for LFF/LFR primer pairs indicated that amplification of the expected size was possible only with the DNA of target species while no cross reaction was observed with other tested DNA samples (figure 4.3).
- Sensitivity test of LFF/LFR primer pairs to amplify DNA of *L. fabarum* in singleplex PCR showed a lower detection limit of 72 pg (figure 4.4)
- It was proved that the species specific primer could be used as a powerful tool to detect *L. fabarum* as an endoparasitoid wasp within its hosts.
- The *L. fabarum* eggs can be detected within *Aphis fabae* (Hemiptera: Aphididae) 12 hours since oviposition.
- A pair of species specific primers designed for *L. fabarum* can be used to monitor the wasp populations under field conditions.

Table 4.3. Species Specific Primer Sequences Designed from the ATPase 6 mtDNA of *L.fabrum*, ptimal PCR Annealing Temperature, Amplication Size and % GC

Primers	Sequence	Annealing temp.	Fragment size	% GC[a]
Forward (LFF)	5′-AGGTTTAATAATTTTTGGGTGAG-3′	61	148	30.4
Reverse (LFR)	5′-ACGAATAGATAAAGTAAAAGGACG-3′	—	—	33.3

[a]means the percentage of guanine-plus-cytosine

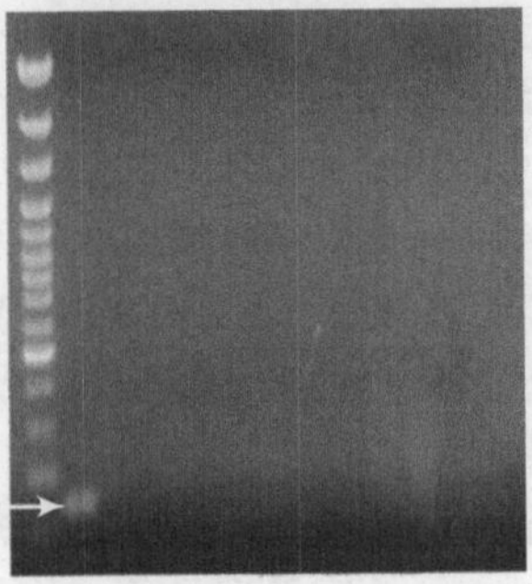

Fig. 4.3: Diagnostic PCR using the species specific primer for *L.fabarum, L.confusus, Aphidius Matricariae, Diaeretiella rapae, Ephedrus niger, Trioxyx angelicae, Aphis craccivora, A. fabae, A.ruborum and Coccinella septempunctata*. Lane 1 = 100 bp DNA marker, Lane 12 = Negative control (No DNA).

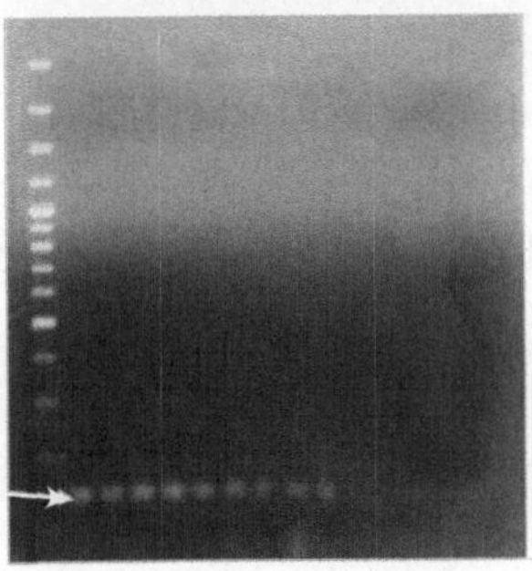

Fig. 4.4: Diagnostic singleplex PCR using 18.4, 9.2, 4.6, 2.3, 1.15, 0.6, 0.3, 0.14, 0.072, 0.036, 0.018, 0.0090 and 0.0045 (ng/ul) of DNA template from *L.fabarum* adults. Lane 1 = 100 bp DNA marker, Lane 15 = Negative control (No DNA).

Molecular Identification of *Trichogramma* Species using the Sequencing of the ITS2 Region of Ribosomal DNA (Santos *et al.*, 2013)

- Due to the importance of its use, to succeed in a biological control program with the Trichogramma species, correct identification is essential, so one can check if they respond to the climatic conditions of the region and culture that they will be applied to (Borba *et al.*, 2005)
- The *T. pretiosum, T. exiguum* and *T. galloi* species, morphologically similar, differ genetically with a high level of dissimilarity.
- Identification and differentiation of *Trichogramma exiguum* , *T. pretiosum* and *T. galloi* using sequences of the ITS2 (Internal transcribed spacer) region of ribosomal DNA inferred the differences between species by the results of the multiple alignments of all sequences obtained.
- With the results of the search for similarities by BLAST (Basic local Alignment Search Tool) tool in the GenBank database (NCBI – National Center for Biotechnology Information), it was found that they all correspond to the desired regions, consistent with the sequences

of *Trichogramma* species, obtaining similarities 95% similarity to *T. pretiosum*, 91% for *T. galloi* and 92% for *T. exiguum* (table 4.4)

- Using the genetic distance matrix it is inferred that species *T. galloi* and *T. exiguum* were more genetically distant with 0.238 and *T. exiguum* and *T. pretiosum* were closer having a genetic distance of 0.189. (table 5.5)
- According to the dendrogram obtained from the genetic distance matrix using the neighbor-joining method, the presence of three groups can be verified: the first formed by *T. exigum*, the second by *T. pretiosum*, and the third, by *T. galloi* which suggests a strong inter-specific variation among species (figure 5.5).

Table 4.4: Identification of Trichogramma spp by Comparing the Consensus Sequence with Sequences Obtained from NCBI

Samples	Primer	Access number	Maximum identification	Blast species
T. pretiosum	ITS-2-R	DQ525178.1	95%	*T. pretiosum*
T. galloi	ITS-2-R	AY182764.1	91%	*T. galloi*
T. exiguum	ITS-2-R	AY182769.1	92%	*T. exiguum*

Table 4.5: Genetic Distance Matrix of ITS2 Ribosomal DNA for Three Species of *Trichogramma*

Species	T. exigum	T. galloi	T. pretiosum
T. exiguum	0	—	—
T. galloi	0.238	0	—
T. pretiosum	0.189	0.215	0

Fig. 5.5: Dendogram for three species of *Trichogramma*

Polymerase Chain Reaction Techniques for Distinguishing Three Species and Two Strains of Aphelinus from Diuraphis noxia and Schizaphis graminum (Zhu and Greenstone, 1999)

- Biological control of the Russian wheat aphid, *Diuraphis noxia* in North America with numerous exotic parasitoids released of *Aphelinus* Spp. (*A. albipodus, A. asychis and A. varipes*).

- The *A. asychis* individuals released compose a group of geographical isolates that may constitute a sibling species complex.
- Ribosomal DNA sequences for the internal transcribed spacer 2 (ITS2) were cloned and sequenced from *Aphelinus albipodus, A. varipes* and 2 strains of *A. asychis,* all endoparasitoids that have been released against the Russian wheat aphid, *Diuraphis noxia.*
- The polymerase chain reaction (PCR) using primers designed on the basis of these rDNA sequences, followed by agarose gel electrophoresis, successfully distinguishes all 4 *Aphelinus* populations from each other and from the Russian wheat aphid and another economically important cereal aphid, the greenbug, *Schizaphis graminum* (figure 4.6).
- *A. asychis* DNA is detectable in a parasitized Russian wheat aphid 24 h after parasitization. The sensitivity is 1023 adult wasp DNA equivalent.

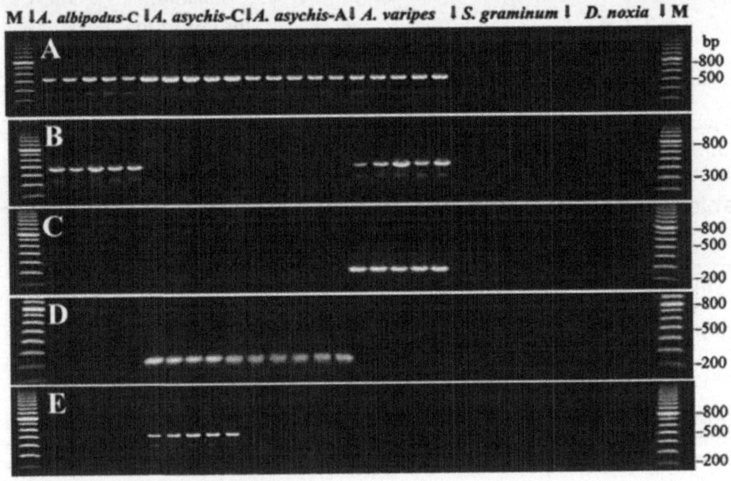

Fig. 4.6: PCR amplifications for distinguishing 4 Aphelinus populations from each other and from the greenbug and the Russian wheat aphid

A PCR amplification of 530 bp fragments in *Aphelinus species to separate the wasps from S. graminum* and *D. noxia using primer 58S-F and 28S-R.*

B *Approximately 480 bp fragments were ampliÞed from A. albipodus and A.varipes using primer 58S-F and Aalv-R for separating A. albipodus and A. varipes from A. asychis and aphids.*

C *300 bp* fragments were amplified from *A. varipes only using primer Ava-F and Aalv-R.*

D *202 bp fragments were amplified from* both Chinese and Antibes strains of *A. asychis using primer Aas-F and 28S-R for separating A. asychis from other Aphelinus* species and aphids.

E 95 bp fragments were ampliÞed from Chinese strain *A. asychis using primer 58S-F and Aas-CRG* M, 100 bp DNA marker from Pharmacia; -C, Chinese strains; -A, Antibes strain.

A Simple PCR-RFLP Method to Distinguish between Species and Strains of *Microctonus* Parasitoids (Vink, 2012)

- *Microctonus* spp (Hymenoptera: Braconidae) are bioagents against weevils in fodder crops.

- Two strains of M. *aethiopides are introduced in Newzealand. One against Sitonia discoidus* (Lucerne pest) and another against *S. lepidus* (Clover pest).
- Intraspecific genetic variation in *M. aethiopides* is strongly associated with weevil host species than geographic origin which has 3 COI halotypes.
- Another species of *M. hyperodae* against *Listronotus bonaricnsis (clover pest) was also introduced which has* 3 COI halotypes.
- Another species M. zealandicus attacks *Ireninus* spp.
- All of the *Microctonus* sps introduced to control forage pests also attacks non target weevil hosts.
- A polymerase chain reaction and restriction fragment length polymorphism (PCR-RFLP) method is used for distinguishing between the two strains of *M. aethiopoides, M. hyperodae* and *M. zealandicus* was developed.Through Molecular markers PCR RFLP the difference of larvae of *Microctonus* spp were identified and adult strains of *M. aethiopoidus* were separated.
- The initial PCR amplification for one of the *M. hyperodae* specimens (East haplotype) was not strong and the 117 bp fragment is barely visible.
- All *Microctonus* species and *M. aethiopoides* strains were differentiated using the Ase1 PCR-RFLP method which is used to identify species and strains of *Microctonus* found in New Zealand (figure 4.7).

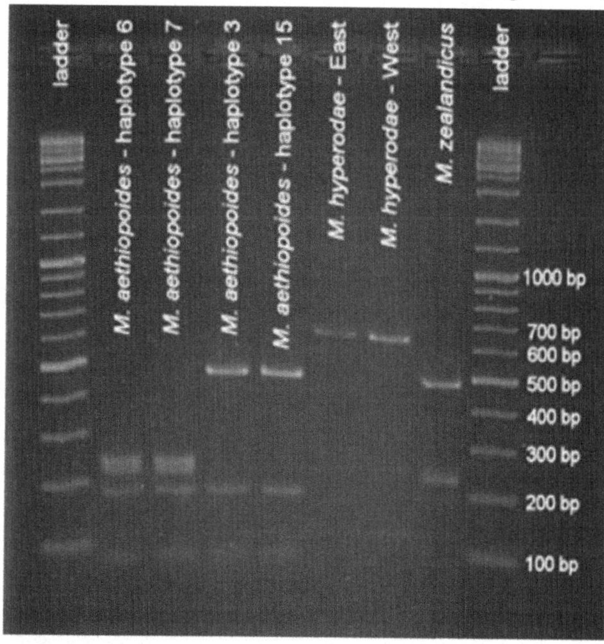

Fig. 4.7: Photograph of agarose gel using ethidium bromide fluorescence to visualise the RFLP analysis of the COI PCR products from *Microctonus* species and their strains

A Single-step Multiplex PCR Assay for the Detection of *Peristenus* spp Parasitoids of *Lygus* spp. (Tara *et al.*, 2005)

- Species of *Lygus* (Hemiptera: Miridae) are serious pests of crops grown in agricultural and greenhouse environments throughout North America.
- Feeding damage by Lygus nymphs and adults cause flower bud and fruit abortion, side shoot abscission, leaf tissue perforation and deformation or death of meristem tissue.
- Release and establishment of European *Peristenus digoneutis* against *Lygus lineolaris*) populations in northeastern USA, renewed interest in the intended liberation of European parasitoids for Lygus control in Canada.
- Accurate identification of natural enemies is the cornerstone of biological control but conventional methods for identifying *Peristenus* species and estimating parasitism rates rely on tedious and time-consuming dissection and rearing methods.
- Although molecular diagnostics have previously been used in the identification of parasitoids and estimation of parasitism rates, this is the first time a single-step multiplex PCR protocol described.
- Species-specific PCR primers for three species of *Peristenus,* and the use of a multiplex PCR assay to detect the eggs and larva of *P. digoneutis* and *P. stygicus* from *Lygus rugulipennis* nymphs (table 4.6).
- Results indicate that the primers amplify uniquely sized, species-specific PCR products for the three species and are capable of detecting single eggs in parasitized nymphs within 3 days post-parasitism.
- Using a multiplex PCR assay, the primers maintain specificity and sensitivity, and allow detection of each of the three species in a single reaction (figure 4.8).
- Multiplex PCR results indicated the occurrence of multiparasitism in some *Lygus* nymphs by the presence of *P. digoneutis* and *P. stygicus* specific PCR products in single nymphs. The relative proportions of above species are similar in the overall species composition
- The single-step multiplex PCR assay described here would be useful in conducting pre-release studies in the area of origin; nymphs can be screened to determine *Peristenus*/host associations as well as the distribution of ***parasitoids*** species besides facilitating studies relating to post-release monitoring.

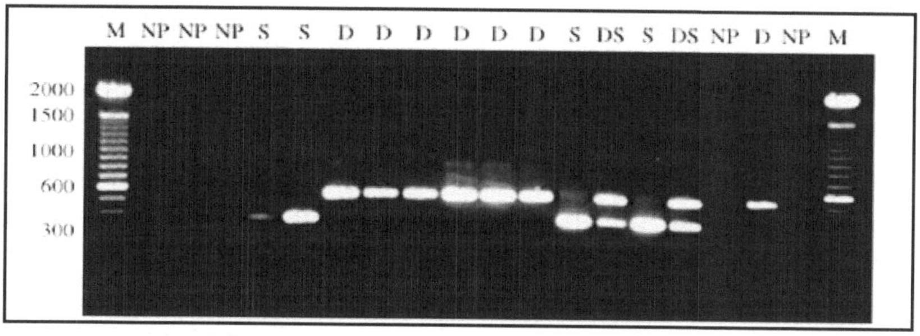

Fig. 4.8: Application of the multiplex PCR assay to ûeld collected *Lygus rugulipennis* nymphs. PCR products specific to *P. digoneutis* (515 bp) and *P. stygicus* (330 bp) are indicated by D and S, respectively. Lanes with no bands indicate nymphs that are not parasitized (NP), and lanes showing both 515- and 330-bp products simultaneously indicate multiparasitism (DS). M, 100-bp marker (Invitrogen)

Table 4.6: Peristenus Species-specific Primers, their Respective Sequences, and Fragment Sizes when Used in Combination with a Genus-specific Reverse Primer (Per R1)

Species	Primer	Primer Sequence	Size
Peristenus spp.	Per R1	5′	—
P. digoneutis	dig F1096	5′	515
P. reliclus	sty F1230	5′	330
P. pallipes	pal F517	5′	1060

1.2 Molecular genetic identification of two bracon species based on RAPD-PCR and 16S rRNA genes (Bark *et al.*, 2013)

- *Bracon* spp is minute and indistinguishable morphologically, further, the environmental factors influence significantly its morphology and physiology. So, identification of the wasp is problematic and its systematic needs to be clarified.
- Random amplified polymorphic DNA (RAPD)-PCR genomic finger printing and partial sequencing of the 16S rRNA gene were evaluated on *B. hebetor* and *B. brevicornis* to investigate their genetic relatedness and to establish the value of techniques for their identification using 20 specific primers.
- Nearly identical RAPD-PCR profiles and identical 467 bp fragments of the 16S rRNA genes indicated genetic diversity.
- The low levels of similarity (78.21% in the partial 16S rRNA genes and 86% in RAPD-PCR) appeared between *B. hebetor* and *B. brevicornis*.
- The produced bands polymorphisms varied from primer to another. Among these primers, only 5 did not reveal any polymorphic bands and they produced the highly monoymorphic percentage (100%), these are identified as B18, A05, Q16, C13 and A02.

- On the other hand, A16, A18, A19, B15, C04 and C05 showed highest percentage of polymorphism (46%, 40%, 50%, 44%,50% and 56%), respectively. Generally,the polymorphic percentage mean was 23.05%. (table 4.7)
- Clear identification of the insects was done by sequencing of mitochondrial 16S rDNA. 467 bp fragment of the mitochondrial 16S rRNA gene for the two insects (figure 4.9).
- BLAST analysis of 467 bp from the two insects which could belong to *Bracon hebetor* Egypt and Bracon brevicornis Egypt (presented in Egypt, figure) showed significant homology with *Bracon hebetor, Callibracon limbatus and Bracon phylacteophagus.*
- A phylogenetic tree constructed from 16S rDNA sequences showed that *B. hebetor* egypt clustered with the B. hebetor with a degree of similarity 92%, but B. brevicornis Egypt clustered in a separated group.
- The phylogenetic UPGMA tree was carried out using MEGA 4 software (figure 4.10). The UPGMA tree was constructed based on the multiply aligned sequence data for five types of insects. The tree separates the genomes into two distinct groups, whereas the insects *Bracon hebetor, Callibracon limbatus, B. phylacteophagus* and *B. hebetor* Egypt were presented in one group but only the insect *B. brevicornis* Egypt was found in another group.
- 16S rRNA gene sequence informatics is one of the most attractive potential tools to provide genus and species identification and reclassification for the two insects under study.
- The RAPD-PCR results revealed genetic variations between *B. hebetor* Egypt and *B. brevicornis* Egypt. The polymorphic percentage mean and the similarity were ~23% and 86%, respectively.

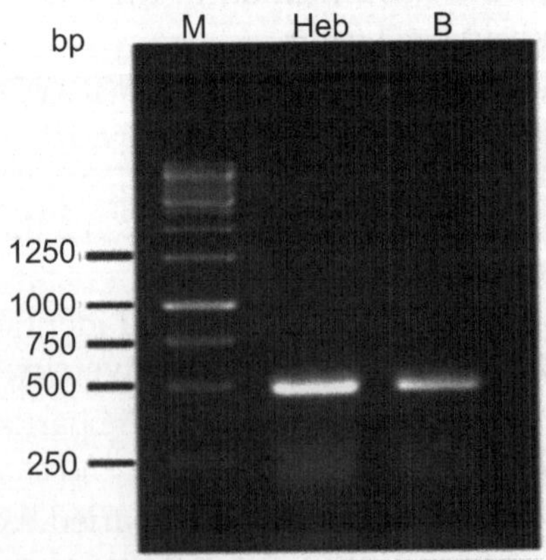

Fig. 4.9: Polymerase chain reaction (PCR) amplified 467bp of 16S rDNA fragments from to species *B. hebetor* egypt and *B. brevicornis* egypt.

- These results suggested that *B. hebetor* Egypt and *B. brevicornis* Egypt have a common ancestor but this percentage of polymorphism due to environment.

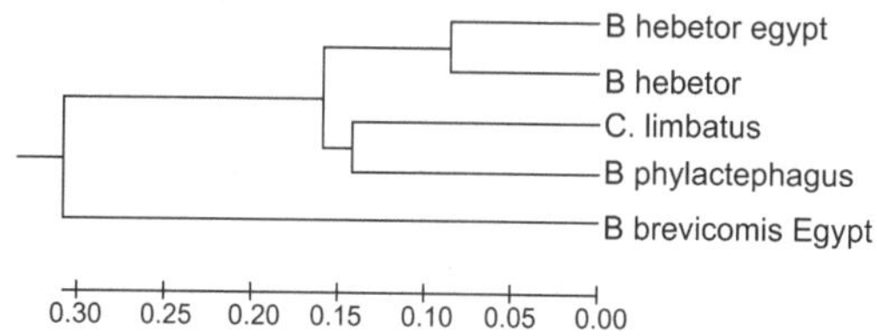

Fig. 4.10: The UPMA tree based on multiply aligned sequences collected from various spp published in the NCBI-Gene Bank database.

Table 4.7: Polymorphisms and F Value were Revealed by the Twenty Primers that Used for the Identification of Two Bracon Species

Primer	Total Ampli-fication products	Total bands		Mono-morphic bands	Polymorphic bands		Polymorphic bands sized with hp	Polymor-phis in percen-tage	F value %
		brevi-cornis	hebe-ctor		brevi-cornis	hebetor			
A01	7	6	7	0	0	1	220	14%	92%
A02	4	4	4	4	0	0	—	0%	100%
A04	7	7	6	6	1	0	80	14%	92%
A05	10	10	10	10	0	0	—	0%	100%
A09	15	11	15	11	0	4	189-200-260-350	27%	85%
A11	10	8	10	8	0	2	40-250	20%	89%
A16	11	8	9	6	2	3	110-140-370-400-460	46%	71%
A18	10	7	9	6	1	3	170-240-350-540	40%	75%
A19	12	7	11	6	1	5	280-330-360-380-410-460	30%	67%
A20	8	8	7	7	1	0	220	13%	93%
B15	9	8	6	3	3	1	130-200-240-420	44%	21%
B16	9	7	8	6	1	2	690-760-870	33%	80%
B18	10	10	10	10	0	0	—	0%	100%
B20	7	7	6	6	1	0	120	14%	92%
C04	10	9	6	5	4	1	120-180-230-200-390	50%	67%
C05	11	7	9	5	2	4	210-260-290-320-410-440	56%	63%
C13	6	6	6	6	0	0	—	0%	100%
C16	10	9	9	8	1	1	300-370	20%	89%
C19	10	9	9	8	1	1	360-390	20%	89%
Q16	8	8	8	8	0	0	—	0%	100%
Total	184	156	165	137	19	28	—	—	—
Mean	—	—	—	—	—	—	—	23.05%	86%

Transgenic Plants

Genetically modified (GM) plants are plants derived from organisms whose genetic material (DNA) has been modified in a way at does not occur naturally, *i.e.* through the introduction of a gene from a different organism (WHO, 2002). GM Crops are described as Genetically Engineered Crops (GE) or Transgenic or Biotech crops.

Molecular Tools Employed for Transgenic Plants

(*a*) *Agrobacterium* mediated method
(*b*) Gene gun method
(*c*) Electroporation
(*d*) Microinjection method

(a) *Agrobacterium mediated method*

- Agrobacterium-mediated transformation is most commonly used method for transgenesis.
- *A. tumefaciens* is a rod shaped Gram negative soil bacterium found in the rhizosphere.
- It contains Ti plasmid (tumor-inducing) which causes crown gall disease in dicot plants.
- It mainly infect the wound site and causes disease symptoms.

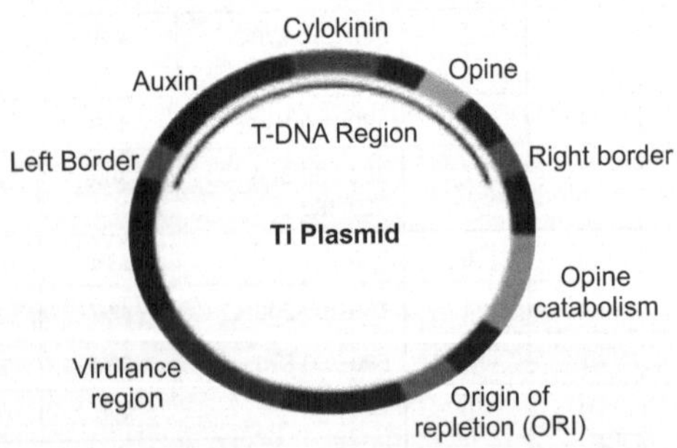

Ti plasmid
- Ori
- T-DNA regions
- Vir region
- A region enabling conjugative transfer
- Genes for catabolism of opines

(b) *Gene gun method*

- The method was first used by Klein *et al.*, (1987) to transform epidermal cell of *Allium cepa.*
- This method is mainly used for cereals transformation.
- Good for plants that cannot be transformed by *Agrobacterium*.
- DNA is bound to tiny particles of gold or tungsten which are subsequently shot into plant tissue or single plant cells under high pressure. The particles penetrate both the cellwall and membranes.

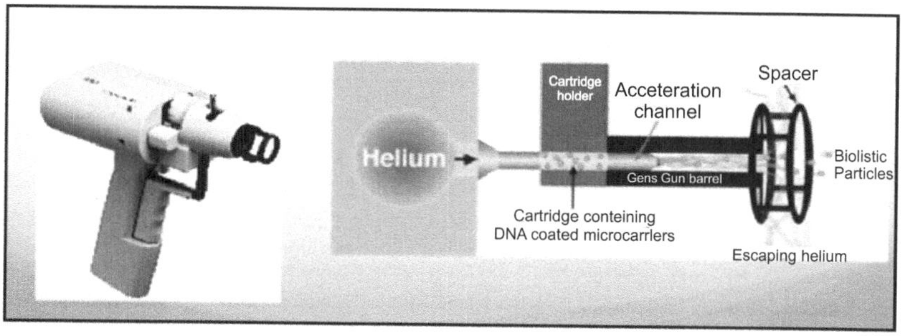

(c) Electroporation

In this technique, short pulses of high voltage are applied to protoplasts which make temporary pores in the plasma membrane to increase their permeability and facilitate the uptake of foreign gene.

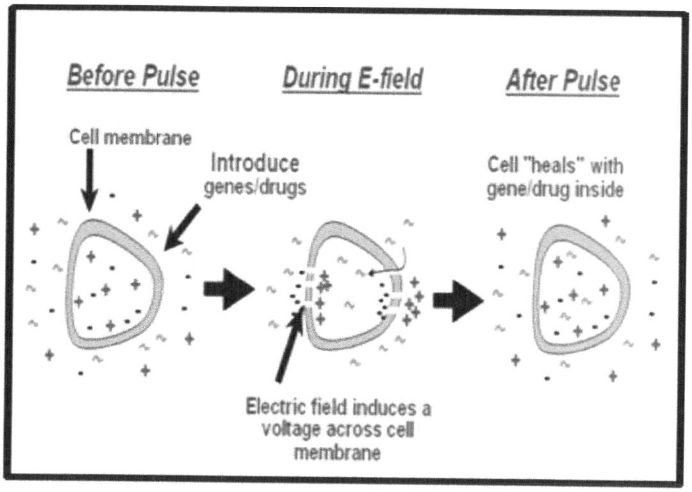

(d) Microinjection method

- Microinjection involves direct physical approach in depositing DNA into specific target cells.
- The protoplasts are immobilised in agarose or on glass slides coated with polylysine or by holding them under suction by a micropipette.
- The exogenous DNA of interest is taken in microinjector and then directly delivered inside the cell.
- Micromanipulator is used for microinjection of the DNA.
- A maximum of 40-50 protoplasts can be microinjected in one hour.
- Successful transformation by microinjection of cells has been achieved in tobacco, alfalfa etc.

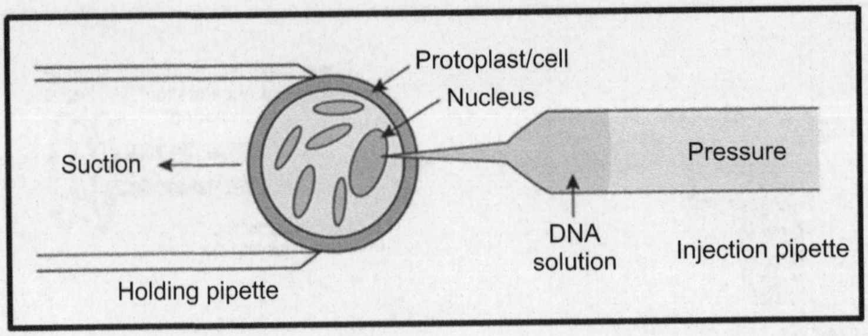

Table 4.8: Transgenic Plants Expressing Foreign Gene for Insect Resistance

Crop	Foreign gene	Origin of gene	Target Insect Pest (s)
Cotton	Cry1Ab, Cry1Ac, Cry2Ab	*Bacillus thuringiensis*	*Helicoverpa zea Spodoptera exigua Trichoplusia ni*
Brinjal	CryIIIb	*B. thuringiensis*	*Leptinotarsa decemlineata*
Maize	Cry1Ab	*B. thuringiensis*	*Ostrinia nubilalis*
Rice	Corn cystatin (cc)	Corn	*Sitophilus zeamais*
	Pin 2	Potato	*Chilo suppressalis*
	CpTi	Cowpea	
	Cry1Ab	*B. thuringiensis*	*C. suppressalis, Cnaphalocrosis medinalis Scirpophaga incertulas*
Potato	*Cry1Ab*	*B. thuringiensis*	*Phthorimaea operculella*
	Oryza cystatin 1 (oc1)	Rice	*L. decemlineata*
Sugarcane	*Cry1Ab*	*B. thuringiensis*	*Diatraea sachharalis*
Tobacco	*Cry1Ab*	*B. thuringiensis*	*Heliothis virescens*
	α-ai	Pea	*Tenebrio molitor*
	CpTi	Cowpea	*H. virescens, Manduca sexta*

Table 4.9: Crystal Protein of *Bacillus thuringiensis* and their Specificity in Developing Pest Resistance Transgenic Plants Include

Crystal proteins	Order(s) specific
Cry-I	Lepidoptera
Cry-II	Lepidoptera & Diptera
Cry-III	Coleoptera
Cry-IV	Diptera
Cry-V	Lepidoptera & Coleoptera

Table 4.10: Genetically Modified Herbicide Resistant Crop Plants

Crop	Global area of GM crops (million ha)	% GM
Herbicide-resistant soybean	21.6	54
Bt maize	7.5	19
Herbicide-resistant oilseed rape	3.5	9
Bt/herbicide-resistant maize	2.1	5
Herbicide-resistant cotton	1.6	4
Herbicide-resistant maize	1.5	4
Bt cotton	1.3	3
Bt/herbicide-resistant cotton	0.8	2
Total	39.9	100

(James, 2000)

The dependence of a worldwide industry on one insect resistance trait has led to the development of Bt-resistant insects. This in turn has led to a search for new insecticidal proteins and their encoding genes that have commercial potential for plant protection.

Alpha amylase inhibitors (Carlini *et al.*, 2002; and Franco *et al.*, 2002), vegetative insecticidal protein (Bhalla *et al.*, 2005, and Fang *et al.*, 2008), chitinases (Kabir *et al.*, 2006) and protease inhibitors (Ferry *et al.*, 2005; and Maheswaran *et al.*, 2007), as well as several other proteins directed to targets in the insect gut.

Manipulation of chemical plant defence Production of plant secondary chemicals is under strong genetic control. Molecular biology gives possibilities for engineering the biosynthesis of these compounds in plants and "programming" to attract the natural enemies of pest before the pest outbreak. However, such genetically modified cultivars are not suitable for organic farming, but can be used in conventional farming to decrease the use of pesticides.

In organic agriculture compounds extracted from plants can be used as biopesticides to kill or repel pest insects or as suppressants for fungal pathogens. Also combinations of specific monoterpenes of plant essential oils like limonene and carvone in different ratios can be sprayed on crop plants to attract natural enemies and to repel the pest insect during the attack period.

Some natural plant extracts act as elicitors and activate direct and indirect defence of crop plants simulating the processes that occur in nature when plants are attacked by pests or pathogens. Methyl jasmonate (MeJa) is a typical fragrance compound of jasmine (*Jasminum officinale*) flowers. MeJa is also an important signal compound (volatile plant hormone) in damaged plants. It mediates the information from the damaged tissues to intact plant parts of the plant or even to the neighbouring plants to activate the production of defence compounds like phenolics or glucosinolates. Furthermore, plants sprayed with MeJa in low concentrations (0.1% solution) started to emit the homoterpenes and sesquiterpenes typical to the emissions of plants attacked by pest insect. This observation suggests that MeJa can be used to activate indirect defence of crop plant in organic agriculture. E.g. the primary parasitoids (*Cotesia plutellae*) of Diamond Back Moth (Plutella xylostella) can be attracted to crop plants already when the moth larvae hatch from the eggs and thus the feeding damage can be nearly totally avoided. (Holopainen, 2005)

Table 4.10: Use of Transgenes and their Mode of Action

Transgene	Source and mode of Action	Example of Use
Bacillus thuringlensis (Bt) endotoxin	The bacillus thuringlensis endotoxin	The *Bacillus thuringiensis* endotoxin"
Vegetative insecticidal protein (VIP)	VIPs are produced by *Bacillus cereus* and *Bacillus thuringiensis.* They have similar activity to endotoxins from Bt. Vip1/Vip2 are toxic to coleopteran insects and Vip3 is toxic to lepidopteran insects.	Highly toxic to *Agrotsi* and *Spodoptera* species. VIP induced gut paralysis, complete lysis of the gut epithelial cells and resulted in larval mortality.
		VIP3Ac1 had insecticidal activity against larvae of *S. frugiperda, Hellcoverpa zea* and *Trichoplusia ni*
Chitinase (enzyme)	Chitinase catalyses the hydrolysis of chitin, which is one of the vital components of the lining of the digestive tract in insects and is not present in plant and higher animals.	Transgenic rapessed (Brassica napus) expressing *M. sexta* chitinase and scorpion insect toxin increased mortality and reduced growth of *Plutella maculipenis*
Cholesterol oxidase (enzyme)	Cholesterol oxidase is a bacterial enzyme that catalyzes the oxidation of cholesterol and other 3-hydroxysterols, resulting in production of the corresponding 3 hydroxysterols and hydrogen peroxide. Functions by damaging midgut membranes.	Cholesterol oxidase from Streptomyces caused stunting of *H. virescens, H. zea* and *Pectinophora gossypiella* when incorporated into an artificial diet.
Lipoxygenase (enzyme)	Dioxygenase enzymes are widely distributed in plants and catalyse the hydroperoxidation of cis-cis-pentadiene moleties in unsaturated fatty acids. Functions by damaging midgut membrans.	Lipoxygenase from soybean retards the growth of *Manduca sexta* when incorporated into artificial diet.

Alpha-amylase inhibitors	Alpha-amylase inhibitors block starch digestion.	Development of pea wevil larvae (*Bruchus pisorum*, Coleoptera) was blocked at an early stage after ingestion of transgenic peas expressing an lpha amylase Inhibitor from the common bean (*Phaseolus vulgaris*)
Trypsin modulating Ostatic factor (TMOF)	A peptide that blocks trypsin biosynthesis in mosquitoes (*Aedes aegypti*, Diptera [AeaTMOF] and fleshflies (*Sarcophaga*, Diptera)	Injection or oral ingestion of Aea-TMOF caused inhibition of trypsin biosynthesis and larval growth in *H. girescens*. Mortality of *H. virescens* increased when fed transgenic tobacco plants expressing Aea-TMOF (Stevens J et al., 2012)

(**Tabashnik *et al*., 2008**)

Transgenic Insects (Genetically modified insects)

- Insects with newly expressed characteristics as a biological component so as to suppress their influence on crops.
- New characters–as a result of manipulation of DNA in laboratory.
- Changes-passed on to next generation.
- Fusion of chromosome and transgene is promoted by transposable elements that cut and repair chromosomes.
- Transgenes used for recognition of transgenic insects are called markers.
- Promoters are used to drive the expression of markers.

Sterile Insect Technique

The sterile insect technique (SIT) is an environmentally friendly method for the biological control of pests using area-wide inundative release of sterile insects to reduce reproduction in a field population of the same species (IPPC, 2007).

- X-rays caused sterility in male insects (1916).
- Dr. Edward Knipling (1954) in screw-worm fly (*Cochliomyia hominivorax*) - subtropical America livestock in Florida.
- Melon fly (*Bactrocera cucurbitae*) from Okinawa in Japan (1972-1993).
- Tse-tse fly (*Glossina austeni*) from Unguja Island in Zanzibar, Tanzania.

Genetic transformation of insects that involves introduction of DNA from external sources was first tried on a scale-less mutant of the stored-grain pest, *Ephestia khuniella1, in 1965. Injection of* wild-type DNA resulted in the production of adults with wing scales.

Initial attempts to genetically modify the fruit fly, *Drosophila melanogaster, resulted in somatic* transformations with extra chromosomal inheritance.True genetic transformation of *D. melanogaster was achieved* after the discovery of the transposon2, P-element. The discovery of other transposons like *hermes, hobo, minos, mosI and piggy Bacs.*

Some Success stories of SIT

Screwworm fly	*Cochliomyia hominivorax*
Mexican fruit fly	*Anastrepha ludens*
Tsetse fly	*Glossina austeni*
Medfly	*Ceratitis capitata*
Sweet potato weevil	*Cylas formicarius*
Spotted pod borer	*Maruca vitrata*

Transgenic Insect Technology is an Improvement over SIT

- The first genetically modified insect is Drosophila melanagaster (1982); Mediterranean fruit fly (1995).
- A transgene is a gene or genetic material that has been transferred naturally, or by any of a number of genetic engineering techniques from one organism to another. The introduction of a transgene has the potential to change the phenotype of an organism.

Gene Manipulation Requirements for developing transgenic insects: Gene of interest, Vector, Marker gene, Promoter.

Vector Plasmid

- Lacks transposase enzyme.
- Contains a transposable element to be incorporated in to host genome under control of a promoter or a marker gene.

Helper (promoter) Plasmid

- Catalyses the excision of the exogenous DNA plus marker gene from the vector plasmid and inserted in to the host genome.

Markers

- Universal Markers (Green fluorescent protein-GFP).
- Eye colour genes.

Protocol for insect transformation

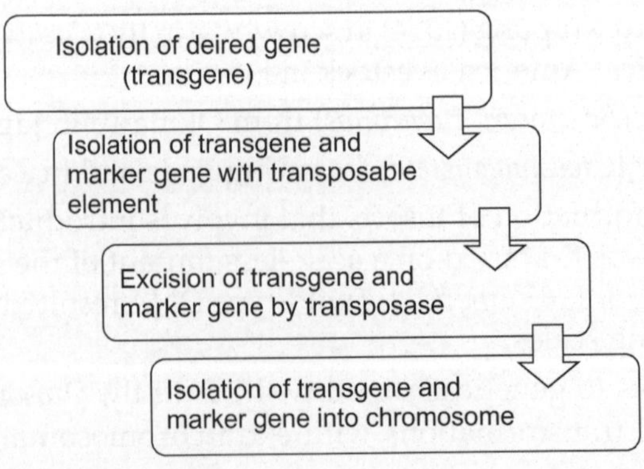

Genetic Modification of Insects is done through *Molecular Vehicles to Deliver the Gene of Interest*

Transposons are characterized by the presence of left and right terminal inverted repeats (TIR) and the gene of interest is placed between the TIR. For stable integration, two separate transposons, one carrying the gene of interest and a visible detectable marker within the functional TIR and another encoding a transpose with defective TIR are used. The most employed transposon is *piggyback* which was discovered in insects that belonged to the order Lepidoptera.

Methods of Gene Transfer

Biological	**Physical**
Transposable elements	Microinjection
Sperm mediated transformation	Biolistics
Paratransgenesis	Lipofection
	Electroporation

Biological Method: Transposable Elements

For genetic modification of insects, the transgene of interest has to be introduced into the germline of an egg and transposons are generally employed for delivering the gene of interest in insects.

Transposans are independently mobile segments of DNA (mobile genetic elements)-move from one site to another in the genome).

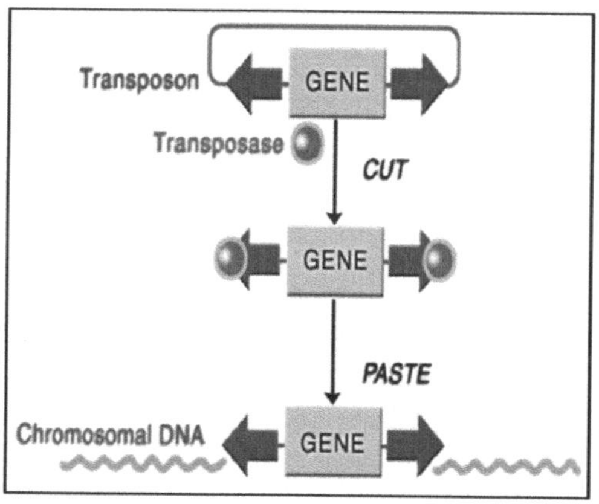

The transposon - used extensively, acts as a gene transfer vector for a number of unrelated insects.

Transposons are related to viruses but lack the ability to be packaged virus capsule.

The general mechanism of action of transposon is by cut and paste, which is aided by the transposon encoded enzyme called transpoase.

In addition to the above, Other mechanisms like replicative transposition, copy and paste are also common.

Since transposons can move around the genome, they are called jumping genes.

Table 4.11: Genetically Modified Insects

Mosquitoes	Insect Species	Transposable element
Control for Vectors transmitting dengue, malaria	Yellow fever mosquito or Denge mosquito (Aedes acgypti)	*Mariner* *Hermes* *PiggvBac*
	Asian tiger mosquito (Aedes albopictus)	*piggyBac*

	Aedes fluvlatilis	*piggyBac*
	New World malaria mosquito (Anopheles albimonis)	*piggyBac*
	A. frican malaria mosquito (Amopheles gambiae)	*piggyBae*
	Indo-Pakistan malaria mosquito (Anopheles stephensi)	*Minos*
	Culex quinques fasciartus	*Hermes*

(Beech et al., 2012)

Fruit flies Developmental biology, Genetics and protein production	Mexican fruit fly (*Anastrepha iudens*) Caribbean fruit fly (*Anastrepha suspense*) Olive fly (*Bactrocera oleae*) Queensland fruit fly (*Bactrocera tryoni*) Meditermanean fuit fly (*Ceralitis capitata*)	*piggy Bac* *PiggyBac* *Minos* *PiggyBac* *piggyBac* *Hernites* *Minos*
	House fly (*Musca domestica*) Common green bottle fly (*Lucilia sericata*) Stable fly (*Stomoxdys calcitrans*) Australian sheep blowfly (*Lucilia cuprina*) Stalk-eyed fly (*Teleopsis dalmanni*)	*piggy Bac* *PiggyBac* *Minos* *PiggyBac* *piggyBac* *Hernites* *Minos*
Wasps, bees	Saw fly (*Atholia rosae*) Honey bee (*Apis mellifera*)	*PiggyBac*
Beetle Protein production, Insecticide resistance and comparative genomic	Hariequin lady bird (*Harmonia axyrids*) Red flour beetle (*Tribolium castameun*)	*piggyBac* *piggyBac &* *Hermes* *Minos*

Butter flies and moths	Pink bollworm (*Harmonia axyrids*)	*piggyBac*
	Squinting bush brown butterfly (*Bicyclus anyona*)	*piggyBac & Hermes*
	Cabbage looper moth (*Trichoplusia ni*)	*piggyBac*
	Silkworm (*Bombyx mori*)	*piggyBac Minor*

(Beech et al., 2012)

Hermes element, mariner element Mos1, Minos and TTAA-specific element, piggybac are commonly used Transposans (piggyBac-discovered in cell cultures of the moth *Trichoplusia).*

Sperm Mediated Transformation

Factors like low reproductive rates and egg properties prevent DNA introduction.

Virgin queens are inseminated with a mixture of linearized DNA and semen (Robinson, 2000).

Paratransgenesis

Paratransgenesis was first conceived by Frank Richards (1996).

Paratransgenesis is a technique that attempts to eliminate a pathogen from vector populations through transgenesis of a symbiont of the vector. The goal of this technique is to control vector-borne diseases.

Microinjection

The procedure involves aligning the needle with the micromanipulator and moving the mechanical stage to orient the micropyle end of the egg to the needle. Most effective stage of insects for transformation : Eggs.

Modifications in Microinjection Technique

Injection into ovarian egg follicles prior to oviposition

Injection into female haemocoel for uptake of DNA into egg follicles along with vitelline.

The DNA carrying the gene of interest flanked by TIR and transpoase are delivered into the region of early embryos that contain germplasm.

During embryonic development, the transpoase will mediate the transposition of the transgene onto a chromosome that results in the production of genetically modified insects.

Microinjection of Embryos

- Delivery of gene through microinjection of embryos.
- This technique requires egg collection and processing.

- It is not feasible for parasitoids and viviparous insects.
- Microinjection of eggs resulted in substantial mortality and little success.

Maternal Microinjection

- Enables DNA injection directly into gravid females and maturing eggs of females.
- Adopted in western predatory mite, *Metaseilus occidentalis* where Gravid females were injected with pesticide 'R' gene.
- *M. occidentalis* - eggs develop one at a time and visible through cuticle. DNA persisted in transgenic mites > 150 generations.

Lipofection

Mostly used for DNA delivery into in vitro cultured cells.

It is process by which DNA or RNA which is encapsulated in an artificial phospholipid vesicle is delivered in to eukaryotic cells.

Biolistics

Involves coating DNA with gold or tungsten microparticles and bombarding into cells or tissues.

Electroporation

The use of high-voltage electric shocks to introduce DNA into cells—can be used with most cell types, yields a high frequency of both stable transformation and transient gene expression, and, because it requires fewer steps, can be easier than alternate techniques.

Table 4.12: Genes Modified in Insects : Economic Importance

Insects	Genes	Character modified
Anopheles	SM 1	Disease causing ability destroyed
Culex	Defensin	Disease spreading ability is lost
Silkworm	Spider flagelliform silk	Enhances quality of silk protein
Wolbachia	Attacin and Cecopin	Infective capacity is lost
Xylella	S1	Disease causing capacity is absent

Genetically Modified Insects (GM Pests)

(a) Pink Bollworm (Pectinophora gossypiella)

- Male pink boll worm moth were sterilized by irradiation.
- Moths are engineered to contain gene from jelly fish (GFP).
- A lethal gene (tTa) is introduced from bacteria.
- It alters the metabolism of the moth larvae.
- (Germ line transformation).
- The gene is a combination of DNA from a virus and a bacterium.

- The captive males carrying the gene eradicated communities of non-GM moths.
- Brood sizes were similar, but female offspring died before reproducing the gene itself disappears after a few generations, requiring ongoing introductions of GM cultivated males.
- Modified moths can be identified by their red glow under ultraviolet light, caused by a coral transgene. *(Briggs, 2001)*

(b) Mediterranean fruit fly (Ceratitis capitata)

- Males are sterilized by irradiation prior to release (Lobo, 1999).
- Sterile males mate with feral females hindering female reproduction.
- GM-males which have a lethal gene that interrupts female development and kills them in a process called "pre-pupal female lethality".
- After several generations, the fly population diminishes as the males can no longer find mates. To breed the flies in the laboratory, the lethal gene can be "silenced" using the antibiotic tetracycline. *(Lobo, 1999).*

(c) Red flour beetle (Tribolium castaneum)

- It is a worldwide pest of stored products.
- Genes responsible for regulating pheromone secretion are mutated.
- Specific gene expression is knocked out by RNA interference *(Dabron, 2002).*

Table 4.13: Some Cloned Resistance Genes Possibly Useful for Genetic Manipulation

Resistance Gene	Source(s)
Acetylcholinesterase (Ace) (pesticide 'R')	*D. melanogaster*
γ-Aminobutyric acid A ($GABA_A$) (dieldrin 'R')	*D. melanogaster*
Cytochrome P450-B1 (DDT 'R')	*D. melanogaster*
Esterase β1 amplification core (OP 'R')	*Culex* species
GST (Dmgst 1-1) (DDT 'R')	*D. melanogaster*
Glutathione-S-Transferase (MdGST 1-1) (OP 'R')	*Musca domestica*
Parathion hydrolase (opd) (parathion, paraoxon 'R')	*Pseudomonas minuta, Flavobacterium sp.*

Genetic Improvement of Natural Enemies

The major constraints in limiting the effectiveness of natural enemies (NE) is Global warming and indiscriminate use of pesticides.

Genetic selection could make natural enemies more effective- First discovered by Mally in 1918.

1st experimental field release of a transgenic natural enemy Strain predatory mite *Metaseiulus occidentalis* carry molecular marker (lacz construct with Drosophila heatshock 70 promoter) in March 1996.

Table 4.14: Genetically Modified Natural Enemies

Natural enemy	Target pest	Trait
Dhalbominus fuscipennis	Pine saw flies	Increased Fecundity
Macrocentrus ancylivorus	Oriental fruit moth	DDT 'R'
Metasieulus occidentalis	Two spotted Spider mite	Permethrin & carbaryl 'R'
Typhlodromus pyri	Apple Red spider mite	Cypermethrin 'R'
Trichogramma chilonis	Eggs of several lepidopteran	Endosulfan 'R'
Anisopteromalus calandrae	*Sitophilus oryzae*	Malathion 'R'
Aphytis melinus	*Aonidiella aurantii*	Carbaryl 'R'
Chrysoperla carnea	Aphids/eggs	Carbaryl 'R'

Limitations of Transgenic Insects

Instability of the introduced genes: Transgenes were reported to get rapidly lost under field conditions. Experimental release of transgenic predatory mites showed that very few individual contained the transgene only after three generations while in laboratory strains, it was persistent for over one fifty generations.

Geography: The eradication zone must have either natural barrier to prevent the immigration of the target pest from outside.

Economics: Cost of rearing, sterilizing, and releasing a large numbers of insects can be very high.

Desirability of sterile males: The lab-reared and sterilized males must be equally or more competitive than the native males in mating with the native females. They may become less desirable after many generations and need renewal.

Limited knowledge about the pest relating to reproductive behavior, population dynamics, dispersal, and ecology of the insect. Accurate estimation of the native population density is not possible

Timing: The development of the lab-reared colony must be synchronous with that of the wild population.

Resistance: Native females may be able to recognize and refuse to mate with sterile males.

Increasing Virulence of Entomopathogens

Improving the Insecticidal Activity of *Bt* Cry Toxins

Bacillus thuringiensis (Bt) is a gram-positive spore-forming soil bacterium that is distributed worldwide. Originally recognized as a pathogen of the silkworm, several strains were found on epizootic events in insect pests. In the 1960s, Bt began to be successfully used to control insect pests in agriculture, particularly because of its specificity, which reflects directly on their lack of cytotoxicity to human health, non-target organisms and the environment.

Since the introduction of transgenic plants expressing Bt genes in the mid-1980s, numerous methodologies have been used to search for and improve toxins derived from native Bt strains. These improvements directly influence the increase in productivity and the decreased use of chemical insecticides on Bt-crops. Recently, DNA shuffling and *in silico* evaluations are emerging as promising tools for the development and exploration of mutant Bt toxins with enhanced activity against target insect pests. In this report, we describe natural and *in vitro* evolution of Cry toxins, as well as their relevance in the mechanism of action for insect control.

Moreover, the use of DNA shuffling to improve two Bt toxins will be discussed together with *in silico* analyses of the generated mutations to evaluate their potential effect on protein structure and cytotoxicity.

Sugarcane giant borer *Telchin licus licus* (Lepidoptera: Castiniidae) is important crop pest without an effective management for its control. Therefore, variants of Cry1Ia12 toxin targeting this insect pest have been generated using DNA shuffling and phage display techniques.

The Cry1Ia12 toxin exhibits considerable toxicity against the Lepidoptera fall armyworm (*S. frugiperda*) and its potential for toxicity against another Lepidoptera species has been confirmed in a study in which a DNA shuffling-generated Cry1Ia variant exhibited toxicity to *T. l. licus (Lucena et al., 2014).*

Improving the Insecticidal Activity of Baculovirus

In general action of baculoviruses is slow. Introduction of foreign gene may increase the virulence of viruses i.e., Baculovirus expression vector system (BEVS).

To Improve the Speed of Action of Baculovirus Insecticides

- Incorporating genes encoding insect specific toxins, insect hormones and enzymes into the virus genome (Establishing cell insect, figure 4.11).

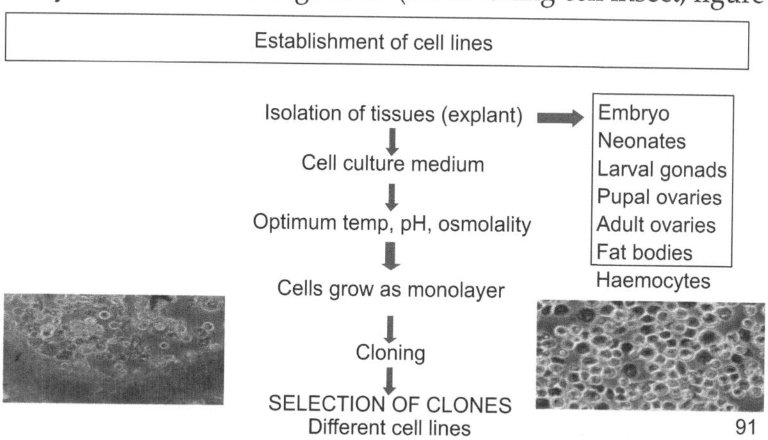

Fig. 4.11: Incorporation of genes by establishing cell lines

- Deletion of a baculovirus gene (figure 4.12).

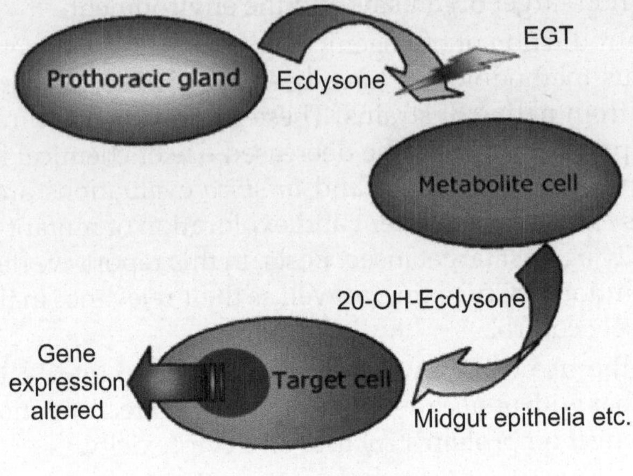

Fig. 4.12: Gene Deletion

- Incorporation of toxin into the OB (figure 4.13).

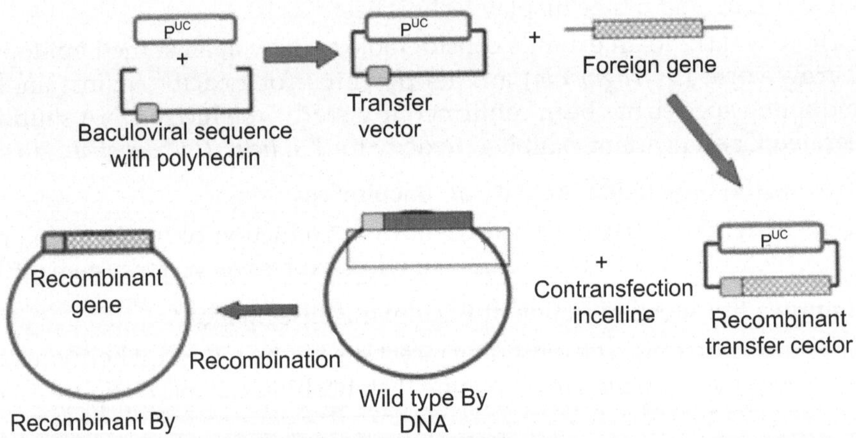

Fig. 4.13: Gene exchange between genetically compatible baculoviruses When two closely related baculoviruses co infect the same host *Eg: Galleria mellonella* larvae with two closely related baculoviruses(Au ca MNPV and Ga me MNPV)

(Stephens *et al.*, 2010)

Improving the Insecticidal Activity of Entomopathogenic Fungi

Biotechnology of EPF as bioagents has importance in studies from identification to formulation. Pathogenicity depends on enzymatic ability of the fungus. Cuticle Penetration is the result of combined action of mechanical force and enzymatic action.

EPF Secrete enzymes that aid in breakdown of insect integument viz., Lipases, Proteases, Chtinases.

Table 4.15: Engineered BV with Increased Virulence

Virus	Foreign gene	Host insect	Percent increase in speed of kill
B.mori NPV	*Andractonus australis* toxin	*B. mori*	40%, paralysis, reduced feeding
	Diuretic hormone from *Manduca sexta*	*B.mori*	LT_{50} reduced by one day, water imbalance
Heliothis zea NPV	*Pymotes tritici* toxin	*H. zea*	47%
A.californica NPV	*Heliothis virescens* JHE	*Trichoplusia ni*	16%, moulting regulation, reduced weight
A.californica NPV	Black widow spider toxin	*H. virescens*	12%
A.californica NPV	Chitinase gene from *Manduca sexta*	*S. frugiperda*	23%

Lipases

Aids in cuticle penetration and initial nutrients release and improves the adhesion of spores to the epicuticle.

In *Spodoptera litura* larval mortality increases due to significant improvement in Conidial germination of *N. rileyi* fungus (combined with 8.13 kDa lipase produce *N.rileyi)* (Supakdamrongkul *et al.*, 2010).

CYP52 (Cytochrome P450 monooxygenase) increases the enzymatic activity in breaking down of insect epicuticle (Silva *et al.*, 2010).

In B. Bassiana the gene encodes the lipase activity is Bbcyp52x1 corresponding to the enzymatic complex CYP52X1 which involves degradation of hydrocarbons (Zhang *et al.*, 2010).

In *M. robertsii*, Mr CYP52 gene from Cytochrome P450 was identified (Lin *et al.*, 2011).

Proteases

Degrades the proteinaceous material in procuticle. Plays important role in pathogenicity and also virulence (Mustafa and Kaur, 2009). Protease Pr1 is a virulence indicator for the entomopathogenic fungi (Moguel *et al.*, 2007).

Proteolytic Enzymes: subtilisin-like serine-protease Pr1 and trypsin-like protease Pr2 (Leger *et al.*, 1994)

The activities of Pr1 and Pr2 have been determined in *B. bassiana, M. anisopliae, Lecanicillium lecanni, Nomuraea rileyi and M. flavoviride* (Bidochka and Meltzer, 2010) protease Pr1 is the key extracellular involved in the cuticle penetration and that, without this enzyme the infection process cannot be achieved (Sun and Liu, 2006).

M. anisopliae was transformed with the introduction of gene *aaIT,* which encodes a neurotoxin of the *Androctonus australis* (scorpion), regulated by the gene *mcl*1 promoter. (Wang and Leger, 2007).

Chitinases

Act synergically with proteases in order to degrade insect cuticle and are associated with germination, hypal growth, morphogenesis, nutrition and defense against competitors (Leger *et al.*, 1994; Adams, 2004).

Chitinases have been recognized as powerful biological control agents due to antifungal activity in *Fusarium equiseti* and as bioinsecticides in the diamond-back moth reducing the time of death. (Prasanna *et al.*, 2013)

The first molecular characterization of a chitinase was for the chit1 gene in *M. anisopliae,* CHIT1 protein present a molecular weight of 42 kDa and it is homologue to the *Aspergillus* album and *Trichoderma harzianum* chitinases. (Bogo *et al.*, 1998)

The Molecular and Genomics of M. anisopliae and B. bassiana at Enzyme Level were Studied

M. anisopliae is a fungus of considerable metabolic and ecological versatility, being a potent insect pathogen that can also colonize plant roots.

M. anisopliae adheres to insects and plants using two different proteins, MAD1 and MAD2 that are differentially induced in insect hemolymph and plant root exudates, respectively.

Expression of Mad1 and Mad2 in *yeast* allowed to adhere to insect and plant surface respectively.

The disruption of Mad1 in EPF delayed germination, suppressed blastospore formation, and greatly reduced virulence to caterpillars.

The disruption of Mad2 blocked the adhesion to plant epidermis but no effects on fungal differentiation and entomopathogenicity.

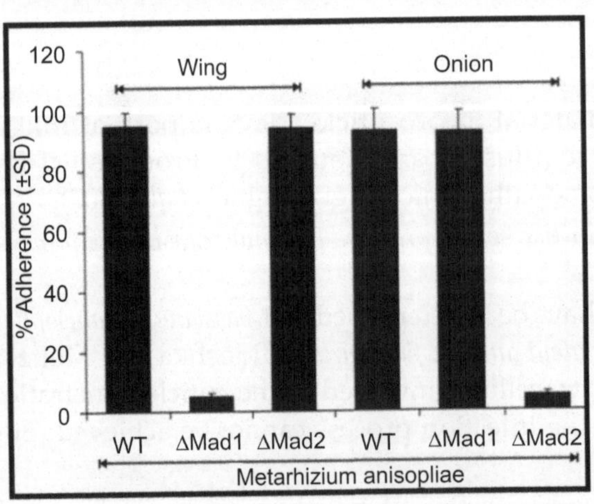

Disruption of *Mad1 and Mad2* blocks adhesion of *M. anisopliae* to insect and plant surfaces Adhesion assays 90% of the parental Wild Type conidia adhered to either locust cuticle or onion epidermis and could not be washed off with 0.05% Tween 20 Only 5.3% ± 1.2% of the ΔMad1 conidia adhered to locust cuticle, ΔMad2 conidia were as adherent as the Wild type

Fig. 4.14: Disruption of Mad1 and Mad2 blocks adhesion of M. anisopliae to insect and plant surfaces

Thus it is inferred that regulation, localization, and specificity controls the functional distinction between Mad1 and Mad2 and enable *M. anisopliae* cells to adapt their adhesive properties to different habitats (figure 4.14) *(Wang and Leger, 2007)*.

Genetic Diversity of EPF

The parasite may be highly virulent in a new parasite host system, but may become less virulent in a long term system.

Depending on the costs of resistance and the phylogenetic longevity of the relationship, host may also become more or less resistant (Restif and Koella, 2004).

EPF with a wide range of hosts such as *Beauveria* spp. the isolates of diverse geographical origin obtained from the same host species show a greater similarity in the genetic structure than the isolates from the same site but isolated from different host species (Castrillo and Brooks 1998, Glare and Inwood 1998).

Due to this fact, the entomopathogenic fungi enzymes production systems are established. The Solid State Fermentation (SSF) is an adequate technology which is employed in the bioprocess development, facilitating its production at great scale.

The ability to degrade protein and chitin rich insect cuticle by any pathogen determines the pathogenesis Expansion or contraction of protein family size has occurred in different fungal species in association with evolutionary adaptations for different hosts and lifestyles.

Accordingly plant pathogens have expanded families of glycoside hydrolases, carbohydrate esterases, cutinases, and pectin lyases to degrade (figure 4.15)

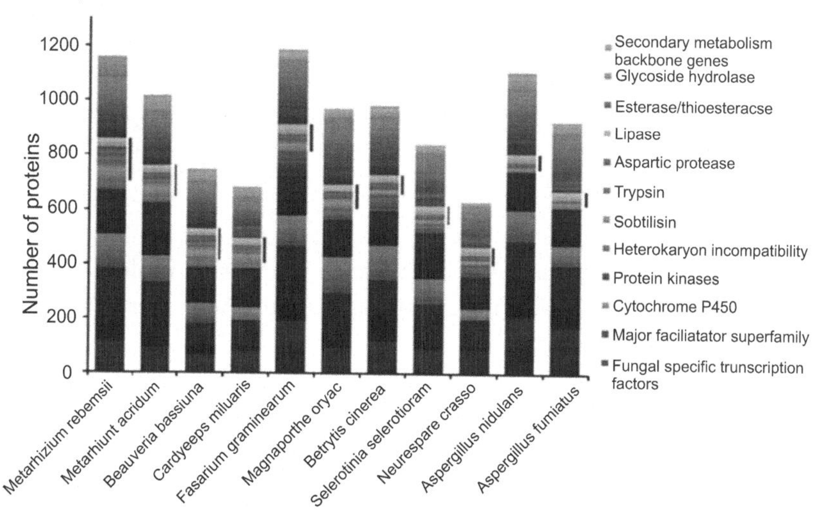

Fig. 4.15: The protein family size of insect pathogens relates to their insect killing strategies

B. bassiana genome resembles *Metarhizium* spp. and *C. militaris* (Gao, Jin, *et al.*, 2011; Zheng, Xia, *et al.*, 2011), in the expansion of gene families of proteases, chitinases, lipases, fatty acid hydroxylases, and acyl-CoA dehydrogenases (for β-oxidation of fatty acids), which all have potential targets in insect hosts (Xiao, Ying, *et al.*, 2012).

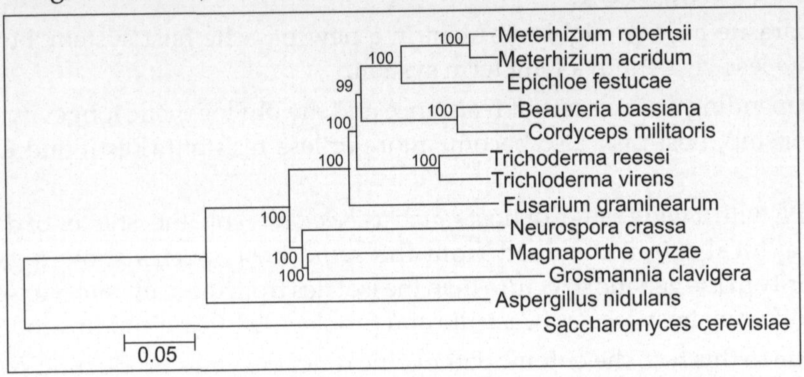

Fig. 4.16: ***Phylogenomic relationships of insect pathogenic fungi (branches highlighted in thicker lines) with other fungi. B. bassiana and C. militaris*** **are closely related and evolved into insect pathogens independently of the** ***Metarhizium*** **lineage (Wang and Raymond, 2014)**

EPF as Bioagents

There is a correlation between pathogenicity and enzymes production in interactions of hosts and EPF. Hence a new potentiality in relation to enzymes as biocontrol agents in insects is being used.

The enzymes efficacy has been proved against cotton aphid (Aphis gossypi). The insecticide action is mainly caused by chitinases (Kim *et al.*, 2010).

In larvae of Diamond back moth enzymes application significantly affects its growth and metamorphosis (Ali *et al.*, 2010; Shaib *et al.*, 2012).

Due to this fact, the entomopathogenic fungi enzymes production systems are established. The Solid State Fermentation (SSF) is an adequate technology which is employed in the bioprocess development, facilitating its production at great scale (Perez *et al.*, 2014).

CONCLUSION

The natural enemies are host specific hence studies at molecular level for detection, differentiation, identification and evaluation leads to successful biological control programme.

Transgenic plants and insects (Pests/Natural enemies) with increased fitness (maintaining gene stability and overcoming gene silencing) may be developed through molecular studies.

Regarding increased virulence of entomopathogens, further molecular studies are still needed for evaluations relating to environmental biosafety.

REFERENCES

Attathom T. (2002): Biotechnology for Insect Pest Control. Pesticides—Advances in Chemical and Botanical Pesticides. *Proc. Sat. Forum, "Sustainable Agricultural System in Asia,"* Nagoya: 73-84.

Bakr R F A, Gesraha Md, Mohamed Guneidy N A, Elatief Farag, Ebeid A R, Elbehery H H A and Ellail Md. (2013): Molecular Genetics Identification of Two Bracon Species Based on RAPD-PCR and 16S rRNA genes. *Egypt Academic Journal of Biological Science,* 5(2): 99-107.

Beech C J, Koukidou M, Morrison N I and Alphey L (2012): Genetically Modified Insects: Science: Use, Status and Regulation, International Centre for Genetic Engineering and Biotechnology (ICGEB), Padriciano, 99:349149 Trieste, Italy. *Collection of Biosafety Reviews,* 6: 66-124.

Benedict M Q. (2014): Transgenic Insects: Techniques and Applications, CABI.PP:399.

Davis G A, Havill N P, Adelman Z N, Caccone A, Kok L T and Salom S M (2011): DNA Barcodes and Molecular Diagnostics to Distinguish an Introduced and Native *Laricobius* (Coeloptera: Derodontidae) Species in Eastern North America. *Biological control,* 50: 53-59.

Hagedorn H H, Hildebrand J G, Kidwell M G and Law J H. (1990): Molecular Insect Science. Proceeding of the International Symposium on Molecular Insect Science, 22-27 1989, Arizona, pp. 401.

Hoffman K F (2014): Insect Molecular Biology and Ecology. CRC Press, pp. 428.

Holopainen J. K. (2005): Improvement of Biological Control by Volatile Plant Compounds. FORSKNINGSNYTT : 18-19.

James C. (2000): Global Status of Commercialized Transgenic Crops 1999. ISAAA Briefs No. 17. ISAAA, Ithaca, New York.

Jenkins C, Chapman T A, Jessica L. Micallef and Reynolds O L (2012): Molecular Techniques for the Detection and Differentiation of Host and Parasitoid Species and the Implications for Fruit Fly Management. Insects, 3: 763-788.

Kaldeh S R, Hosseini R, Hajizadeh J and Sohani M M (2012): Molecular Identification and Detection of Lysiphlebus fabarum (Hym: Braconidae): A Key Parasitoid of Aphids, by Using Polymerase Chain Reaction. Journal of Agriculture Science and Technology, 14: 1453-1463.

Lucena W A, Pelegrini P B, Martins D, Fonseca F C A, Gomes, J E, Leonardo L. P. de Macedo, Maria Cristina Silva, Oliveira R S and Grossi-de-Sa M F (2014): Molecular Approaches to Improve the Insecticidal Activity of *Bacillus thuringiensis* Cry Toxins. *Toxins (Basel),* 6(8): 2393–2423.

Pérez S L, Barranco-Florido, J E, Rodríguez-Navarro, Cervantes M J F and Ramos L M Á (2014): Enzymes of Entomopathogenic Fungi, Advances and Insights. Advances in Enzyme Research, 2: 65-76.

Rechcigl J E and Rechcigl N A (1998): Biological and Biotechnological Control of Insect Pests. Lewis Publishers, pp. 359.

Rosen, D (1986): The Role of Taxonomy in Effective Biological Control Programs. Agriculture Ecosystems and Environment 15: 121-129.

Rukshana K and Sebastiana C D (2015): Molecular Barcoding and Phylogeny Analysis of *Goniozus nephantidis* (Hymenoptera: Bethylidae), A Larval Parasitoid of Coconut Black Headed Caterpillar, *Opisina arenosella* (Lepidoptera: oecophoridae). International Research Journal of Pharmacy, 2015, 6(4): 239-241.

Stevens J, Kerry D, Jennifer, Shelley Evans and Marilyn Anderson (2010): Biotechnological Approaches for the Control of Insect Pests in Crop Plants (12th Chapter); Pesticides–Advances in Chemical and Botanical Pesticides, pp. 271:308.

Tabashnik BE, Gassmann AJ, Crowder DW, Carriere Y (2008): Insect Resistance to Bt Crops: Evidence versus Theory. *National Biotecology,* 26: 199-202.

Talukdar D. (2013): Modern Biotechnological Approaches in Insect Research. *International Research Journal of Science and Engineering,* 1(3): 71-78.

Tara D G, Kuhlmann U, Haye T, Gillott C, and Erlandson M (2005) : A Single-step Multiplex PCR Assay for the Detection of European *Peristenus* spp., Parasitoids of Lygus spp. *Biocontrol Science and Technology,* 15(5): 481-495.

Trang T T K, Malathi V Jand Debjani D (2013): DNA Barcode for Identification of *Chelonus blackburni* (Hymenoptera: Braconidae), A Biocontrol Agent in Cotton Crop. *Omonrice,* 19: 61-68.

Vink, C J (2012) : A Simple PCR-RFLP Method to Distinguish between Species and Strains of *Microctonus* Parasitoids Found in New Zealand. *New Zealand Plant Protection,* 65: 186-191.

Wang C.S., St Leger R.J (2007): The MAD1 Adhesion of *Metarhizium anisopliae* Links Adhesion with Blastospore Production and Virulence to Insects, and the MAD2 Adhesion Enables Attachment to Plants. Eukaryot. Cell, 6:808–816.

Zhang, S., Wideman, E., Bernard, G., Lesot, A., Pinot, E., Pedrini, N., *et al.,* (2012). CYP52X1, Representing New Cytochrome P450 Subfamily, Displays Fatty Acid Hydroxylase Activity and Contributes to Virulence and Growth on Insect Cuticular Substrates in Entomopathogenic Fungus *Beauveria bassiana. Journal of Biological Chemistry,* 28: 13477-13486.

Zhu Y C and Greenstone M H (1999): Polymerase Chain Reaction Techniques for Distinguishing Three Species and Two Strains of *Aphelinus* (Hymenoptera: Aphelinidae) from *Diuraphis noxia* and *Schizaphis graminum* (Homoptera: Aphididae). *Annals of the Entomological Society of America,* 92(1): 71-79.

Plant Biotechnology and Industrial Applications
Edited by: Alka Chauhan and Pawan Kumar 'Bharti'
ISBN: 978-93-5056-884-2
Edition: 2017
Published by: Discovery Publishing House Pvt. Ltd., New Delhi (India)

5 Utilization of Different Wastes for Enzymes Production and their Utilization in Industry

[1]Nivedita Sharma and [1]Shruti Pathania

INTRODUCTION

Environmental issues and concerns aimed at reducing the ambient pollution have boosted the search for "Clean Technologies" to be used in the production of commodities of importance to chemical, energy and food industries. This practice makes use of alternative materials, requires less energy, and diminishes pollutants in industrial effluents, as well as being more economically advantageous due to its reduced costs.In today's world, there has been a shift in focus to regeneration of supplies from wastes, which are found in abundance as a by-product ofany process. India's population is widely expanding. Technological advancement or innovation focused on enhancement of supplies to meet the then growing demands (Bhindey, 1994). Booming industrialization presents to the world a perennial need for raw materials for the produce and if the generated material can satisfy the requirement the cost of enzyme can be reduced (Madhumithah *et al.*, 2011). Regarding enzymes, the high price is still one of the major concerns for industrial application (Kang *et al.*, 2004; Maciel *et al.*, 2008). Enzymes are considered by their biotechnological importance. Their use has increased markedly in recent years (Graminha *et al.*, 2008).

Enzymes occur in every living cell, hence are present in all microorganisms. Each single strain of organism produces a large number of enzymes which may be hydrolyzing, oxidizing or reducing and metabolic in nature. But the absolute and relative amounts of the various individual enzymes produced have been found to vary markedly between species and even between strains of the same species. Hence, it is customary to select strains for the commercial production of specific enzymes which have the capacity for producing highest amount of the particular enzymes desired.

The concerns to reduce environmental pollution have encouraged the use of forestry, agro-industrial and urban waste sources through bioprocesses. The

[1] Dr. Y.S. Parmar University of Horticulture and Forestry, Nauni, Solan, Himachal Pradesh, 173230, India

utilization of such materials as substrates in microbial cultivations to produce mushrooms, digestible cell proteins, organic acids, secondary metabolites, enzymes, fermentable sugars for the production of second-generation ethanol, among others, have been reported (Nigam and Singh 1996; Sánchez, 2009). Lignocelluloses are the building blocks of all plants and are ubiquitous to most regions of our planet. Their chemical properties make it a substrate of enormous biotechnological value. The basic chemistry of cellulose, hemicellulose, and lignin has a profound effect on lignocellulose tertiary architect (Malherbe and Cloete, 2002).

Fig. 5.1: The different source of isolation of potential microbes: (*a*) compost, (*b*) soil, (*c*) decaying wood, (*d*) sludge

Submerged fermentation is the cultivation of microorganisms containing soluble carbon sources and nutrients maintained under agitation. The use of submerged culture is advantageous because of the ease of sterilization and process control rendering it easier to design these systems. Depending on the strain and culture conditions, the enzyme can be constitutive or inducible, showing different production level and is a preferable method for enzyme production for bacterial fermentations (Vidhayalakashmi *et al.*, 2009). On the other hand, SSF is a highly attractive and alternative process needs to be exploited for generation of cellulase/xylanase enzymes with the use of cheaply available lignocellulosic residues and low input of process engineering. SSF has an edge over SmF due to low capital investment and operating cost, higher product yield, better product quality, cheaper product recovery and cheaper technology (Pandey *et al.*, 2003). Among different microorganisms evaluated so far, molds being best suited microorganisms to SSF for commercial cellulase and xylanase production.

Solid-state fermentation isespecially suited to growth of fungi because of theirlower moisture requirements compared with bacteria. (Ogawa, 1995) Solid-state fermentations are simple, low cost, andprovide high yields of appropriate enzymes (Wang *et al.*, 2005). Theenzymes produced are more concentrated than thosefrom submerged cultures. Problems with solid-statefermentation include incomplete utilization of thenutrients because of poor oxygen and heat transfer in the substrate (Sangsurasak P and Mitchell, 1995) Solid-state fermentations can useinexpensive and widely available agricultural residuesas substrates.Fungi are mostlypreferable, because they generally produce extracellularenzymes which facilitate recovery of the enzymes from thefermentation broth (Amin *et al.*, 2014). Some of theseapplications are in the production of detergent, starch, beverages, food, textile industry, animal feed, pulp andpaper, leather, chemical and biomedical products (Elisashvili, 2006 and Dumsday, 2004).

Table 5.1: Different Enzymesand their Microbial Sources

Some	Enzyme	Microroganisms
Fungal	Amylase	*A.oryzae*
	Glucosidase	*A.flavus*
	Protease	*A.niger*
	Glucose oxidase	*P.notatum*
	catalase	*A.niger*
	Pectinase	*A.niger*
Bacterial	Amylases	*Bacillus subtilis*
	Protease	
	Peniciliinase	
Yeast	Invertase	*S.cerevisiae*

BIOMASS AVAILABLE FOR ENZYME PRODUCTION

Biomass comprising forestry, agricultural and agro-industrial wastes are abundant, renewable and inexpensive energy source, including variety of materials such as sugarcane bagasses, waste paper, brewer spent grains, switch grass and straw, stems, stalk, leaves, husks, shell and peels from cereals like rice, wheat, corn sorghum and barley and forest waste. Waste accumulated every year in the large quantity causing larger environmental problems. Due to their chemical composition based on sugars and other compound of interest they could be utilized for the production of value added products such as ethanol, food additives, enzymes, organic compounds and other. Therefore beside the environmental problems caused by their accumulation in the nature, the non use of these materials constitutes a loss of potentially valuable source (Mussatto and Teixeira, 2010). Lignocellulose is the world's main source of renewable organic matter and the chemical properties of its components make it a material of great biotechnological value. Therefore, a few years ago, the concept of lignocellulose biorefinery emerged, which has received growing attention due to the potential of conversion of this material into many high added value products such as chemical compounds, fermentation substrates, feedstock and biofuels (Ragauskas *et al.*, 2006; Demirbas, 2008).

In nature a variety of bacteria and fungi produces cellulase and xylanase to hydrolyze the insoluble polysaccharides into soluble oligomers and subsequently to oligomers. This conversion is quite difficult and owing to the complex structure of plant cell wall degradation (Moiser *et al.*, 2005).

Fig. 5.2: Different waste utilized for enzymes production under solid state fermentation.

Abbreviations: a = Forest residues b = Wood chips c = Pine needles d = Waste apple pomace e = Rice gran f = Sugarcane baggaseg= Wheat straw h = Fruit waste i = Orange pulp j = Cassava waste k = Coconut waste l = Fish industrial waste

Substrates and their Enzymes Involved in their Degradation

Cellulose

Biomass comprises on average of 50% cellulose, 30% hemicelluloses and 20% lignin by dry weight. Hemicellulose is an important biomass reservoir in the plant cell wall (Hongpattarakre, 2002).

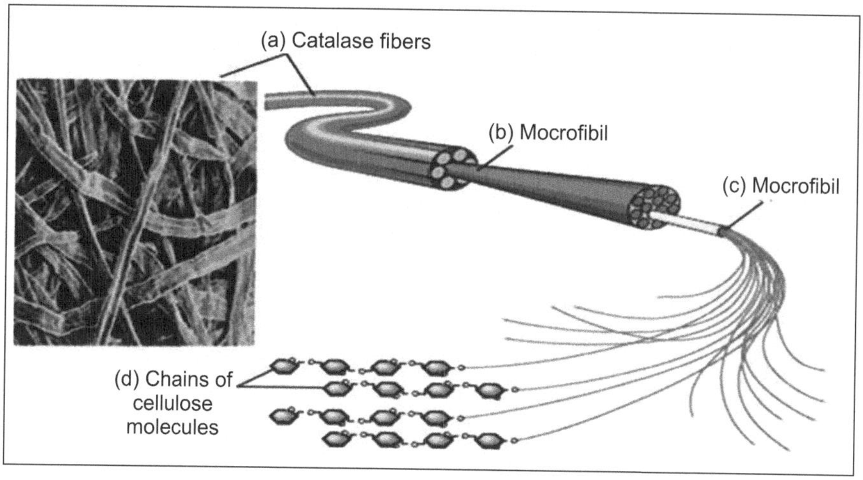

Fig. 5.3: Composition of cellulose fibre

Cellulosesare the most common carbohydrate occurring in plant throughout the world. In fruits and vegetables cellulose comprising of almost 50% of carbohydrates while hemicelluloses comprise 15-34% (Das and Singh, 2004). Cellulose is an unbranched linear homopolymer of glucose units linked by β-1,4-D-glucosidic bonds, forming an insoluble, crystalline microfibrils which are highly resistant to enzymatic hydrolysis (Hongpattarakre, 2002).

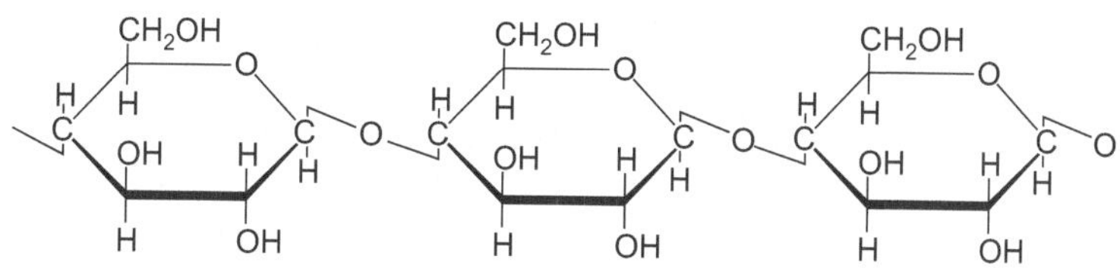

Fig. 5.4: Structure of cellulose (Simon and Scherage, 1988)

Cellulose fibers, crystaline and amorphous regions alternate. The crystaline regions are very cohesive, with rigid structure, formed by the parallel configuration of linear chains, which results in the formation of intermolecular hydrogen bonds, contributing to cellulose's insolubility and low reactivity, at the same time making it more resistant to acid hydrolysis, making water entrance difficult and modifying fiber elasticity. The amorphous regions are formed by cellulose chains with weaker organization, being more accessible to enzymes and susceptible to hydrolysis (Bobbio & Bobbio, 2003; Nelson & Cox, 2006).

(i) Biochemistry of cellulose degradation

Cellulases are a group of hydrolytic enzymes capable of hydrolyzing cellulose to smaller sugar components of β-glucose units. Cellulase, a complex of sequentially acting component enzymes are found to be synthesized by a variety of microbes (Karmakar and Ray, 2011). The cellulose-hydrolysing enzymes (i.e. cellulases) are divided into three major groups:

(*a*) *Endoglucanase* (endo-1,4-β-D-glucanase, EC 3.2.1.4): These catalyse random cleavage of internal bonds of the cellulose chain.

(*b*) *Cellobiohydrolase or Exoglucanase* (exo-1, 4-β-D-glucanase, EC 3.2.1.91): These attack the chain ends, releasing cellobiose.

(*c*) β-*glucosidase or cellobiase* (1, 4-β-D-glucosidase, EC 3.2.1.21): They are only active on cello-oligosaccharides and cellobiose, and release glucose monomers units from the cellobiose, for instance.

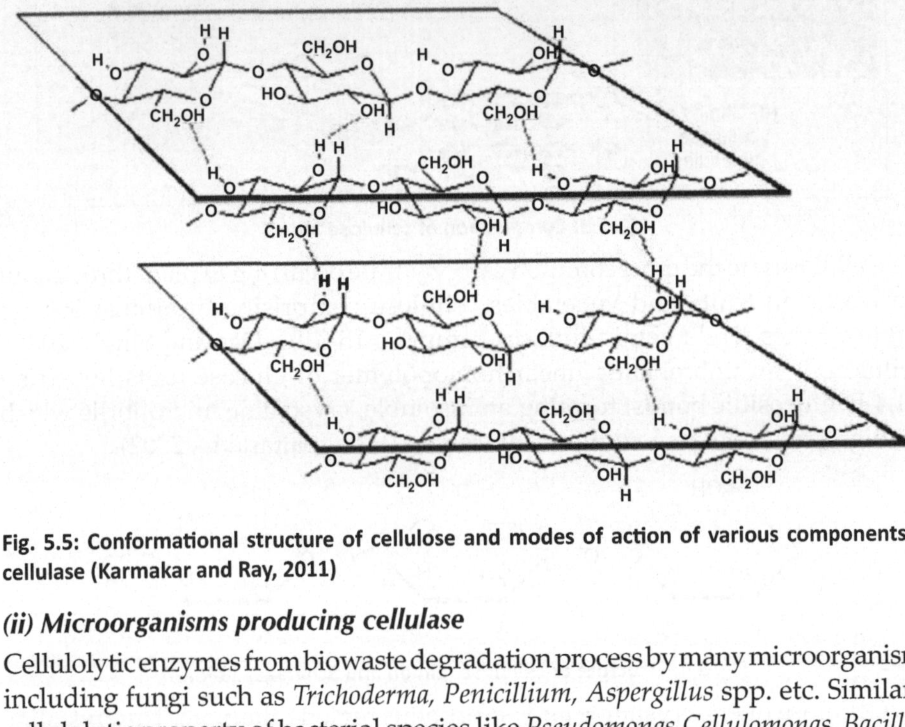

Fig. 5.5: Conformational structure of cellulose and modes of action of various components of cellulase (Karmakar and Ray, 2011)

(ii) Microorganisms producing cellulase

Cellulolytic enzymes from biowaste degradation process by many microorganisms including fungi such as *Trichoderma, Penicillium, Aspergillus* spp. etc. Similarly cellulolytic property of bacterial species like *Pseudomonas,Cellulomonas, Bacillus, Micrococcus, Cellovibrio and Sporosphytophaga* spp. were also reported.

Thermophilic fungi i.e., *Chaetomium thermophile, Humicolainsolens (syn. Scytalidiumthermophilum), Sporotrichum thermophile, Thermoascusaurantiacus,* etc. (Bhat 2000; Maheshwari *et al.,* 2000).

(iii) Different wastes for cellulase production

Agroindustrial waste: Wheat straw, rice bran, forest residue, pines, coconut shell, fruit peels, grape marc, orange peel, bagasse.

Hemicellulose

Xylan(group of hemicellulose) are the heteropolysaccharides consisting of a β-1,4-xylopyranosyl backbone with branches of acetyl arabinosyl and glucuronyl residues. Xylan is a heteroploymer composed primarly of β-1,4-linked xylose with various amount of arabinose, glucose, galactosides, uronic acid and other sugars as side group depending on the plant source. In some higher plants and agricultural wastes, xylan constitutes from 20-40% of the dry weight (Rifaat *et al.*, 2005), hemicelluloses has different classification, depending upon the sugar residue e.g. xylans, mannans, glucans, glucouronoxylans, arabonoxylans, glucomannans, galactomannnans, galactoglucomannans, β-glucans and xyloglucans. When compared to cellulose, hemicelluloses differ by composition of sugar residue units, by presence of shorter chain, a branching of main chain molecules and the amorphous structure, which made its structure easier to hydrolyse than cellulose (Butt *et al.*, 2008).

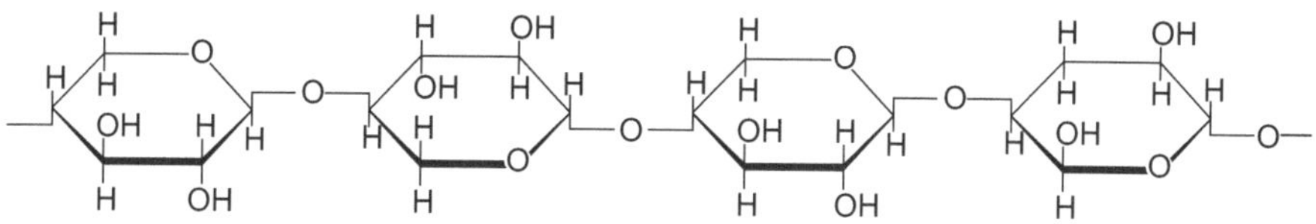

Fig. 5.6: Structure of xylan (Roubroeks *et al.*, 2001)

I. Xylanase in degradation of xylan

Xylans are linear homopolymers that contain d-xylose monomers linked through β-1-4-glycosyl bonds (Garg *et al.*, 2009). In order to efficiently depolymerisexylan to the components monosaccharides, a mixture of different enzymatic functionalities are required including:

1. Endo-1,4-β-xylanase (EC3.2.1.8)
2. β-D-xylosidase (EC 3.2.1.37)
3. α-L-arabinofuranosidase (AFs) (EC 3.2.1.55)
4. α-glucuronidae (EC 3.2.1.139)
5. Acetyl xylan esterase (EC 3.1.1.72)
6. Ferulic/coumarc acid esterase (EC 3.1.1.73) (Dodd and Cann, 2009).

II. Microorganisms producing xylanase

Xylanase occur widely in bacteria and fungi. Many reports on xylanases from *Bacillus* spp., *Clostridium* spp., *Streptomyces* spp., *Aspergilus* spp., and other microorganisms are available (Bastawde, 1992; Wong *et al.*, 1988). Cellulase-free xylanases have been purified and characterized from *Ascomycete Thielaviaterrestris* (Gilbert *et al.*, 1992), *Aspergillus niveus* RS2 (Sudan and Bajaj, 2007), *Acrophialophoranainiana* (Cardoso and Filho, 2003) and from different species of *Bacillus* (Ayyachamy and Vatsala, 2007; Knob and Carmona, 2009).

III. Different wastes utilized for xylanase production

Wheat bran, Soya oil cake, bagasse, tomato pomace, apple pomace, rice bran, wheat husk, rice straw.

Lignin

Lignin is the third major component of lignocellulosic biomass and its concentration ranges for 20 to 35 %. It is a complex polymer of phenyl propane units (coumaryl, coniferyl and sinapyl alcohol) (Bishnu *et al.*, 2011). Lignin acts as cementing agent and an impermeable barrier for enzymatic attack (Howard *et al.*, 2003). Lignin provides plants with the structural support and impermeability they need as well as resistance against microbial attack and oxidative stress (Bishnu *et al.*, 2011). These properties of lignin may be attributed to its amorphous nature, water insolubility and optical inactivity. The latter properties also make it tough to degrade (Fengel and Wegener, 1984). Lignin forms a lignocellulosic comlex with the carbohydrates and proteins (Oziel *et al.*, 2008). Lignin, which provides the structural component of the plant cell wall, is a heterogeneous and complex biopolymer that consists of phenyl propanoid units linked by various non-hydrolyzable C-C and C-O bonds (Gellerstedt, 1989). The main limitation of all hemecontaining peroxidases is their low operational stability, mostly due to their rapid deactivation by hydrogen peroxide.

(i) Ligninases

Laccase (EC 1.10.3.2) is a multicopper blue oxidase that couples the four electron reduction of oxygen with the oxidation of a broad range of organic substrates, including phenols, polyphenols, anilines, and even certain inorganic compounds by aone-electron transfer mechanism (Piontek, 2002). Laccase is widely distributed in higher plantsand fungi (Messerschmidt, 1990) and has been found also in insects and bacteria. Recently a novelpolyphenol oxidase with laccase like activity was mined from a metagenome expressionlibrary from bovine rumen microflora (Beloqui, 2006). Laccases are extracellular phenol oxidases that catalyse the oxidative degradation of aromatic compounds in lignin, while reducing oxygen to water. They are relatively non-specific enzymes. Laccase isoforms vary between species and within species (Oziel *et al.*, 2008). The broad substrate specificity of laccases permits their use in multiple biotechnological and industrial applications as inexpensive biologically and environmentally friendly tools for the pretreatment of lignocellulose for bioethanol production, pulp bleaching, dye degradation, and xenobiotic transformation and detoxification.

Laccases are glycoproteins with molecular weight of 50-130 kD. The carbohydrate moiety of the majority of laccases consists of mannose, N-acetylglucosamine, and galactose and constitutes about 45% of the protein mass in laccases of plant origin. Fungal laccases have lower carbohydrate contents (10-20%). In laccases from the basidiomycete P. eryngii the carbohydrate moieties are 1 and 7% (Munoz, 1997), whereas in laccases from *C. fulvocinerea* and *B. cinerea* carbohydrate contents are 32 and 49%, respectively, i.e. are high for fungal laccases. Many researchers think the carbohydrate moiety of the molecule is responsible for the stability of the protein globule: deglycosylation of laccase from Ganodermalucidum completely inhibited the activity (Ko *et al.*, 2001). The carbohydrate moiety has also been supposed to protect the enzyme molecule against proteolysis and inactivation by free radicals (Yoshitake, 1993).

Laccases produced by some wood-rotting fungi from the genus Basidiomycete play a major role in the biodegradation of lignin (Coll, 1993) and have the capability to oxidize recalcitrant aromatic compounds with redox potentials exceeding their own with the help of natural or chemical mediators (Camarero, 2005). Because of their wide reaction capabilities as well as the broad substrate specificity, the laccase and the LMS possess great biotechnological potential. Promising applications include textile-dye bleaching (Kierulff, 1997), pulp bleaching (Palonen, 2004), food improvement, bioremediation of soils and water, polymer synthesis, and the development of biosensors and biofuel cells (Minussi, 2002).

(ii) Microorganisms producing laccase

Laccases is widely distributed in plants, bacteria i.e. *S. lavendule, S. cyaneus, Marinomonasmediterranea* and *Marinomonasmediterranea,* fungi i.e. *Phanerochaetechrysosporium, theiophoraterrestris* and *Lenzites, Betunia* and white rot fungi such as *Phlebia radiate, pleurotusostreatus* and *Trametes versicolor* and *Trichoderma* such as *T. atroviride, T. harazianum, T. longibrachiatum* and insects. They have been isolated from Ascomycetous, Deuteromycetous and Basidiomycetous fungi to which more than 60 fungal strains belong. The white rot basidiomycetes fungi efficiently degrade the lignin in comparison to Ascomycetes and Deuteromycetes which oxidize phenolic radicals and quinines.

(iii) Different waste utilized for liginase production

Rice bran, oil palm waste, empty fruit bunches (EFB), rice straw, rice husk and corn cob rice bran, wheat, sugarcane bagasse, pulse husks, municipal solid waste, tea production waste, agro food waste.

Pectin

Pectinases are a big group of enzymes that break down pectic polysaccharides of plant tissues into simpler molecules like galacturonic acids. It has long been used to increase yields and clarity of fruit juices. Since pectic substancesare a very complex macromolecule group, various pectinolytic enzymes are required to degrade it completely. These enzymes present differences in their cleavage mode and specificity being basically classified into two main groups that act on pectin "smooth" regions or on pectin "hairy" regions. Pectinases are one of the most widely distributed enzymes in bacteria, fungi and plants. This review describes the pectinolytic enzymes and their substrates, the microbial pectinase production and characterization, and the industrial application of these enzymes.Three major pecticpolyssacharides groups are recognized, all containing D-galacturonic acid to a greater or a lesser extent.

Homogalacturonan (HG): HG is a linear polymer formed by D-galacturonic acid which can be acetylated and/or methyl esterified. It can be called smooth regions of pectin. The molecule is classified according to its esterification level:

pectin has at least 75 % of the carboxyl groups methylated; pectinic acid has less than 75% of the carboxyl groups methylated; pectic acid or polygalacturonic acid has no methyl esterified carboxyl groups. Frequently the word pectin is used as a generic name for pectic substances.

Rhamnogalacturonan I (RGI): RG I is composed of the repeating disaccharide rhamnose-galacturonic acid. The galacturonic residues can be acetylated and both residues can carry side chains of neutral sugars as galactose, arabinose and xylose.

Rhamnogalacturonan II (RGII): Despite its name, RGII is a homogalacturonan chain withcomplex side chains attached to the galacturonic residues. Vincken and coworkers have proposed a pectin moleculestructure model in which HG and RGII are long side chainsof RGI backbone (figure 5.1). Both RG chains are also calledhairy regions of pectin molecule. In unripe fruit, pectin is found as a water insoluble pecticsubstance, the protopectin, bounded to cellulose microfibrils conferring rigidity on cell walls. During ripening the fruitenzymes alter the pectin structure by breaking the pectin backbone or side chains, resulting in a more soluble molecule.

(i) Pectinase

Pectinesterases: Pectinesterase (PE; E.C. 3.1.1.11) is responsible for hydrolysis of pectin by removal of methoxyl esters, resulting in acid pectins and methanol (Whitaker, 1984). Sources of PE can be plants, bacteria and fungi (Hasunuma *et al.*, 2003). According to Jayani *et al.*, (2005), PEs are stable at a temperature range of 40-50°C and have a pH range between 4.0-8.0 with fungal PE having a lower pH optima than bacterial PE.

Polygalacturonases: Polygalacturonases (PGs) hydrolyze the polygalacturonic acid chain. Endo PGs (E.C. 3.2.1.15) are found in bacteria, yeast and fungi (Sakai *et al.*, 1993 while exo-PGs (E.C. 3.2.1.67) can be of fungal origin (with monogalacturonic acid as the end product) as well as of bacterial origin (with digalactouronic acid as the end product; Luh and Phaff, 1951). PGs perform best within a pH range of 3.5-5.5 and temperature range of 30-50 °C (Jayani *et al.*, 2005).

Pectate lyases: Pectate lyases (PLs) depolymerize pectic substances by a trans-eliminative split at C-4 and simultaneous removal of H atom at C-5 (Sakai *et al.*, 1993). They can be endo PL (E.C. 4.2.2.2), exo PL (E.C. 4.2.2.9), endopolymethylgalacturonatelyase (E.C. 4.2.2.2) and exopoly-methylgalactouronatelyase (E.C. 4.2.2.9; Jayani *et al.*, 2005). Commercial PLs can be of both fungal and bacterial origins have pH optima of 7.5-10.0 and temperature optima of 40-50°C.

(ii) Microorganisms producing pectinase

Bacteria: Agrobacterium vitis, Actinidiadeliciosa, A. chinesis, bacillus licheniformis, B.halodurans, B.subtilis, campylobacter consisus, Clostridium butyricum.

Fungus: Alternaria alternate, Colletotrichum lupine, Fusarium sp, rhizopussp, Penicillum sp.

(iii) Different wastes utilized for pectinase production

Orange peel, cocoa, banana, mango peel, raw papaya andlemon peel.

Protease

Proteases are the efficient executioners of a common chemical reaction: the hydrolysis of peptide bonds. These enzymes are widely distributed in nearly all plants, animals and microorganisms (Supuran *et al.*, 2002; Mosolov and Valueva, 2005). Proteolytic enzymes belong to the hydrolase class of enzymes (EC 3) and are grouped into the subclass of the peptide hydrolases or peptidases (EC 3.4). Proteases represent the class of enzymes which occupy a pivotal position with respect to their physiological roles as wellas their commercial applications. They perform both degradativeand synthetic functions (Raq *et al.*, 1998). Proteases regulate the fate, localization, and activity of many proteins, modulate protein-protein interactions, create new bioactive molecules, contribute to the processing of cellular information, and generate, transduce, and amplify molecular signals.

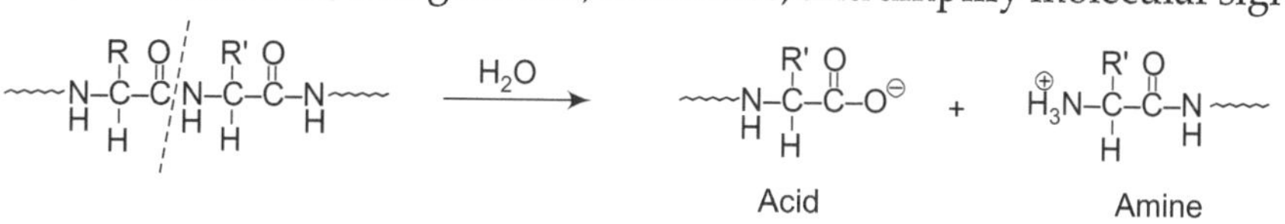

Fig. 5.8: The breakdown of protein by protease

(i) General classification of proteases

According to the Nomenclature Committee of the International Union of Biochemistry and Molecular Biology, proteases are classified in subgroup 4 of group 3. Due to their huge diversity, mechanism of action and structure they do not easily complied under general system of enzyme (Rao, 1998).

Currently proteases are classified on the basis of three major criteria that include:

- Type of reaction catalyzed,
- Chemical nature of catalytic site, and
- Evolutionary relationship with reference to structure (Barrett *et al.*, 1995).

Various other classifying criteria followed are:

(a) Depending upon the optimum pH proteases are named as

Acid proteases: These are active in the pH range 2.0 – 3.5. Fungus are the main source of acidic protease called aspergillopepsin i.e. *Aspergillus niger* (O'Donnell *et al.*, 2001), *A. oryzae* (Tsujita *et al.*, 1978), *A. awamori* (Moralejo *et al.*, 2002), *A. fumigates* (Reichard *et al.*, 1995) and *A. saitoi* (Tello-Solis *et al.*, 1995), they are mostly extracellular in production and are being commercially available.

Neutral proteases

These are active in the pH between 6.5 and 7.5.

Alkaline proteases

These are active in the pH between 7.5 and 10.5. An alkaline protease from alklophilic *Bacillus* so 221 has been reported by Horikoshi (1971) as the first enzyme with alkaline pH optimum produced by an alkalophilic microorganisms.

(b) Proteases are broadly classified as endoor exo-enzymes on the basis of their site of action on protein substrates

Exopeptidases: Exopeptidases cleave the peptide bond proximal to the amino- or carboxy-termini of the substrate. The exopeptidases act only near the ends of polypeptide chains. Based on their site of action at the N or C terminus, they are classified as amino- and carboxy-peptidases, respectively (Neurath, 1957).

Endopeptidases: Endopeptidases are characterized by their preferential action at the peptide bonds in the inner regions of the polypeptide chain away from the N and C termini (Ward, 1986).

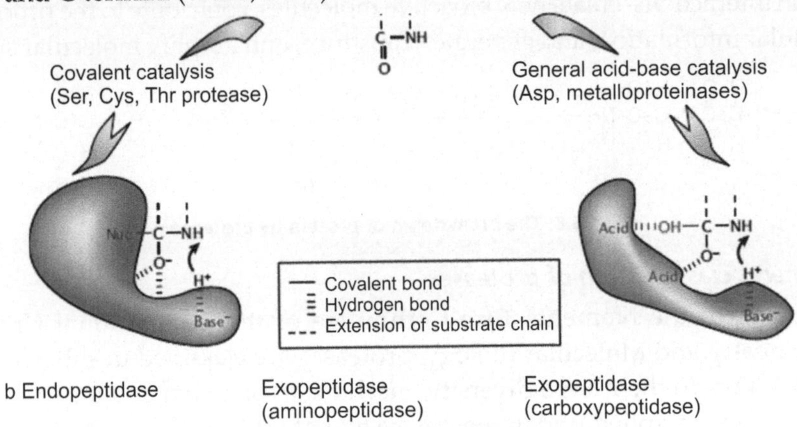

Fig. 5. 9: Action of endopeptidases

(c) Based on the functional group present at active site and their catalytic mechanisms, proteases are further classified into four prominent groups.

1. Serine proteases, with a serine and histidine.
2. Cysteine proteases, with a cysteine.
3. Aspartic proteases, with an aspartate group and
4. Metalloproteases, with a metallic ion (Zn^{++}, Ca^{++} or Mn^{++}) in their active site.

Table 5.2: List of Protease Production from Bacterial Strain

B. firmus	Landau *et al.*, 1992
B. acidophilus	Sharma *et al.*, 1994
B. proteolytices	Boyer and Hyung, 1996
Bacillus sp KSM-K 16	Kobayashi *et al.*, 1996
Bacillus sp Y	Shimogaki *et al.*, 1991

(ii) Different wastes utilized for protease production

Rice mill waste, vegetable waste, cake potato, pumpkin, cauliflower, cabbage, brinjal, bran, gram husk, rice bran, mustard oil, cassava waste, tapioca peel.

Keratin

Keratin is a fibrous structural protein found in human skin, hair and nails, it is also a part of theanimal kingdom and found in birds, reptiles, amphibians and mammals. It is used in hair care products, animal feed and fibres for textiles. Keratins are insoluble proteins from feathers, wool, hooves, scales, hair, nails (hard keratins) and stratum corneum (soft keratins). These proteins which belong to the scleroprotein groups are compounds that are extremely resistant to the action of physical, chemical and biological agents. Mechanical stability and high resistance to proteolytic degradation of keration are due to their disulfide bonds, hydrogen bonds, salt linkages and cross linkings (Kaluzewska *et al.*, 1991).

(i) Keratinase: Keratinase [E.C.3.4.21/24/99.11] are proteases able to degrade the scleroprotein keratin. Hugeamount of this protein are available as feathers, a waste by product generated by the poultry production. The mechanical stability of keratin and its resistance to biochemical degradation depends on tight packing of the production chains. In α-Helix (α-keratin), or β-Sheet (β-keratin) structure are linked by disulfide bonds which fold into initial 3-dimensional form. The enzymes capable of degrading keratin are known as keratinolytic enzymes (Alexandre *et al.*, 2005).

(ii) Microorganisms producing keratinase: They are general species of fungi, actinomyces and bacteria viz., *Doratomycesmicrosporus, Aspergillus sp, Alternariaradicina, Trichurus spiralis, Stachybotrysatra, Onygenasp, Absidiasp, Rhizomucor*sp (Friedrich *et al.*, 1999), *Streptomyces pactum, S. albs, S. thermoviolaceus, S. fradiae* (Noval and Nickerson, 1959), *S. thermonitrificans* (Mohamedin, 1999), *Flavobacteriumpennavorans, Bacillus sp* (Suntornsuk and Suntornsuk, 2003), *Stenotrophomonas*sp (Yamamura *et al.*, 2002), *Bacillus licheniformis* and *B. pumilus* (Nitisinprasert *et al.*, 1999) and *Vibrio*sp (Sangali and Brandelli, 2000). *Bacillus halodurans*PPKS-2, *Bacillus sp* Serine 32 8.0 50 [19], *Bacillus sp.* JB 99 Serine protease 66, *Pseudomonas sp.,* MS 21 Serine 30 *Pseudomonas aeruginosa* Serine, *Vibrio sp.* Kr 2 Serine *Doratomyces microspores, Streptomyces sclerotialus-Streptomyces strain* BA 7, *Aspergillus oryzae* NRRL-447, *Penicilliumsp, Chrysobacterium sp. strain* Kr 6.

(iii) Different wastes utilized for protease production: Feather of chicken (Poultry waste), wool waste, feather meal, raw feathers, chicken nails, hair and wool.

Chitin

Chitin is a long chain structural polymer composed of N-acetylglucosamine (GlcNAc) monomers connected via β (1-4) linkages. It is the second most abundant organic polysaccharide in nature after cellulose. In nature this homopolysaccharide is present in the shells of crustaceans, exoskeleton of insects, fungal and algal cell wall, zooplankton and several phytoplankton species Chitin is often tightly bound with other compounds like protein, lipids, pigments and calcium carbonate. Conversion of these chitinous wastes to useful chitin and related oligomers involves processes like demineralization, deproteinization or hydrolysis, which was earlier carried out with strong acid and bases that involves high cost, low yields and corrosion problem. The probable alternative to solve this problem is utilization of chitinolytic enzyme, chitinase and β-N-acetyl hexosaminidase.

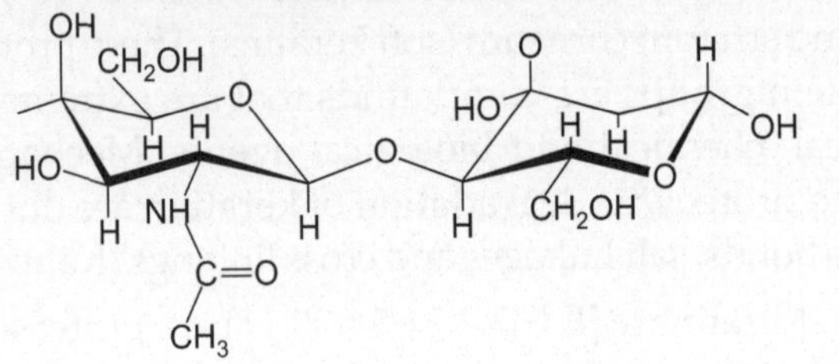

Fig. 5.10: Structure of chitin

(i) Chitinase in degrading chitin: Chitinases catalyze the hydrolysis of chitin, a b(1,4)-linked N-acetyl-glucosamine (GlcNAc) polysaccharide (Figure 5.1), and are critical for the normal development of insects (Fukamizo & Kramer, 1995) and fungi (Bartnicki-Gracia, 1968). Structurally diverse chitinases have been isolated from plants, where they may act as a defense against fungal pathogens (Boller *et al.*, 1983; Collinge *et al.*, 1993). The ®ve known classes of chitinases are grouped into two glycosyl hydrolase families (Henrissat & Bairoch, 1993). Family 18 consists of class III and class V chitinases found in a wide range of organisms including bacteria, plants, animals and fungi. Family 19 consists of class I, II and IV chitinases, and are found only in plants. The enzyme structures and hydrolysis mechanisms for the two families appear to be quite different.

Chitinases (EC 3.2.1.14) are produced by several bacteria, actinomycetes, fungi and also by higher plants.

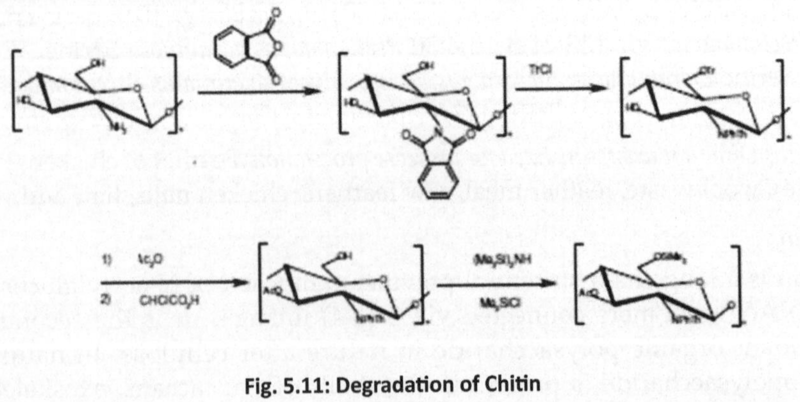

Fig. 5.11: Degradation of Chitin

(ii) List of microorganisms producing chitinase: Bacteria: *Flavobacterium, Bacillus, Cytophaga, Pseudomonas.*

Fungi: *Aspergillus, Mucor and Mortierella.*

Aerobic *Aeromonas, enterobacter, Chromobacterium, arthobacter, Flavobacterium Serretia, Bacillus Erwinia, Vibrio.*

(iii) Different wastes utilized for chitinase production: Prawn waste, shellfish waste, shrimp shell, marine waste, sea food, fish processing waste, flake chitin, fungal cell wall crab shell, food and agricultural industrial waste, crustacean *waste.*

Starch

Starch is a polymer of glucose linked to one another through C1 oxygen by a glycosidic bond. At the end of the polymeric chain, a latent aldehyde group is present. This group is known as the reducing end. Pure starch consists predominantly of α-glucan in the form of amylose and amylopectin. While amylopectin is soluble in water, amylose and the starch granule itself are insoluble in cold water. Amylose is a linear polymer consisting of up to 6000 glucose units with α, 1-4 glycosidic bonds (figure 5.1). The relative content of amylose and amylopectin varies with the source of starch. Average amylose content in most common starches is 20-30% (Marc *et al.,* 2002). Amylopectin consists of short α, 1-4 linked linear chains of 10–60 glucose units and α, 1-6 linked side chains with 15–45 glucose units (figure 5.2). The average number of branching points in amylopectin is 5% (Thompson, 2000). The complete amylopectin molecule contains about 20,00,000 glucose units, thereby being one of the largest molecules in nature (Marc *et al.,* 2002).

Starches are defined as waxy when the ratio of amylose to amylopectin is low (~15%), normal when amylase represents ~16-35% and high-amylose (or amylo-) when amylose exceeds ~36%. Starch depolymerization by amylase is the basis for several industrial processes such as preparation of glucose syrups, bread making and brewing.

(i) Amylase in degradation of starch: Amylases are a class of enzymes that are capable of digesting glycosidic linkages found in starches. These enzymes are classified as endoamylases and exoamylases according to the manner in which the glycosidic bond is attacked. The α-amylase family, *i.e.* the clan GH-H of glycoside hydrolyses, is the largest family of glycoside hydrolases, transferases and isomerases comprising nearly 30 different enzyme specificities.

Endoamylases are able to cleave α, 1-4 glycosidic bonds present in the inner part (endo-) of the amylose or amylopectin chain. α-amylase (EC 3.2.1.1) is a well-known, classical calcium containing 1,4 α D glucan glucanohy-drolase endoamylasewhichcatalyzeshydrolysis of starch and related carbohydrates byrandomly cleaving internal α D (14) glycosidiclinkage, yielding glucose, maltose, maltotriose, and other oligosaccharides. It belongs to familythirteen in the classification of glycosidehydrolases. This family is the most varied of allglycoside hydrolase families, containing manyenzymes able to catalyze various reactions, suchas hydrolysis, transglycosylation, condensationand cyclization (Senthil kumar *et al.*, 2012).

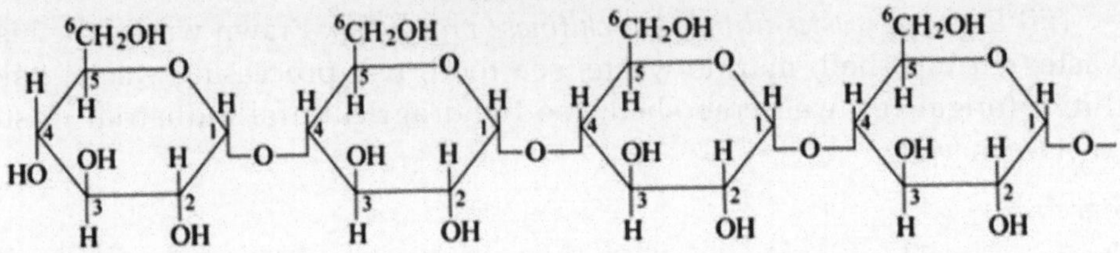

Fig. 5.12: Structure of amylase

Enzymes belonging to the second group, the exoamylases, either exclusively cleave α,1-4 glycosidic bonds such as β-amylase (EC 3.2.1.2) or cleave both α,1-4 and α,1-6 glycosidic bonds like amyloglucosidase or glucoamylase (EC 3.2.1.3) and α-glucosidase (EC 3.2.1.20). Exoamylases act on the external glucose residues of amylose or amylopectin and thus produce only glucose (glucoamylase and α-glucosidase), or maltose and β-limit dextrin. Glucoamylase and α-glucosidase differ in their substrate preference: α-glucosidase acts best on short maltooligosaccharides and liberates glucose with α-configuration while glucoamylase hydrolyzes long-chain polysaccharides best. α-amylases and glucoamylases have also been found in a large variety of microorganisms (Pandey *et al.*, 2000a).

(ii) Microorganisms producing amylase: Production of α-amylase is usually performed by bacteria strains such as *Bacillus subtilis, B. polymyxia, B. mesentericus, B. vulgarus, B. megaterium and B. licheniformis.*

(iii) Different waste for utilized for cellulase production: Agro-industrial waste: wheat bran (WB), corn flour (CF), rye straw (RS), wheat straw (WS), banana waste, coffee waste, banana peel, potato waste, fruit waste, cassava fibres.

ENZYME PRODUCTION

Enzymes of industrial interest have traditionally been obtained from submerged fermentation (SmF) dueto easy handling and control. In recent years, solid state fermentation (SSF) has received renewed interest since SSF can produce higher yields or better product characteristics than SmF. SSF has been recently reassessed, especially because of the possibility of usinglow-cost agro-industrial residues as raw materials (Pérez-Guerra *et al.*, 2003; Malilas *et al.*, 2013).

Substantial cost reduction may be possible by exploring ways of cellulose conversion using micro-organisms that produce cellulolytic/xylanolytic enzymes.

Solid state fermentation is an attractive process to produce cellulase and xylanase economically due to its lower capital investment and lower operating expresses (Xen and Cen, 1999). To reduce the cost of enzyme, selection of a cheap and easily available substrate appears to be essential (Beg *et al.*, 2000 & Senthi Kumar *et al.*, 2005). The lignocellulosic biomass especially agricultural wastes are known to be excellent carbon source for microbial enzyme production (Yang *et al.*, 2006). It is an attractive method for fungal enzymes production because it stimulates the natural growth of micro-organisms on a moist insoluble substrate in the absence or near absence of free liquid (Pandey, 2002). This cultivation technique is acquiring a special relevancy in the field of biotechnology processes, as an alternative to the traditional submerged fermentation, because has lower energy requirement, produces less waste water, gives high product concentrations, avoids the foaming and has lower risks of contamination (Gessesse and Mamo, 1999 & Suryanarayan, 2003).

Classification

(*i*) Solid Substrate Fermentation

(*ii*) Submerged Fermentation

(i) Solid substrate fermentation: Micro-organisms are cultivated on a solid substrate with a high content of nutrients and a large surface area, such as wheat germ, wheat bran, rice bran and cereal meal, with the addition of mineral salts. The low water content of the medium considerably lowers the threat of bacterial infections. Also, the enzyme solution obtained is more concentrated in comparison to that obtained in a submerged fermentation process. The major downside of this method of production is that it is not possible to feed ingredients to the medium during cultivation. As a result, the changes in pH and carbohydrate concentration cannot be controlled during the process and are predetermined by the composition of the medium and inoculum.

(ii) Submerged fermentation: In this case, microorganisms are cultivated in a liquid medium in which contains the required nutrients in the required concentrations. Nutrients are generally supplied in the form of cheap and readily available materials such as rice bran and wheat bran (sources of carbohydrates) or in pure and concentrated forms such as bacteriological peptone (source of proteins) which are either dissolved or suspended in water to form the growth medium. The medium is fed into a CSTR (Continuous Stirred Tank Reactor) where it is incubated at a specified temperature and pressure with constant aeration and agitation, until sufficient concentration of product is reached. The advantage of this process is the ease with which various parameters can be monitored (by periodic sampling of broth) and controlled if necessary by the addition of further nutrients or reagents. Surface-active agents are often used to prevent foaming and to cause increased excretion of extra-cellular enzymes.

Table 5.3: Comparison of Submerged Fermentation and Solid State Fermentation

Advantages	Consequences	Problems to be solved
Biological advantages		
Low water demand	Less waste water	Building of moisture gradients
High concentration of the endproduct	Lower downstream costs	
Catabolite repression significantly lower or missing	Fermentation in the presence of glucose	
Utilisation of solid substate	High concentration of the growth substrates	Building of substrate gradients Building of pH gradients
Lower sterility demands Solid support for microorganism	Mixed cultures of fermenting microorganisms	—
Simulation of the natural environment	Better performance of cultivated microorganisms	—
Fermentation of water-insoluble solid substrates		
Mixed culture of microorganisms	Synergism of metabolic performance	—
Processing advantages		
High-volume productivity	Smaller fementer volumes	
Low energy demand for heating	—	Building of temperature gradients
Easy aeration	—	Building of oxygen gradients on a large scale
Utilisation of otherwise unusable carbon sources	Cheap and abundant carbon sources	—
No anti-foam chemicals	No lost of microorganisms during fermentation	—

Trichoderma harazium, cellulose degrading filamentous fungi, having tremendous ability to biomass degradation (Ahmed *et al.*, 2009) the partial purification of three cellulose enzymes exoglucanase (EXG), endoglucanase (EG) and β-glucosidase (BGL), the optimal pH, temperature and incubation time of cellulase production is found to be 120 h at 25°C, pH 5.5.

Table 5.4: Examples of Different Fungi Producing Different Lignocellulolytic Enzymes and their Substrates

	Group	Fungal strain	Enzymes	Substrate
Aerobic fungi	Ascomycetes	*T. reesci*	Cellulases (CM Case, CBH, BGL), Hemicellulase (xylanase)	Wheat straw
		T. harzianum	Cellulases (CM Case, CBH), b-1,3-glucanases	Wheat bran, wheat straw
		A. niger	Cellulases, Xylanases	Sugar cane bagases
(Extra cellular lignocellulolytic enzymes	Basidiomycetes	*Pestalotiopsis sp.*	Cellulases (CMCase, CBH), Laccase	Forest litter of Quiercus variabilis
		P. chrysosporium	Cellulases (CMCase, CBH, BGL), CDH, LiP, MnP, Hemi-cellulases (CMCase, CBH, BGL)	Red oak, grape seeds, barley bran, woodchips
		F. palustris	Cellulases (CMCase, CBH, BGL)	Orchard grase hay
Anaerobic rumen fungi (Chytridio-mycetes)	*Anacromyces*	*Anacromyces mucronatus 543*	Cellulase (CMCase), Hemicel-lulase (xylanase)	Orchard grass hay
	Caecomyces	*Caecomyces communis*	Cellulases, Hemicellulases (xylanase, β-D-xylosidase)	Maize stem
	Cyllamyces	*Cyllamyces aberensis*	Cellulases, Xylanases	Grass oilage
(Cell-wall associated lignocellulolytic enzymes, "cellulosome")	*Neocallimastix*	*Neocallimastix frontalis*	Cellulases, Hemicellulase (xylanase, β-galactosidase)	Cotton fiber, wheat straw
	Orpinomyces	*Orpinomyces sp.*	Cellulase (CmCase, CBH, β-glucosidase), Hemicellulases (xylanase, mannanases)	Wheat straw
	Piromyces	*Piromyces sp.*	Cellulase (CmCase, CBH, β-glucosidase), Hemicellulases (xylanase, mannanases)	Maize stem

The pretreated corn cobs samples were tested for hydrolytic enzyme production from *Aspergillus niger*-IR01. In 250 ml conical flask 25 ml of Vogel's media with 2% pretreated substrates were used for enzyme production with 2% inoculum size for 96 h of fermentation period. Maximum CMCase activity (40.1 ± 1.3 IU/ml) was achieved at 2.5% NaOH treated corn cob for 30 min of autoclaving time. Highest xylanase and FPase activities of 140.3 ± 1.36 IU/ml and 10.1 ± 0.54 IU/ml was noted with 0.5% NaOH (for 15 min of steaming time) and 15min steam hydrolyzed corn cobs (Irfan *et al.*, 2010).

Raza *et al.*, (2011) reprted the production of β-glucosidase for selection of co-culture of *Aspergillus* sp., and optimization of cultural conditions for the biosynthesis of β-glucosidase by solid state fermentation. For this purpose, mono and co-cultures of *Aspergillus niger, A. awamori* and *Aspergillus oryzae* were tested and co-culture of *Aspergillus niger* and *Aspergillus oryzae* gave comparatively better production of β-glucosidase. The enzyme production was optimal when agricultural by product wheat bran (10 g) was used as solid substrate for fungal growth. Among 10 different diluents tested, M-2 containing (g/l, w/v) KH_2PO_4 2.0, $(NH_4)_2SO_4$ 1.4, urea 0.3, $MgSO_4.7H_2O$ 0.3, $ZnSO_4.7H_2O$ 0.0014, $FeSO_4.7H_2O$ 0.005, $MnSO_4$ 0.0016, $CoCl_2$ 0.002, $CaCl_2$ 0.002, polypeptone 1.0 and Tween-80 2.0 ml gave relatively higher enzyme production. The maximum production of β-glucosidase (2975 ± 5.3 U/g/min) was obtained after optimization of cultural conditions such as incubation period 72 h, initial pH 5.5, substrate to diluents ratio (1:1) and inoculum size (2 ml of spore suspension i.e., 3:1 ratio of *Aspergillus niger* and *Aspergillus oryzae*).

Table 5.5: Different Enzymes and the Substrate Utilized by Them

Enzyme	Fungi	Substrate	Reference
Endoglucanase	*Trichoderma reesei* QM9414	Rice bran	Rocky-Salimi & Hamidi-Esfahani, 2009
	Aspergillus terreus M11	Wheat bran and straw, corn cob, reedstraw, sugarcane bagasse	Gao *et al.*, 2008
	Myceliophthorasp. IMI 387099	Rice straw	Badhan *et al.*, 2007
Laccase	*Coriolopsisbyrsina*	Wheat bran	Gomes *et al.*, 2009
	Lentinustigrinus BAFC 197	Wheat straw	
	Pleurotusostreatus	Peanut shell	Mishra & Kumar, 2006
	Trametes versicolor	Sugarcane bagasse	Pal *et al.*, 1995
Xylanase	*Campomanesiapubescens*	Fruit waste	Silva *et al.*, 2013
	Bacillus brevis	Lignocellulosic substrate	Goswani and Rawat, 2015
	Aspergillus niger (CH)	Agave tequilana	Huitron *et al.*, 2008

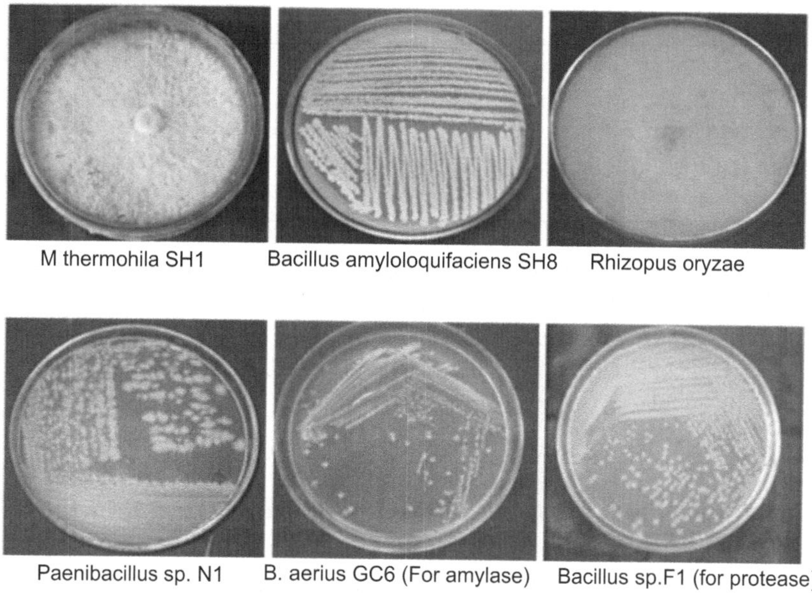

Fig. 5.13: Potential bacterial isolates capable of secreating commercial enzymes

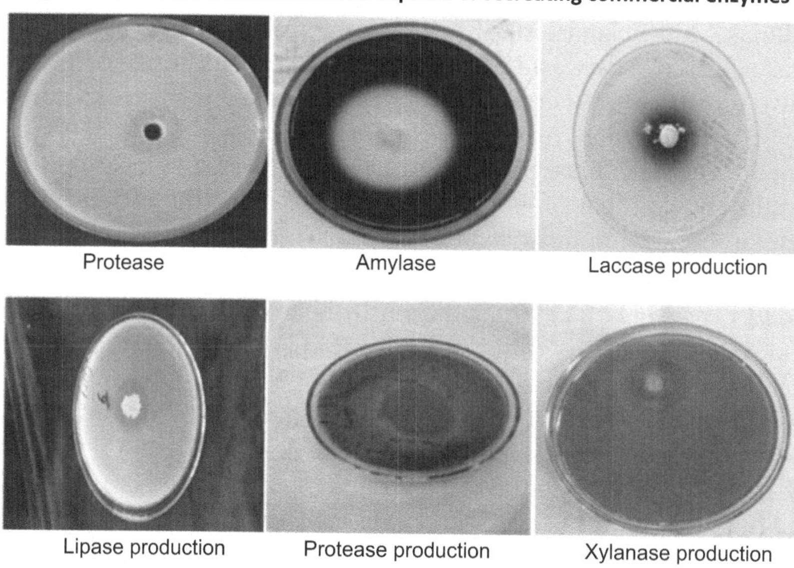

Fig. 5.14: Selection of industrially important microorganisms on the basis of their zone of hydrolysis

Geotrichum sp. F3 revealed maximum xylanase titers in Nakamura medium, pH 4.0, temperature 55°C, inoculum size 10%, substrate concentration 2.25 % after 7 days of incubation. Optimization of fermentation conditions enhanced the enzyme production to 77.54 IU/ml, as compared to initial production i.e. 10.12 IU/ml. When enzyme production mode was switched over to SSF from submerged fermentation using microwave irradiated sawdust of *C. deodara* by

Geotrichum sp. F3 using Nakamura medium, pH 4.0 and with inoculum size of 10 % at 25°C, xylanase production was enhanced dramatically to 112.890 U/g (Sharma *et al.*, 2012).

Aspergillus niger F7 isolated from soil was found to be the potent producer of cellulase and xylanase residue of forest species *Toonaciliata, Celtrisaustralis, Cedrusdeodara* and *Pinusroxburghii* was selected as substrate for biodegradation Highest extracellular enzyme activity of 2201±23.91 U/g by *A. niger* was shown in pretreated *C. australis*wood resulting in 6.72±0.20 percent hydrolysis and 6.99±0.23 biodegradation index (BI). In BSM mediated degradation of forest waste with *A. niger*, extracellular enzyme activity was increased up to 4089±67.11 U/g of dry matter in turn resulting in higher BI of 15.4±0.41 and percent hydrolysis of 19.38±0.81 in pretreated *C.australis* wood (Kaushal, 2012).

The potential fungus *Alternaria alternate* was isolated from humus rich soil of Himalayan forest grew at 30°C and producing maximum extracellular cellulase and xylanase in dubos medium under submerged fermentation. To further enhance the enzyme production under SSF, mixed substrate was alkali pretreated giving enzyme activity of 24.56 IU/ml cellulase and xylanase activity of 23.71 IU/ml (Dolma *et al.*, 2014).

Cellulase and xylanase production from rice straw using *M. thermophila* SH1 was assessed. The waste was dried, grinded to mesh size of 2.0 mm and microwave pretreated. Fermentation was carried out in flasks containing pretreated and untreated rice straw, vogel's medium, cultured at 50°C initially for 8 days to verify cellulase production and for 5 days for xylanase production. The results showed that *M. thermophila* SH1 produced the highest amount of cellulase i.e. 43.07U/gds and xylanase of 281.07U/gds using pretreated rice straw under SSF (Pathania *et al.*, 2015).

Bacillus coagulans B30 isolated from forest soil of northern Himalayan of India, explored for its cellulase free-xylanase production using physio-chemically pretreated forest biomass as a substrate. Maximum xylanase production was observed in microwave pretreated mixed biomass producing 281.63 U/g of xylanase under solid state fermentation. Xylanase was purified having molecular weight of 66.54 kDa by using SDS Page. Purified xylanase showed high temperature (503C) and pH (9.00) optimum (Sharma *et al.*, 2013).

Fungus *Myceliophthorathermophila* SH1 under solid state fermentation. Pretreated lignocellulosic biomass has emerged as a suitable substrate for cellulase and xylanase production by *M. thermophila* SH1 reaching upto 35.32 U/g cellulase and 203.20U/g of xylanase in NaOH + H_2O_2 pretreated *Populusdeltoides* wood. Different ethanologenic yeasts and bacteria were employed under monoculture and co-culture combinations for fermentation. The highest ethanol yield of 13.40 g/l was obtained in method IV by monoculture of *S. cerevisiae* II (Sharma and Sharma, 2013).

Raghavendra and Geeta (2007) reported that the agricultural crop residues such as paddy straw, wheat straw and sugarcane bagasse are abundantly available having rich source of sugars. In the present study, pretreatment process was developed for hydrolyzing paddy straw, wheat straw and sugarcane bagasse into fermentable sugars. The powdered substrates were delignified with 3 per cent NaOH and subjected for microbiological and commercial cellulase enzyme pre-treatment. Among the fungal cultures *Trichoderma reesei* has yielded maximum reducing sugar of 22.30 mg/g in paddy straw, 25.56 mg/g in wheat straw and 28.56 mg/g in sugarcane bagasse. In case of commercial cellulase enzyme sugarcane bagasse has yielded maximum reducing sugar 136.86 mg/g after hydrolysis with 2.5 percent enzyme concentration at 45°C for 24 h incubation.

Akhtar *et al.,* (2001) produced cellulases by *Bacillus subtilis* used for saccharification of wheat straw, rice straw and bagasse. Wheat straw, rice straw and bagasse were separately pretreated with (1-4% w/v) NaOH for 4 h. It has been seen that saccharification level has been increased to 33 in comparison to 4% sachharification of untreated wheat straw when the substrate was pretreated with 2% NaOH for 4h at room temperature. Sherief *et al.,* (2010) investigated bioprocessing of lignocellulosic biomass for production of bioethanol using Thermotolerant *Aspergillus fumigatus* under Solid State Fermentation conditions. Alkali pretreatment was given to rice straw twenty grams of milled dried rice straw was suspended in 160 mL 1% (w/v) NaOH and pretreated in an autoclave at 121°C for 1 h. The residues were collected and washed extensively with water until washings turned neutral. The residues were dried at 65°C for two days. Dried biomass is grinded to ensure more uniform particle size distribution.

Production of cost effective cellulase-free xylanase from a newly isolated *Geotrichum* sp. F3 using cheap and easily available forest wood residue of Cedrusdeodara has been explored in place of conventional and highly expensiveat spelt xylan. The main objective of this research was to determine the best cultivation conditions in the submerged process for xylanase production followed by solid state fermentation (SSF) from *Geotrichum* sp. F3 aiming towards optimization of enzyme production. *Geotrichum* sp. F3 revealed maximum xylanase titers in Nakamura medium, pH 4.0, temperature 55°C, inoculum size 10%, substrate concentration 2.25% after 7 days of incubation. Optimization of fermentation conditions enhanced the enzyme production to 77.54 IU/ml, as compared to initial production i.e. 10.12 IU/ml. When enzyme production mode was switched over to SSF from submerged fermentation using microwave irradiated sawdust of C. deodara by Geotrichum sp. F3 using Nakamura medium, pH 4.0 and with inoculum size of 10 % at 25°C, xylanase production was enhanced dramatically to 112.890 U/g.

Industrial Application of Enzymes

(i) Cellulase: Cellulases have wide range of industrial applications such as starch processing, animal feed production, grain alcohol fermentation, malting and brewing, extraction of fruit and vegetable juices, pulp and paper industry and textile industry.

Pulp and Paper Industry

Mixtures of cellulases (endoglucanases I and II) and xylanases have also been used for bio modification of fiber properties with the aim of improving drainage and beat ability in the paper mills before or after beating of pulp. Mansfield *et al.*, (1996) studied the action of a commercial cellulase preparation on different fractions of Douglas fir kraft pulp and observed that the cellulase treatment decreased the defibrillation reducing the fibre coarseness.

The main advantages of enzymatic deinking are reduced or eliminated alkali usage, improved fiber brightness, enhanced strength properties, higher pulp freeness and cleanliness, and reduced fine particles in the pulp. Moreover, deinking using enzymes at acidic pH also prevents the alkaline yellowing, simplifies the deinking process, changes the ink particle size distribution, and reduces the environmental pollution. Although enzymatic deinking can lower the need for deinking chemicals and reduce the adverse environmental impacts of the paper industry the excessive use of enzymes must be avoided because significant hydrolysis of the fines could reduce the bond ability of the fibers.

Textile Industry

Traditional stonewashing of jeans involves amylase-mediated removal of starch coating (desizing) and treatment (abrasion) of jeans with pumice stone (1-2 kg/ pair of jeans) in large washing machines. Cellulases have been successfully used for the biostoning of jeans and biopolishing of cotton and other cellulosic fabrics. During the biostoning process, cellulases act on the cotton fabric and break off the small fiber ends on the yarn surface, thereby loosening the dye, which is easily removed by mechanical abrasion in the wash cycle. The advantages in the replacement of pumice stones by a cellulose-based treatment include less damage of fibers, increased productivity of the machines, and less work-intensive and environment benign by Karmakar and Ray (2011).

Bioethanol Industry

Enzymatic saccharification of lignocellulosic materials such as sugarcane bagasse, corncob, rice straw, *Prosopisjuliflora, Lantana camara,* switch grass, saw dust, and forest residues by cellulases for biofuel production is perhaps the most popular application currently being investigated. Bioconversion of lignocellulosic materials into useful and higher value products normally requires multistep processes (Kuhad *et al.*, 2010).

Wine and Brewery Industry

Microbial glucanases and related polysaccharides play important roles in fermentation processes to produce alcoholic beverages including beers and wines by. These enzymes can improve both quality and yields of the fermented products. Glucanases are added either during mashing or primary fermentation to hydrolyze glucan, reduce the viscosity of wort, and improve the filterability. In wine production, enzymes such as pectinases, glucanases, and xylanases play an important role by improving color extraction, skin maceration, must clarification, filtration, and finally the wine quality and stability. B-glucosidases can improve the aroma of wines by modifying glycosylated precursors. Macerating enzymes also improve pressability, settling, and juice yields of grapes used for wine fermentation.

(ii) Xylanase: Applications of xylanases (11,46) can be found in the food and beverage industries (bakery goods, coffee, starch, plant oil, and juice manufacture), feedstock improvement, and the quality improvement of lignocellulosic residues. Often, use of xylanases permits such processes to be run with fewer chemicals, under less harsh conditions, and with less disturbing side reactions. Thus, the use of xylanases is beneficial for society as well as for the environment. Pulp and paper manufacture are currently the industrial sectors in which xylanases have received their highest-profile application. These enzymes play an important ecological role in the process of pulp bleaching, since they can be used to minimize the need for pollutant and environmentally aggressive chemicals (particularly chlorine-containing compounds) to degrade the lignins in pulp.

De-inking of Newsprint

Cellulase blended with xylanase in specific ratios is used for deinking newsprint. At optimum ratio, brightness of deinked pulp is higher, ink removal ratio is lower and breaking length, bursting index and tearing index are higher than for chemically deinked pulp. This process also gives a higher yield than chemical deinking.

In Poultry Industry

Xylanase is added to poultry feed material such as rice/wheat bran along with various other enzymes to improve absorption of nutrients by the birds and to reduce the quantity and nutrient concentration of the birds' droppings.

In Wine Production

It is used to break down xylans, pectin and hemicellulose present in fruits into simpler molecules such as xylose and glucose. By breaking down cell walls, it helps extract more juice from the fruit.

In Baking

Xylanase breaks down glycosidic linkages in arabinoxylans (in endo or exo fashion), producing smaller fragments. This improves the handling properties of dough, the over-spring and the bread volume.

In Forage Digestions

Xylanase along with other fibrolytic enzymes is sprayed onto forages in specific total mixed ratios and fed to lactating dairy cows to enhance FCM and milk production.

Bioethanol Production

Xylanase enzyme found effective in production of bioethanol as they hydrolyse the complex structure and thereby releasing the sugars that can be converted by yeast into ethanol.

(iii) Pectinase: Pectinase production occupies about 10% of the overall manufacturing of enzyme preparations. These enzymes are widely used in the food industry in the production of juices, fruit drinks and wines.

Acid pectinases, which are widely used in extraction, clarification, and removal of pectin in fruit juices, in maceration of vegetables to produce pastes and purées, and in winemaking, are often produced by fungi, especially *Aspergillus niger.*

Pectinase addition in the extraction process improves the fruit juice yield through an easier process, decreases the juice vicosity and degrades the gel structure, thus improving the juice concentration capacity. In the case of fruit juice, extraction by enzymatic maceration can increase yields by more than 90% compared to conventional mechanical juicing, besides improving the organoleptic (color, flavor) and nutritional (vitamins) properties and technological efficiency (ease of filtering).

Pectinolytic enzymes have been applied to the degumming of jute, sunn hemp, flax, ramie and coconut fibers for textile application. Degumming can be done by adding pectinolytic mixtures or by fiber fermentation (dewretting) using pectinase-producing microorganisms. In order to remove the non-cellulosic gummy material composed mainly of pectin and hemicellulose, Kapoor and coworkers had run three treatments on ramie and sunn hemp bast fibers: enzymic, chemical and chemical associated with enzymic treatment. Of the three treatments, the third one was the most promising for degumming. The scanning electron microscopic studies revealed a complete removal of non-cellulosic gummy material from the surface of ramie and sunn hemp fibres. Enzymes involved in the breakdown of plant cell wall polyssaccharides can be used to extract vegetal oils, coconut germ, palm, sunflower seed, rape seed olives and kernel oils which are traditionally produced by extraction with organic solvents, such as the potentially carcinogen hexane. By degrading cell wall components like pectin enzymes promote the oil liberation.

(iv) Protease: Proteases have a large of applications mainly in the detergent and food industries (Chaplin, 2010). In view of the recent trend of developing

environmentally friendly technologies, proteases are envisaged to have extensive applications in leather treatment and in several bioremediation processes.

Detergent Industry

Alkaline proteases have contributed greatly to the development and improvement of modern household and industrial detergents. They are effective at the moderate temperature and pH values that characterize modern laundering conditions in industrial & institutional cleaning. Alkaline protease find a major application as detergent additives because of their ability to hydrolyze and remove proteinacious stains like blood, egg, gravy, milk etc in high pH conditions (Saeki *et al.*, 2007).

Leather Industry

Soaking, dehairing of hides and skins and bating have traditionally being carried out by using different chemicals which poses a high tannery waste pollution threat. Hence, proteases with a pH optimum around 9–10 are widely used in soaking to facilitate the water uptake of the hide or skin. Alkaline proteases with elastolytic and keratinolytic activity are used for dehairing and bating process to obtain a desired grain, softness and tightness of leather in a short time (Giongo *et al.*, 2007).

Chemical Industry

A high stability in the presence of organic solvents is a feature which is highly desired in applications involving biocatalysis in non-aqueous medium for peptide synthesis. Alkaline proteases from *Aspergillus flavus, Bacillus pseudofirmus* SVB1, *Pseudomonas aeruginosa* PseA have shown promising results for potential of peptide synthesis due to their organic solvent stability (Yadav SK *et al.*, 2011). In addition to demonstrating high organic tolerance, alkaline proteases from *B. pumilus* strain CBS *and Streptomyces* sp. strain AB1 are potential strong candidates for use in peptide synthesis in low water systems.

Medical Uses

The use of immobilized alkaline protease from *Bacillus subtilis* possessing therapeutic properties has been studied for development of soft gel-based medicinal formulas, ointment compositions, gauze, non-woven tissues and new bandage materials (Davidenko *et al.*, 1999). Oral administration of proteases from *Aspergillus oryzae* has been used as a diagnostic aid to correct certain lytic enzyme deficiency syndromes.

Pharmaceutical Enhancement of the Nail Treatment

The tropical therapy of Nail disease is limited bythe low permeability of drugs through the nail plate. To increase drug penetration, the integrity of the nail plate must be compromised to a certain extent. Keratinolytic enzymes might decrease the barrier properties of the nail plate by hydrolyzing the nail keratins.

Then the addition of a reducing agent (Dithiothreitol, DTT) would increase the damage caused to the nail plate as it cleaves the disulphide linkages of keratins and increases access of the enzyme substrate. So the enzymatic disruption of nail plate is translated into enhanced drug penetration, into the nail plate.

Feed and Food industry

Alkaline proteases are widely used for production of protein hydrolysates for more than 40 years. Hydrolysates can be used as additives to food and mixed feed to improve their nutritional value. In medicine, they are administered to patients with digestive disorders and food allergies. Protein hydrosylates can be obtained from a variety of substrates such as whey, meat, soy and casein (Neklyudov A *et al.*, 2001).

(v) Keratinase: Keratinase producing microorganisms have the important industrial application in fermentation technology. Submerged fermentation of poultry waste by microorganism producing keratinase helps in the conversion of non-soluble keratin (feather) into soluble protein or polypeptide (Suntornsuk and Suntornsuk, 2003). These protein by product may be used as animal and livestock feed, and as leather filling agents (Sastry *et al.*, 1986). Keratinase has also emerging application in dehairing process in leather industry instead of sodium sulphides (Alexandre *et al.*, 2005) and also used as a detergent to remove strains on cloth (Gessesse *et al.*, 2002). Valorization of keratin containing wastes like feathers from poultry farms and hair from leather industries may have the potential in development of non polluting processes. The scope of this work is to degrade the poultry feather wastes (insoluble protein) to soluble protein.

Degradation of Prion and Prion-like Proteins

The degradation of prion and prion like proteins by microbial keratinase was reported. Prion diseases are a group of progressive condition that effect the brain and nervous system. Misshaped prion production carries the disease between individuals and cause deterioration of the brain. In recent times a type of TSE Transmissible Spongi form Incephalopathies (TSEs) called bovine spongiform encephalopathy (BSE) spread incattle.

Depilation process

Keratinous wastes could be degraded by some microorgnisms in nature. Native human foot skin (NHFS) was used as sole nitrogen source to screen microorganisms with keratin degradating capability. For appromimately 200 strains, a strain of Streptomyces sp strain No 16 was found to possess the strongest keratinolytic activity and the substrate specificity test indicated that the crude keratinase could degrade keratin azure, human hair, cock feathers and collagen.

(vi) Amylase: Food industry: Amylases are extensively employed in processed-food industry such as baking, brewing, preparation of digestive aids, production

of cakes, fruit juices and starch syrups (Couto and Sanroman, 2006). Besides generating fermentable compounds, α-amylases also have an anti-staling effect in bread baking, and they improve the softness retention of baked goods, increasing the shelf life of these products (van der Maarel, 2002 and Gupta *et al.*, 2003).

Table 5.5: Uses of Amylases in Various Sectors of Industries (Sivaramakrishnan *et al.*, 2006)

Sector	Uses
Food industry	Production of glucose syrups, crystalline glucose
	Production of high fructose syrups
	Production of maltose syrups
	Reduction of viscosity of sugar syrups
	Reduction of haze formation in juices
	Solubilization and saccharification of starch for alcohol fermentation in brewing industries
Biofuel industry	In degradation of starchy substrates for their conversion to bioethanol to be used as power alcohol
Detergent industry	Used as an additive to remove starch based dirt
Paper industry	Reduction of viscosity of starch for appropriate coating of paper
Textile industry	Warp sizing of textile fibres
Pharmaceutical industry	Used as a digestive aid

A thermostable maltogenic amylase of *Bacillus stearothermophilus*is used commercially in the bakery industry (Maarel, 2002). Amylases are also used for the clarification of beer or fruit juices and for the pretreatment of animal feed to improve the digestibility of fibre (Maarel, 2002; Gavrilescu and Chisti, 2005; Ghorai*et al.*, 2009).

(vii) Chitinase: Food industry: Organically rich effluents from food processing plants are characterized by high chemical oxygen demand (COD) or biochemical oxygen demand (BOD) and total suspended solids. Recovery of suspended solids by coagulation and settling may also be cost effective for reducing surcharges in terms of their potential utilization.

Muscle foods: Muscle food products are highly susceptible to favour and rancidity development caused by oxidation of their highly unsaturated lipids. Warmed-over favour in cooked poultry and uncured meat is developed upon storage and results in the deterioration of desirable meaty favour.

Nutritional effect of chitin and chitosan in foods: Multiple action of chitin and chitosan in food systems relate to their effects as dietary fibre and as functional ingredients. The United States Food and Drug Administration (USFDA) approved chitosan as a feed additive in 1983. Chitosan is also used in the food industry as a food quality enhancer in certain countries. Japan produces dietary cookies, potato chips and noodles enriched with chitosan because of its hypocholesterolemic effect. Furthermore, vinegar products containing chitosan are manufactured and sold in Japan, again because of their cholesterol lowering ability.

Purification of Water

Better awareness of the ecological and health problems associated with heavy metals and pesticides and their accumulation through the food chain has prompted the demand for purification of industrial waste waters prior to their discharge or use. Conventional methods for the removal of metals from industrial waste water may be ineffective or expensive, especially when metals are available at low concentrations.

(viii) Laccase: Food industry: Laccases can be applied to certain processes that enhance or modify the colour appearance of food or beverage. In this way, an interesting application of laccases involves the elimination of undesirable phenolics, responsible for the browning, haze formation and turbidity development in clear fruit juice, beer and wine.

Pulp and paper industry: The industrial preparation of paper requires separation and degradation of lignin in wood pulp. Environmental concerns urge to replace conventional and polluting chlorine-based delignification/bleaching procedures (Kuhad *et al.*, 1997). Pre-treatments of wood pulp with ligninolytic enzymes might provide milder and cleaner strategies of delignification that are also respectful of the integrity of cellulose (Kuhad *et al.*, 1997).

Textile industry: The textile industry accounts for two-thirds of the total dyestuff market (Riu *et al.*, 1998) and consumes large volumes of water and chemicals for wet processing of textiles. The chemical reagents used are very diverse in chemical composition, ranging from inorganic compounds to polymers and organic products (Mishra and Tripathy, 1993; Banat *et al.*, 1996; Juang *et al.*, 1996).

Nanobiotechnology: During the past two decades, bioelectrochemistry has received increased attention. Progress on bioelectrochemistry has been integrated into analytical applications, e.g. in biosensors working as detectors in clinical and environmental analysis (Haghighi *et al.*, 2003). Since laccases are able to catalyse electron transfer reactions without additional cofactors, their use has also been studied in biosensors to detect various phenolic compounds, oxygen or azides.

CONCLUSION

The search for "clean technologies", using alternative feedstocks, in order to obtain products of industrial interest, save energy and reduce effluent production is economically advantageous and has been encouraged by environmental issues during the last years. Researches dealing with the use of lignocellulosic wastes in bioprocesses, specially for microorganisms cultivation and cellulases, xylanases, ligninases and other enzymes production, stand out. These enzymes have potential for various biotechnological applications and in recent years special attention has been given to the destructuring, hydrolysis and saccharification of lignocellulosic material in order to obtain fermentable sugars that can be converted into second generation ethanol by fermenting microorganisms. However, for an efficient conversion of lignocellulosic materials into products of industrial interest, some bottlenecks must be overcome. The search for microbial strains suitable for cultivation in large scale, producing enzymes with characteristics appropriate to the biotechnological processes to which they are intended is of great importance.

REFERENCES

Ahmed, S., Bashir, A., Saleem, H., Saadia, M. and Jamil, A. (2009): Production and Purification of Cellulose-degrading Enzymes from a Filamentous Fungus *Trichoderma harzianum. Pakistan Journal of Botany*, 3(1-2): 40-44.

Aikat, K. and Bhattacharyya, B.C. (2001): Protease Production in Solid State Fermentation with Liquid Medium Recycling in a Stacked Plate Reactor and in a Packed Bed Reactor by a Local Strain of *Rhizopusoryzae. Process Biochemistry,* 36:1059–1068.

Amin, H. N., Bhattit, M., Zuber, I. A., Bhatti, A. and Asgher, M. (2010): Use of enzymes in industries. *The Journal of Animal & Plant Sciences,* 24(5): 2014 1430-1437

Beg, Q. K., Bhushan, B., Kapoor, M. and Hoondal, G. S. (2000) Enhanced Production of a Thermostable Xylanase from *Streptomyces* Species QG-11-3 and Its Application in Biobleaching of Eucalyptus Kraft Pulp. *Enzyme and Microbial Technology,* 27: 459-466.

Bhiday, M.R. (1994): Earth Worms in Agriculture. *Indian Farming,* 43(12): 31-34.

Bishnu, J., Megh, R. B., Dinita, S., Jarina, J., Rajani, M., Lakshmaiah, S. (2011): Lignocellulosic Ethanol Production: Current Practices and Recent Developments, *Biotechnology and Molecular Biology Review,* 6(8): 172-182.

Butt M S, Tahir-Nadeem T, Ahmed Z and Sultan M T. 2008. Xylanase in Baking Industry. *Food Technology and Biotechnology* 46(1): 22-31.

Camarero, S., Ibarra, D., Martinez, M.J. and Martinez, A.T. (2005): Lignin-derived Compounds as Efficient Laccase Mediators for Decolorization of Different Types of Recalcitrant Dyes. *Applied Environmental Microbiology,* 71: 1775-1784.

Cao, Y. and Tan, H. (2002): Effect of Cellulase on the Modification of Cellulose. *Carbohydrate Research,* 337: 1291-1296.

Champagne, P. (2007): Feasibility of Producing Bio-ethanol from Waste Residues: A Canadian Perspective Feasibility of Producing Bio-ethanol from Waste Residues in Canada. *Resources, Conservationand Recycling,* 50: 211-230.

Coll, P.M., Fernandez-Abalos, J.M., Villanueva, J.R., Santamaria, R. and Perez, P. (1993): Purification and Characterization of a Phenoloxidase (laccase) from the Lignin Degrading Basidiomycete PM1 (CECT 2971). *Applied Environmental Microbiology,* 59: 2607-2613.

Da-Silva R, Lago E S, Meheb C W, Macchione M M, Park Y K and Gomes E. 2005. Production of Xylanase and CMCase on Solid State Fermentation in Different Residues by *Thermoascusauranticusmiehe. Brazilian Journal of Microbiology* 36(3): 235-241.

Das, A. and Ghosh, U. (2009): Solid State Fermentation of Waste Cabbage by *Penicilliumnotatum* NCIM NO-923 Production and Characterization of Cellulases. *Journal of Scientific and Industrial Research*, 68: 714-718.

Dashtban, M., Schraft, H. and Qin, W. (2009): Fungal Bioconversion of Lignocellulosic Residues; Opportunities & Perspectives. *Internetional Journal of Biological Sciences*, 5 (6): 578-595.

deAzeredo, L.A.I., P.M. Gomes, G.L. Sant'Anna, L. R. Castilho and D.M.G. Freire (2007): Production and Regulation of Lipase Activity from *Penicilliumrestrictum* in Submerged and Solid State Fermentations. *Biofuel*, 11(2): 23-35.

Demirbas, A. (2008): Products from Lignocellulosic Materials via Degradation Processes. *Energy Sources*, 30 (1): 27-37.

Dumsday, G. (2008): Using Biology to Add Value to Waste Lignin Streams. *Microbiology Australia*, 29, 21-24.

Elisashvili, V., Penninckx, M., Kachlishvili, E., Asatiani, M. and Kvesitadze, G. (2006): Use of *Pleurotusdryinus*for Lignocellulolytic Enzymes Production in Submerged Fermentation of Mandarin Peels and Tree Leaves. *Enzyme and Microbial Technology*, 38, 998-1004

Fengel, D., Wegener, G. (1984): Chemical Composition and Analysis of Wood, Wood: Chemistry, Ultrastructure, Reactions, *Berlin*, 26-65.

Gao, J., Weng, H., Zhu, D., Yuan, M., Guan, F. and Xi, Y. (2008): Production and Characterization of Cellulolytic Enzymes from the Thermoacidophlilic Fungal *Aspergillus Terreus* M11 Under Solid-State Cultivation of Corn Stover. *Bioresource Technology*, 99 (16): 122-132.

Gao, J.; Weng, H.; Zhu, D.; Yuan, M.; Guan, F. & Xi, Y. (2008): Production and Characterization of Cellulolytic Enzymes from the Thermoacidophlilic Fungal *Aspergillus Terreus* M11 under Solid-State Cultivation of Corn Stover. *Bioresource Technology*, 99(16):7623-7629.

Gellerstedt, G. and Northy, R.A. (1989): Analysis of Birch Wood Lignin by Oxidative Degradation. *Wood Science and Technology*, 23: 75-83.

Gessesse, A. and Mamo, G. (1999) High Level of Xylanase Production by an Alkalophilic *Bacillus* Species by Using Solid State Fermentation. *Enzyme and Microbial Technology*, 25: 68-72.

Gilbert, M., Xiao, X., Chaitaweesub, P., Kalpravidh, W., Premashthira, S. and Boles, S. (2007): Avian Influenza, Domestic Ducks and Rice Agriculture in Thailand. *Agriculture Ecosystem Environment*, 119:409–415.

Glazer, A.N., Nikaido, H. (2007). Biomass, In: *Microbial Biotechnology: Fundamentals of Applied Microbiology*, 12): 430-455.

Gramina, E. B. N., Goncalves, A.Z.L., Pirota, R.D.P.B., Balsalobre, M. A. A., Da-Silva, R. and Gomes, E. (2008): Enzyme Production by Solid-state Fermentation: Application to Animal Nutrition. *Animal Feed Science and Technology*, 144(1-2): 1-22.

Hongpattarakere, T. (2002): Hyperthermostable Cellulolytic and Hemicelluloytic Enzymes and their Biotechnological Applications. *Songklanakarin Journal of Sciences and Technology*, 24(3): 481-491.

Howard R. L., Abotsi, E., Rensburg J., Howard, S. (2003): Lignocellulose Biotechnology: Issues of Bioconversion and Enzyme Production, *African Journal of Biotechnology*, 2: 602-619.

Immanuel, G., Dhanusa, R., Prema, P. and Palavesam, A. (2006): Effect of Different Growth Parameters on Endoglucanase Enzyme Activity by Bacteria Isolated from Coir Retting Effluents of Estuarine Environment. *International Journal od Environmental Science and Technology*, 3 (1): 25-34.

Irfan, M .S. Q., Gulsher, M., Abbas, S., Muhammed, N. and Baig, S. (2010): Pretreatment of Corn Cob for Production of Hydrolytic Enzymes from *Aspergillus niger*–IR01. *International Journal for Agro Veterinary and Medical Sciences*, 4(3): 81-87.

Kalogo, Y., Habibi, S., MacLean, H.L., Joshi, S.V. (2007): Environmental Implications of Municipal Solid Waste-derived Ethanol. *Environmental Science and Technolology*, 41:35-41.

Kang, S.W., Park, Y.S., Lee, J.S, Hong, S. I. and Kim, S. W. (2004): Production of Cellulases and Hemicellulases by *Aspergillus niger* KK2 from Lignocellulosic Biomass. *Bioresource Technology*, 91(2): 153-156.

Kang, W., Park, Y.S., Lee, J.S., Hong, S.I., Kim, S.W. (2004): Production of Cellulases and Hemicellulases by *Aspergillus niger* KK2 from Lignocellulosic Biomass. *Bioresource Technology*, 91: 153–156.

Karmakar, M. and Ray, R. R. (2010): Extra Cellular Endoglucanase Production by *Rhizopusoryzae* in Solid and Liquid State Fermentation of Agro Wastes. *Asian Journal of Biotechnology*, 2: 27-36.

Kierulff, J.V. (1997): Denim Bleaching. *Textile Horiculture*, 17: 33-36.

Kim, S., Dale, B.E. (2004): Global Potential Bioethanol Production from Wasted Crops and Crop Residues. *Biomass and Bioenergy*, 26:361-375.

Kumar, P., Barrett, D. D. M., Delwiche, M. J. and Stroeve, P. (2009): Method for Pretreatment of Lignocellulosic Biomass for Efficient Hydrolysis and Biofuel Production. *Industrial and Engineereing Chemistry Research*, 48: 3713-3729.

Leite, R.S.R., Alves-Prado, H.F., Cabral, H., Pagnocca, F.C., Gomes, E., Da-Silva, R. (2008). Production and Characteristics Comparison of Crude α-Glucosidases Produced by Microorganisms *Thermoascusaurantiacus*and *Aureobasidium pullulans* in Agricultural Wastes. *Enzyme and Microbial Technology*, 43: 391–395.

Leite, R.S.R.; Alves-Prado, H.F.; Cabral, H.; Pagnocca, F.C.; Gomes, E.; Da-Silva, R. (2008). Production and Characteristics Comparison of Crude-Glucosidases Produced by Microorganisms *Thermoascusaurantiacus*and *Aureobasidium pullulans* in Agricultural Wastes. *Enzyme and Microbial Technology*, 43: 391–395.

Lemos, J. L. S., Bon, E. P. S., Santana, M. D. F. E. and Pereira, N. (2000): Thermal Stability of Xylanase Produced by *Aspergillus awamori*. *Brazallian Journal of Microbiology*, 31(3): 1517-1590.

Machiel, G. M., Vandenberghe, L.P.S., Haminiuk, C. W. I., Fendrich, R. C., Bianca, B.E. D., Brandalize, T. Q. S., Pandey, A. and Soccol, C. R. (2008): Xylanase Production by *Aspergillus niger* LPB 326 in Solid-state Fermentation using Statistical Experimental Designs. *Food Technology Biotechnology*, 46 (2): 183-189.

Malherbe, S. and Cloete, T. E. (2002): Lignocellulose Degradation: Fundamentals and Applications. *Reviews in Environmental Science & Biotechnology*, 1: 105-114.

Malilas, W., S.W. Kang, S.B. Kim, H.Y. Yoo, W. Chulalaksananukul and S.W. Kim (2013): Lipase from *Penicilliumcamembertii* KCCM 11268: Optimization of Solid State Fermentation and Application to Biodiesel Production. *Korean J. Chemical Engineering*, 30: 405-412.

Messerschmidt, A. and Huber, R. (1999): The Blue Oxidases, Ascorbate Oxidase, Laccase and Ceruloplasmin, Modeling and Structural Relationships. *European Journal of Biochemistry*, 187: 341-352.

Minussi, R.C., Pastore, G.M. and Duran, N. (2002): Potential Applications of Laccase in the Food Industry. *Trends Food Science Technol.*, 13: 205-216.

Mosier, N., Wyman, C., Dale, B., Elander, R., Lee, Y. Y., Holtzapple, M. and Ladisch, M (2005): Features of Promising Technologies for Pretreatment of Lignocellulosic Biomass. *Bioresource Technology*, 96: 673-686.

Nigma, P. and Singh, D. (1996). Processing of Agricultural Wastes in Solid State Fermentation of Microbial Protein Production. *Journal of Science and Industrial Research*, 55(5-6): 373-380.

Ogawa, A., Yasuhara, A., Tanaka, T., Sakiyama, T. and Nakanishi, K. (1995): Production of Neutral Protease by Membrane-surface Liquid Culture of *Aspergillus oryzae*IAM2704. *J Ferment Bioengineering*, 80:35–40.

Oziel, D., Enrique, F., Jose, M. G., Jaime, S. C., Rolando R. R. (2008): Use of Pleurotuspulmonarius to Change the Nutritional Quality of Wheat Straw-effect on Chemical Composition, *Interciencia Print Version*, 33(6): 21-34.

Palacios-Orueta, Martinez G., Larrondo, N., Putman, N., Gelpke, M.D.S., Huang, K. ad Chapman, J,.(2004) Genome Sequence of the Lignocellulose Degrading Fungus Phanerochaetechrysosporium Strain RP78. *Nature Biotechnol*ogy, 22:1–6.

Palonen, H. and Viikari, L. (2004): Role of Oxidative Enzymatic Treatments on Enzymatic Hydrolysis of Softwood. *Biotechnology Bioengergy*, 86:550–557.

Pandey, A. (2002): Solid State Fermentation. *Biochemical Engineering Jounal*, 36: 1-4.

Pérez-Guerra, N., A. Torrado-Agrasar, C. López-Macias and L. Pastrana (2003). Main Characteristics and Applications of Solid Substrate Fermentation. *Electronic J. Environ. Agricultural Food Chem*istry, 2: 343-350.

Pionte, K., Antorini, M., Choinowski, T. (2002): Crystal Structure of a Laccase from the Fungus *Trametes versicolor* at 1.90-Å Resolution Containing a Full Complement of Coppers. *Journal of Biochemistry and Engineering*, 277: 37663-37669.

Pokhrel, D. and Viraraghavan, T. (2005) Municipal Solid Waste Management in Nepal: Practices and Challenges. *Waste Managment*, 25:555-562.

Prasand, C., Singh, A. and Joshi, H. C. (2007): Ethanol as an Alterntative Fuel from Agricultural, Industrial and Urban Residue. *Resources Converstion and Recycling*, 50: 1-39.

Ragauskas, A.J.,Williams, C.K., Davison, B.H., Britovsek, G., Cairney, J., Eckert, C.A., Frederick, W.J., Hallett, J.P., Leak, D.J., Liotta, C.L., Mielenz, J.R., Murphy, R., Templer, R. and Tschaplinski, T. (2006): The Path Forward for Biofuels and Biomaterials. *Science*, 311(5760): 484-489

Rani, D. S. and Nand, K. (2001): Purification and Characterization of Xylanolytic Enzymes of a Cellulase Free Thermophilic Strain of *Clostridium absonum*CFR-702. *Process Biochemistry*, 36: 355-62

Raza, F., Raza N A, Hameed U, Ikram-Ul-Haq and Mariam I. (2011): Solid State Fermentation for the Production of b-glucosidase by Co-culture of *Aspergillus niger* and *Aspergillus oryzae*. *Pakistan Journal of Botany*, 43(1): 75-83.

Rifaat, H. M., Nagieb, Z. A. and Ahmed, Y. M. (2005): Production of Xylanases by *Streptomyces* Species and their Bleaching Effect on Rice Straw Pulp. *Applied Ecology and Environmental Research*, 4(1): 151-160.

Rifaat, H. M., Nagieb, Z. A. and Ahmed, Y. M. (2005): Production of Xylanases by *Streptomyces* Species and their Bleaching Effect on Rice Straw Pulp. *Applied Ecology and Environmental Research*, 4(1): 151-160.

Roubroeks J P, Andersson R, Mastromauro D I, Christensen B E and Aman P. 2001. Molecular Weight, Structure and Shape of Oat (1→3),(1→4)-β-D-glucan Fractions Obtained by Enzymatic Degradation with (1→4)-β-D-glucan 4-glucanohydrolase from *Trichoderma reesei*. *Carbohydrate Polymer*46: 275-285.

Sanchez, C. (2009): Lignocellulosic Residues: Biodegradation and Bioconversion by Fungi. *Biotechnology Advances*, 27(2): 185-194.

Sangsurasak, P. and Mitchell, D.A. (1995): The Investigation of Transient Multi-dimensional Heat Transfer in Solid-state Fermentation. *Chemical Engineering Journal*, 60:199–204.

Sa-Pereira, P., Paveia, H., Costa-Ferreira, M. and Aires-Barros, M.R. (2003): A New Look at Xylanases: An Overview of Purification Strategies. *Molecular Biotechnology*, 24: 257-281.

Senthil Kumar, S. R., Ashokkumar, B., Chadra, R. K. and Gunasekaran, P. (2005) Optimization of Medium Composition for Alkali Stable Xylanase Production by *Aspergillus fischeri* Fxn I in Solid State Fermentation using Central Composite Rotary Design. *Bioresouce Technology*, 96: 1380-1386.

Simon, I. and Scheraga, H. A. (1988): Structure of Cellulose: Low Energy Conformations of Single Chains. *Macromolecules*, 21: 983-990.

Subramaniyan, S. and Prema, P. (2002): Biotechnology of Microbial Xylanase: Enzyme System: Biochemistry, Molecular Biology and Application. *Critical Reviews in Biotechnology*, 22:33-64.

Taherzadeh, M.J. and Karimi, K. (2007). Enzyme-Based Hydrolysis Process for Ethanol from Lignocellulosic Materials: A Review. *BioResources*, 2 (4): 707-738.

Taherzadeh, M.J., Gustafsson, L., Niklasson, C. & Liden, G., (1998): Conversion of Furfural in Aerobic and Anaerobic Batch Fermentation of Glucose by *Saccharomycescerevisiae*. *Journal of Bioscience and Bioengeneering*, 87:169-174.

Wang, R., Chau, Sing Law, R. and Webb, C. (2005): Protease Production and Conidiation by *Aspergillus oryzae*in Flour Fermentation. *Process Biochemistry*, 40:217–227.

Wen, Z., Liao, W. and Chen, S (2004): Hydrolysis of Animal Manure Lignocellulosics for Reducing Sugar Production. *Bioresour Technol*ogy, 91:31-39.

Xia, L. and Cen, P. L. (1999): Cellulase Production by Solid State Fermentation on Lignocellulosic Waste from the Xylose Industry. *Process Biochemistry*, 34: 909-912.

Yang, S. Q., Yan, Q. J., Jiang, Z. Q., Li, L. T., Tian, H. M. and Wang, Y. Z. (2006): High-level of Xylanase Production by the Thermophilic *Paecilomycesthermophilia* J18 on Wheat Straw in Solid State Fermentation. *Bioresource Technology*, 97: 1794-1800.

Plant Biotechnology and Industrial Applications
Edited by: Alka Chauhan and Pawan Kumar 'Bharti'
ISBN: 978-93-5056-884-2
Edition: 2017
Published by: Discovery Publishing House Pvt. Ltd., New Delhi (India)

6 Status of Environmental Management System Compliance for Industrial Workplace in the State of Punjab, India

[1]Meenakshi Sharma, [2]Rupinder Singh Litt and [3]A.S. Balgir

ABSTRACT

This paper identifies and evaluates the significant factors related to climate change vis-à-vis compliance of environmental management system in manufacturing units located in Punjab. A comparative study has been made by selecting ISO 14001:2004 units as well as non-ISO 14001:2004 units. The data collection has been done by designing a suitable questionnaire by personal interview method. Through this study an attempt has been made to observe the status between units following ISO 14001:2004 norms and units not following ISO 14001:2004 norms. The findings reveal that certified units have implemented environmental management system in much better way and are contributing in controlling the climate change.

INTRODUCTION

General

The climate change is by reason of global warming, the end product of global warming changes the climatic conditions and in view of global warming the earth is warming. The climate change is also due to the anthropogenic activities of the human beings which start from the manufacturing industries. Many times this source of clime change was ignored. But if these focal points will be focused, the climate conditions would be improved. The manufacturing industries are of small scale, medium scale and of large scale enterprises. The larger industries are managing their environment by implementing the EMS (environmental management system) ISO 14001 and the medium and small scale enterprises are not implementing it by virtue of the financial problem. And the large scale industries which are ISO 14001 certified, if they are implementing it properly then the environment of that industry would be balanced and will not cause

1 Assistant Professor, Amritsar College of Engineering and Technology, Amritsar (Punjab)-143 001, India
2 Professor, Guru Nanak Dev Engineering College, Ludhiana (Punjab)-143001, India
3 Visiting Professor, PEC (Punjab Engineering College) Chandigarh (PB)-160012, India

the climate change, and if they have certification only for the completion in the market and incline the status and not implementing the EMS, then there is a check required. This research examine the status of ISO 14001 certified industries in Punjab state and for the comparison purposes the ISO 14001 non-certified industries has also covered.

Environment protection is a continued process in which continuous improvement over the system is required. For the frequent development of the environment system, EMS ISO14001 is the implementation procedure for the environmental preservation of all. In the manufacturing industries who are implementing the EMS are following the combined method for all the measures i.e. health and safety, quality measures and environmental measures. They prepared the combined annual book which has been distributed to all the departments of the firm, and the responsibility for implementing and continuous checking has given to the head of the department, and has given the authority of changing the control measures, if that causing trembles on environment.

Terms, Definitions and Abbreviations

The following terms and definitions that are in this research are as follows:

IMS: Integrated Management system to direct and control an organization with regard to quality, environment, occupation safety and health.

Responsibility: In this system documentation wherever the word "responsibility appears; to be read together with "authority" i.e. "responsibility and authority".

Weighted average score

WAS: Process of calculating the mean by using weights and frequencies of a value in a sample.

Environmental Management System

EMS objectives are being monitored and measured for fulfilment of desired standards as per their organizational norms stated in their manual and with reference to the state government norms. The various describe the details of this monitoring including the specifications, benchmarks, etc. to be achieved. Wherever the required parameters do not meet the specified criteria, correction and corrective actions was taken by those responsible. All the ISO14001 certified organizations follows the combined system of all i.e. quality management, health and safety management and environmental management, they integrate their management system, which is known as integrated management system. It has been evolved on the basis of company's purpose, their commitments to meet the requirements and continual improvements in the efficacy of IMS. The product requirements, significant environmental aspects, occupational risk of health and safety, relevant to legal and other requirements, with the view of integrated parties have been studied while preparing this policy. The enlightenment on the policy is generated within the organization through a wide publicity and training. The policy is outlined for continuing suitability through the management reviews. The policy is publically available and is delivered to the interested parties on request.

Main Elements of ISO-14001

- Define Environment Policy
- Identify Aspects/analyze their impact
- Set targets and objectives
- Establish Operational control
- Identify and meet Legal Requirements
- Define Management Responsibility & Authority
- Create Competence through training & Awareness
- Internal & External communications
- Control of documents
- Emergency preparedness & response plan

EMS requirements in ISO-14001

Environmental management system, ISO14001 specifies the following requirements:

- Policy
- Plan
- Implementation and operation
- Check
- Review by the management

The correct operation of the EMS at the worksite is conditioned by a vast range of factors, i.e. the resources available to EMS personnel, the experience and training of these personnel, and the conditions in which their duties are performed regarding the environment. For this reason, the previously mentioned variables should be evaluated as a way of determining if EMSs in the production sector are currently being implemented as per ISO 14001.

Then the status of environmental management system from both ISO 14001 certified and non-certified manufacturing industries are collected. Both the details of ISO14001 certified and non-certified manufacturing industries are given below:

EMS Non-certified Industries Selected for this Study

- Friends engineering factory, focal point, Amritsar. Manufactures cutting and printing machines.
- Leela textile mill, Amritsar. This industrial unit is a dying industry.

- Essma Woolen Mills Pvt. Ltd., Amritsar, this industry manufactures woolen cloths and blankets.
- OCM private limited formally known as OCM India Limited Estate, GT road, chhehata. Amritsar. The industry manufactures the cloths.
- SEL manufacturing Co. Ltd., Machiwara road, Nawanshahr. The industrial unit manufactures ready-made garments.
- M/s Ralson (India) Ltd, G.T. Road (NH-1), Ralson Nagar, Ludhiana (Punjab). The industrial unit manufactures bicycle hub with installed manufacturing expanse of ~20000 pieces/day.
- Freedom industry limited, Amritsar. This industry manufactures paints.
- H M textile industry, Amritsar. This industry manufactures clothes.
- Verka milk plant, Ludhiana, manufactures milk.
- Automobile tyres range, G.T. Road, focal point, Amritsar. This industrial unit manufactures motor cycle tyres, e-bikes/scooters, three-wheeler, tractors and LCV. Company's annual turnover is US$ 65.27 Millions.

EMS Certified Companies Selected for this Study

Rail Coach Factory is one of the biggest railway coach manufacturer in India having manufacturing capacity of 1500 coaches per annum. RCF is certified IMS since May' 2009 and the certification is valid up to Jul' 2015. Its certification to ISO 14001:1996 by M/s DET NORSKE VERITAS, New Delhi since July 1999.

Rishab Spinning Mill

Rishab spinning mills limited is a spinning and hosiery unit located in the district of Ludhiana (INDIA). It includes the Quality & Environment Management System obsession as per ISO 9001: 2008 and ISO 14001: 2004 since Sept., 2009 by Bureau of Indian standards (BIS). Last recertification was occurred in 2012.

JCT Limited

JCT limited is a textile mill having spinning, weaving processing facilities located in Phagwara. JCT limited is certified to IMS and certified to ISO14001:2004 in 2007.

Hero Steels

Hero steels commenced its steal operations in 1976. The Ludhiana unit of hero steal is a composite steal unit. HERO Steels is certified to Quality Environmental Management System (QEMS) and certified to ISO14001:2004 in 2008.

Comparative Study

All the ISO14001 certified manufacturing industries follows the EMS procedure in a continuous manner and follow their apex manual with the procedure manual, whereas in case of non-ISO14001 units follows the norms of the state government, but all the selected industries follow the legal compliances as per the government norms.

In the certified organizations, they have more numbers of supervisor's strengths, whereas in non-certified industries, they have very less number of supervisor's strength.

At last it can be concluded that all the manufacturing industries should follow ISO14001, and then only the climate change could be controlled. And need to be added with this that all the manufacturing industries should implement the ISO14001 standards. Because these manufacturing units are the main source of anthropogenic activities causes pollution in the climate, if they all will starts implementing the EMS then only the other hubs of pollution could be focused.

Objectives for Thesis Work

1. To collect the Environmental Management data from industrial workplaces located in the state of Punjab.
2. To analyze the results of the data of industrial workplaces in the state of Punjab.
3. Evaluate the comparison of EMS for certified and non-certified companies.

RESEARCH METHODOLOGY

The sample of this survey is from the state of Punjab.

Researcher has covered only the manufacturing industries of Punjab and not the service units.

The manufacturing industries covered are ISO14001 certified as well as non-certified.

The data has been collected through the questionnaire and personal interview method:

1. Top Management commitments of the organization.
2. Total strength of supervisors in both the ISO14001 certified and non-certified industries.
3. Then from their total strength, number of supervisors involved in environmental management system.
4. Supervisors experience in EMS implementation.
5. EMS supervisors responsibilities during Environmental measurements.
6. The office location of the supervisors.
7. The responsibilities which are assigned to the EMS supervisors.
8. Numbers of technical and non-technical supervisors.
9. Supervisor's educational background.
10. What type of responsibilities they are having in the environmental protection.
11. For checking the proper operational method for control, type of section they select for measuring the effluent.

12. Does their company evaluate the environmental aspects and its subsequent impacts?
13. Has the responsibilities assigned to the supervisors been formally allocated in writing?
14. Environmental monitoring tools they use on-site?
14. (A) does their organization has requisite in-house testing facilities?
14. (B) if No, do they seek assistance from outside testing facilities?
14. C if yes, specify the organization.
15. Document requirements.
16. What measure benefits the certified organizations intend to derive by implementation of EMS in their company?
17. What steps have they taken by implementing EMS in their company?

Design and Method of Questionnaire

The questionnaire has been designed with the help of literature review to get an idea of the questionnaire techniques. The questions have been divided into five. Firstly, "scale" or strength of response, from that the respondent could choose one answer, then comes "second" type of questions with the range of pre-given answers beside which respondent could tick were involved. This type of questions appears simpler for the respondent to complete it and encourage the respondents to continue the rest questions. The "third" type of questions, respondent could choose more than one answer, in this type of questions, respondent has limit to answer more than one and is not bonded to tick one. The "fourth" type of question was yes/no type, in which the respondent could answer either yes or no. And the last type of question includes the comments or free writing, in which the respondent could give his/her comments.

Pilot Testing

A pilot testing is an array referral of the full project, includes the questionnaire and interview. Questionnaire was filled by 5 to 7 respondents, then that responses were obtained, coded and analyzed. Questionnaire that was not providing useful data was put away (attached in annexure 1), and the final review of the questionnaire was made.

Improvement over the Questionnaire

The questionnaire which was not providing useful data was replaced with the questionnaire which provides useful and relevant data; the revised questionnaire has been attached in annexure 2.

Final Questionnaire

The new questionnaire was filled by the respondent and then the responses were obtained, coded and analyzed. This new questionnaire has provided useful data and as per the researcher's requirements.

Interview

With the questionnaire, it has been decided to add the interview of the respondent, which would help in gaining much more knowledge to the respondent about the status of EMS. Because sometimes respondent fails to explain it in writing, for those reasons interview helps in elaborating the things more clearly. The interviews are arranged at the same time as the questionnaires has issued to the respondent, because the interview we're not be used as a "check out". Like that of questionnaire design and procedure of interview session had referred from the literature sources. The types of questions that were used in the interview are unstructured type of interview, where there is a general theme to the interview but freedom in how the discussion develops.

Technique Used for the Data Analysis

Weighted Average Score and Percentage Method.

Weighted average score: The formula for computing a weighted arithmetic mean for a sample or a population is

$$\frac{\sum_{i=1}^{n} w_i x_i}{\sum_{i=1}^{n} w_i}$$

where w_i represents the weight associated with element x_i, this value of w_i equals the number of times that element appears in the data set.

The numerator (the top half of the formula) tells you to multiply each element in the data set by its weight and then add the results together, as shown here:

$$w_1x_1 + w_2x_2 + w_3x_3 + \ldots + w_nx_n$$

The denominator (the bottom half of the formula) tells the addition of the weights together:

$$w_1 + w_2 + w_3 + w_4 + w_5 + \ldots.. + w_n$$

Therefore the weighted arithmetic mean is calculated by dividing the numerator by the denominator.

Percentage method: The percentage method is used for comparing certain feature.

$$\text{Sample Percentage} = \frac{\text{Actual population}}{\text{Sample size}} \times 100$$

RESULTS AND DISCUSSIONS

In this the questionnaire was designed on the basis of the status of environmental management system covering the top management commitments and the resources, roles and responsibilities of the supervisors involved in the ISO14001 certified and non certified manufacturing industries in the state of Punjab. The

ISO14001 certified industries covered are Rail coach factory Kapurthala, Rishab spinning mil, Hero steels and JCT Ltd. Phagwara and the non-ISO 14001 certified industries covered are Friends engineering factory, Amritsar; Leela Textile Mill, Amritsar; Essma Woolen Mills Pvt. Ltd., Amritsar; OCM India limited Estate, GT Road, Chhehata, Amritsar; SEL manufacturing Co Ltd., Nawanshahr; M/s Ralson (India) Ltd, G.T. Road (NH-1), Ralson Nagar, Ludhiana; Freedom Industry Limited, Amritsar; H M Textile Industry, Amritsar; Verka Milk Plant, Ludhiana; Automobile Tyres Range, G.T. Road, Focal Point, Amritsar. The results for both types of industries were analyzed and comparative study was done.

Question 1. Top management commitments.

Table 5.1: Top Management Commitments

S. No.	Top management commitment	Certified industries	Non-certified industries
1.	Top management commitment for environmental management system	5	3.8
2.	Have EMS apex manual and procedure manual been prepared for guidance manual of all?	5	3.7
3.	Responsibility defined to take preventive measures against special/specific processes.	5	3.35
4.	Compliance environmental legal requirements	5	3.1
5.	Allocation of resources for the implementation of environmental management system	5	3
6.	Use of available advanced green technology for construction purpose	5	2.1
7.	Have managers and the staff equipped with requisite responsibility and authority to implement EMS	4.4	3.4
8.	Concern of staff members related to the environmental management system	4.6	2.95
9.	Are operational processes being monitored, evaluated and analyzed on monthly, six monthly and yearly basis	4.6	3.55
10.	Is production given priority over EMS implementation?	4.6	3.5

- It has been interpreted from this evaluation that the ISO14001 certified industries have demonstrated good practices in the following areas:
    1. Top management commitment for environmental management system.
    2. EMS apex manual and procedure manual which have been prepared for guidance manual of all.
    3. Responsibility defined to take preventive measures against special/specific processes.
    4. Compliance environmental legal requirements.

5. Allocation of resources for the implementation of environmental management system.
6. Use of available advanced green technology for construction purpose.

- The following have been identified as potential areas for improvement for the ISO 14001 certified industries:
  1. Have managers and the staff equipped with requisite responsibility and authority to implement EMS.
  2. Concern of staff members related to the environmental management system.
  3. Are operational processes being monitored, evaluated and analyzed on monthly, six monthly and yearly basis.
  4. Is production given priority over EMS implementation?
- Interpretation for the non-ISO14001 units evaluates that these are the following activities, the researcher has given rank 1, on those activities the industries require improvement :
  (*a*) Top management commitment for environmental management system activities on which these companies require improvement.
  (*b*) EMS apex manual and procedure manual which have been prepared for guidance manual of all.
  (*c*) Operational processes are being monitored, evaluated and analyzed on monthly, six monthly and yearly bases.
  (*d*) Production given priority over EMS implementation.
- Interpretation for the non-ISO14001 units evaluates that these are the following activities, the researcher has given rank 2, on those activities the industries require more improvement:
  (*a*) Responsibility defined to take preventive measures against special/specific processes.
  (*b*) Compliance environmental legal requirements.
  (*c*) Allocation of resources for the implementation of environmental management system.
  (*d*) Have managers and the staff equipped with requisite responsibility and authority to implement EMS.
- Interpretation for the non-ISO14001 units evaluates that these are the following activities, Researcher has given rank 3, on those activities the industries requires more improvement:
  (*a*) Use of available advanced green technology for construction purpose.
  (*b*) Concern of staff members related to the environmental management system.

Question 2. Total strength of supervisors in the companies:

Table 5.2: Strength of the Supervisors

Total strength of the supervisors	Certified	Non-certified
less than 100	0%	80%
Between 100 to 500	0%	20%
More than 500	100%	0%

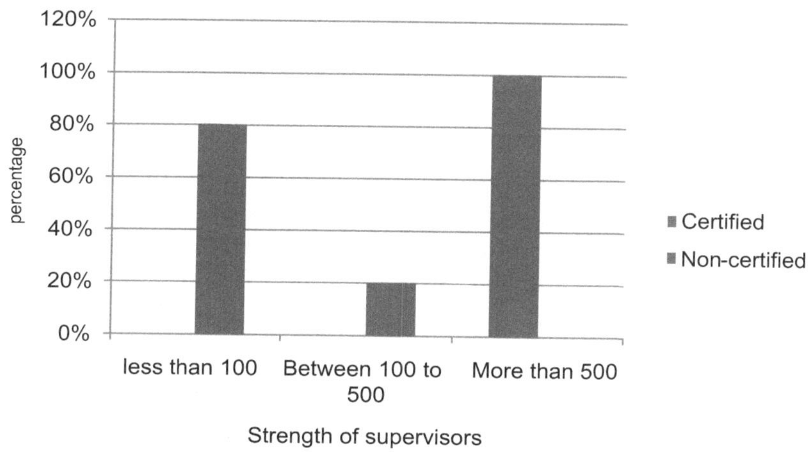

Graph 5.1: Strength of the supervisors.

The evaluation of the total strength of the supervisors in the company shows that there 100% of the ISO14001 certified companies who are having more than 500 number of supervisors and 20% non-ISO14001 certified companies are having number of supervisors in between 100 to 500 and 60% non-ISO14001 certified companies are having their strength of supervisors more than 500.

Question 3. Number of supervisors involved in environmental management system:

Table 5.3: Number of Supervisor Involved in Environmental Management System

Number of supervisor involved in environmental management system	Certified	Non certified
< 10 %	25%	0%
10-30%	25%	0%
>30%	50%	0%

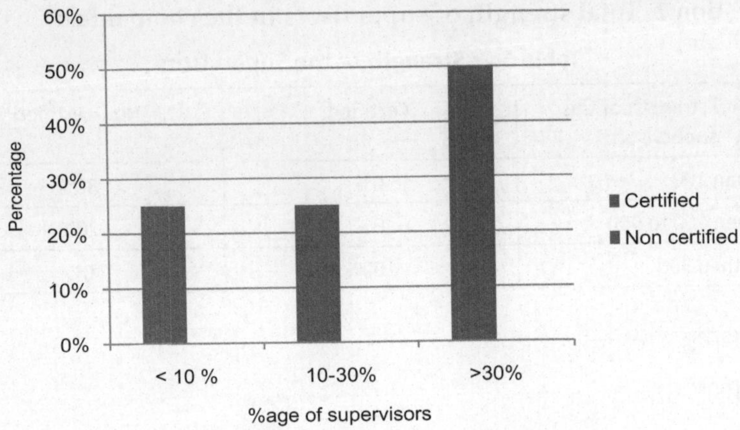

Graph 5.2: Number of supervisor involved in environmental management system

The valuation of the number of supervisors involved in environmental management system shows that 25% of the ISO14001 certified companies having less than 10% of the EMS supervisors, 25% of the ISO14001 certified companies having in between 10 to 30% of the supervisors and 50% of the ISO14001 certified companies having greater than 30% of the EMS supervisors in their companies. Whereas in case of non-ISO14001 units, the evaluation showed that there is no supervisor of non-ISO14001 involved in EMS.

Question 4. Experience of supervisors involved in EMS implementation:

Table 5.4 Experience of Supervisors Involved in EMS Implementation

Experience of supervisors involved in EMS implementation	Certified	Non certified
< 5 years	25%	40%
5-10 years	25%	0%
>10 years	75%	90%

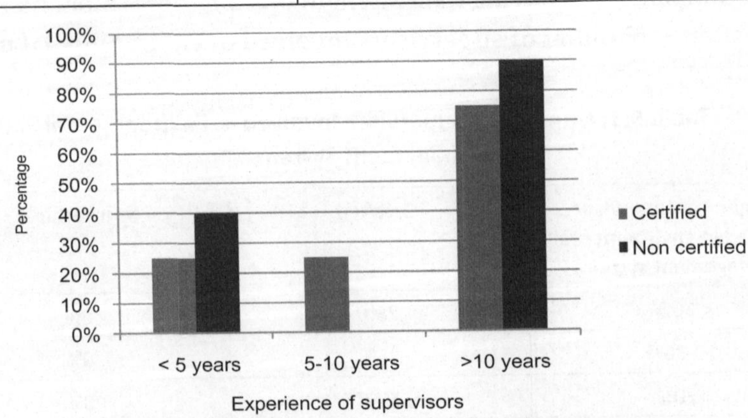

Graph 5.3: Experience of supervisors involved in EMS implementation

The assessment shows that in case of ISO14001 certified companies there are 25% of the supervisor having less than 5 years of experienced supervisors, 25% of the companies having their supervisors experience in EMS is in between 5 to 10 years and 75% of the companies having their supervisor's experience in EMS is more than 10 years. Whereas for non-ISO14001 40% of the companies having their supervisors experience in EMS implementation less than 5 years; no supervisor is having experience in between 5 to 10 years and the companies having their supervisors experience more than 10 years accounts for 90%; that means the non-certified units have EMS experienced supervisors, but not involved in EMS implementation.

Question 5. EMS supervisor's responsibility during environmental measurements:

Table 5.5 EMS Supervisor's Responsibility during Environmental Measurements

EMS supervisors responsibility during environmental measurements	Certified	Non certified
On sites	100%	70%
In office	50%	30%

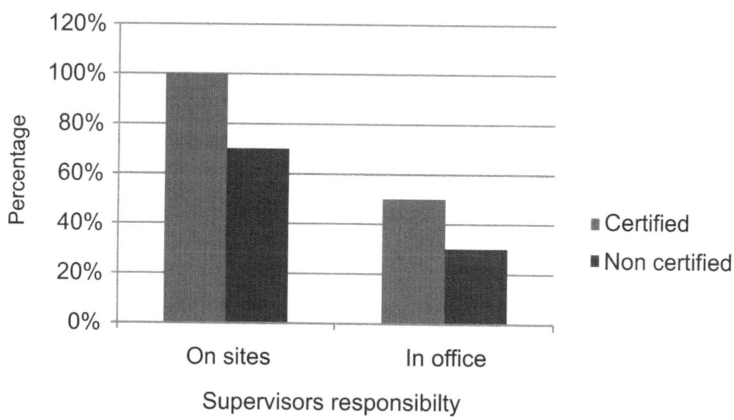

Graph 5.4: EMS supervisor's responsibility during environmental measurements

The results for ISO-14001 certified industries shows that there are 100% of the companies having their supervisor's responsibilities on-site and rest 50% of the companies is having their supervisor's responsibilities in-office only. The non-ISO industries evaluation for the EMS supervisor's responsibility during environmental measurements shows that there are 70% of the companies having their supervisor's responsibility on-site, and rest 30% of the companies having their supervisor's responsibility in office.

Question 6. Their office location:

Table 5.6: Office Location

Office location	Certified	Non-certified
Office at the workplace	100%	60%
Office at the branch of company (remote control)	0%	40%

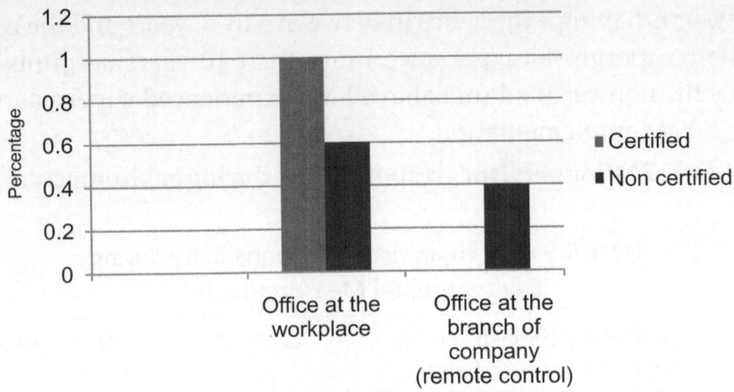

Graph 5.5: Office location

The assessment for office location shows that the 100% ISO14001 certified companies are having office at the workplace, no company having their office at the branch of the company. And for the office location of the supervisors for the non-ISO14001 company's shows that there are 60% of the companies having their supervisor's office location is at the workplace, rest 40% of the companies having their supervisor's office location is at the branch of the company (remote control).

Question 7. Responsibilities assigned to the supervisors other than EMS:

Table 5.7: Responsibility Assigned to Supervisors Other than EMS

Responsibility assigned to supervisors other than EMS	Certified	Non certified
Technical office manager	100%	90%
Safety and health supervisor	100%	70%
Quality assurance supervisor	100%	80%
Production assistant	100%	60%
Supervisor involved in production works	100%	30%
No other role	0	0%
Others	0	0%

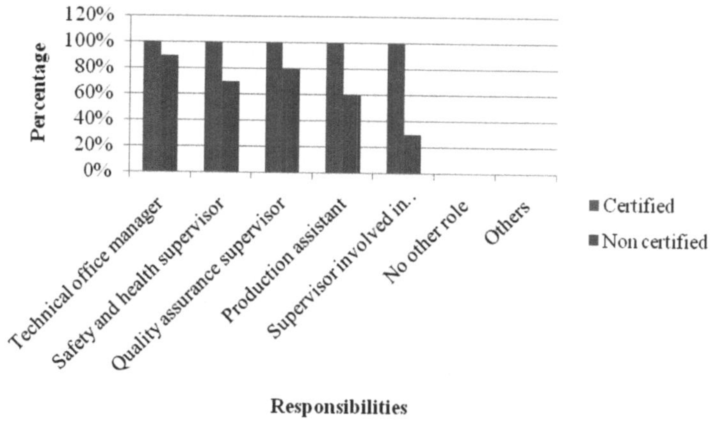

Graph 5.6: Responsibility assigned to supervisors other than EMS

The appraisal of the responsibilities assigned to the EMS supervisors showed that all the 100% of companies having their supervisors which took the responsibilities of technical health manager, safety and health supervisor, quality and health manager, production assistant, production works, other than EMS. Whereas the same pattern was not followed by non-certified companies. 90%, 70%, 60% and 30% of these non-ISO14001 companies have their supervisors which took the responsibility of technical health manager, safety and health supervisor, construction assistant and production works respectively.

Question 8. Number of technical and non-technical supervisors:

Table 5.8: Number of Technical and Non-technical Supervisors

Number of technical and non technical supervisors	Certified	Non-certified
Technical	60%	70%
Non Technical	40%	30%

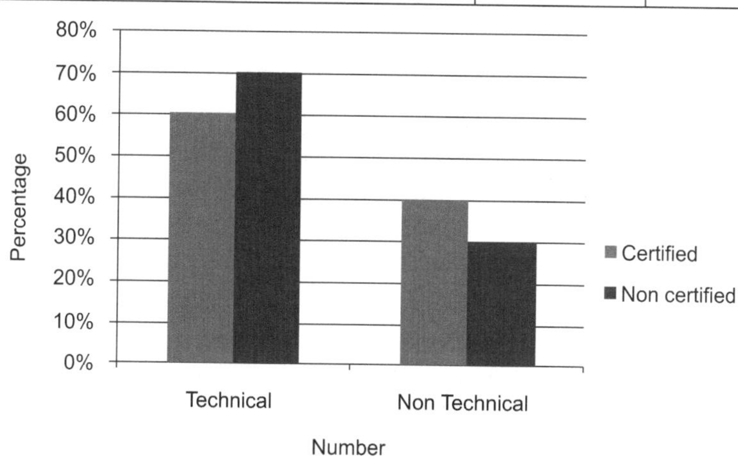

Graph 5.7: Number of technical and non technical supervisors

The valuation of number of technical and non-technical supervisors shows that there are 60% companies having the technical supervisors, and 40% of the supervisors are having non-technical supervisors. And the non-certified industries shows that there are 70% of the companies having technical supervisors, 30% of the companies having non-technical supervisors.

Question 9. Supervisor's educational background:

Table 5.9: Supervisor's Educational Background

Supervisors educational background	Certified	Non-certified
Engineering Degree	40%	20%
Any other Degree	30%	30%
Diploma	60%	70%
No degree, only practical experience	30%	50%

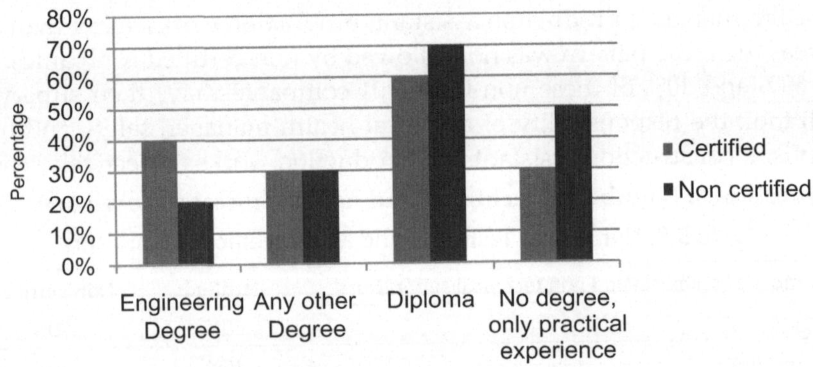

Graph 5.8: Supervisor's educational background

The valuation for the supervisor's educational background shows that there are 40% supervisors in the ISO14001 certified company having engineering degree, 30% of the supervisors having any other degree, 60% of the supervisors in the company having diploma, and there are 30% of the supervisors having no degree, only practical experience. And for the non-certified industries shows that there are there are 20% of the companies having their supervisors educational background is in engineering degree, are 30% of the companies having their supervisors educational background is in any other degree, are 70% of the companies having their supervisors educational background is in diploma, are 50% of the companies having their supervisors educational background is in no degree, only practical experience.

Question 10. Responsibilities they are having in the environmental protection:

Table 5.10: Type of Responsibilities, Supervisors Having in Environmental Protection

Type of responsibilities, supervisors having in environmental protection	Certified	Non-certified
Checking and controlling the environmental rules as per ISO 14001 standards	100%	0%
Checking and controlling the proper operational machines for control and measurements of the effluent	100%	100%

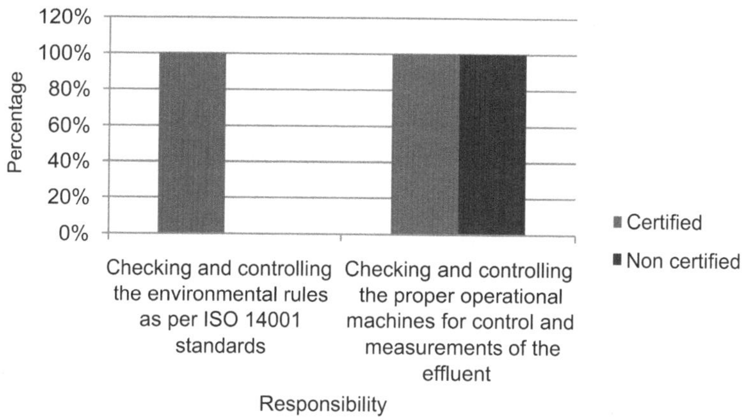

Graph 5.9: Type of responsibilities, supervisors having in environmental protection

The responsibilities of the supervisors shows that there are 100% of the ISO 14001 certified companies checks and controls the environmental rules as per ISO 14001 standards and rest 100% checks the proper operational machines for control and measurement of the effluent waste in all the four companies Rishab spinning mill Ludhiana, Rail coach factory Kapurthala, JCT Ltd. Phagwara and Hero steels. And the non-certified industries show that there is no industry that checks and controls the proper environmental roles as per ISO 14001. 100% of the non-certified industries checks and controls the proper operational machines for control and measurement of the effluent waste.

Question 11. For checking the proper operational method for control, type of section they select they select for measuring the effluent:

Table 5.11: Type of Section they Select for Measuring the Effluent

For checking the proper method for control, type of section they select for measuring the effluent	Certified	Non-certified
Air monitoring	100%	80%
Water testing	100%	40%
Noise monitoring	25%	90%

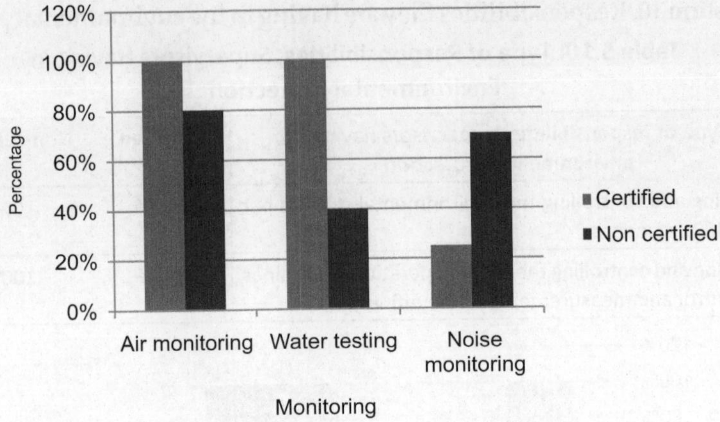

Graph 5.10: Type of section they select for measuring the effluent

For the evaluation of the proper operational method for control, all the companies monitors air and water, where as 25% of the companies monitor the noise. The results for non-certified industries shows that 80% of the companies monitor the air pollution, 40% of the industries monitor the water, 90% of the industries monitors the noise.

Question 12. Does the company evaluate the environmental aspects and its subsequent impacts:

Table 5.12: Company Evaluate the Environmental Aspect and Its Subsequent Impacts

Company evaluate the environmental aspect and its subsequent impacts	yes	No
certified	100%	0%
non-certified	80%	20%

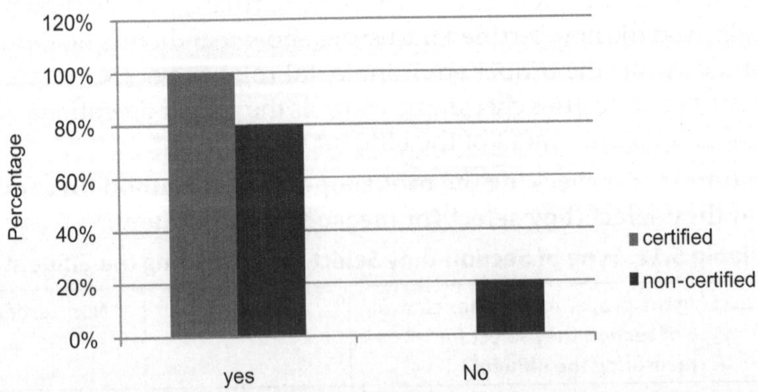

Graph 5.11: Company evaluate the environmental aspect and its subsequent impacts

All the ISO-14001 certified industries evaluate the Environmental Aspects and its Subsequent impacts. Whereas 80% of the non-certified industries evaluates the environmental aspect and its subsequent impacts, rest 20% of the industries does not evaluate the environmental aspect and its subsequent impacts.

Question 13. Has the responsibility been formally allocated in writing:

Table 5.13: Responsibilities Allocated in Writing

Responsibilities allocated in writing	Yes	No
Certified	100%	0%
Non-certified	80%	20%

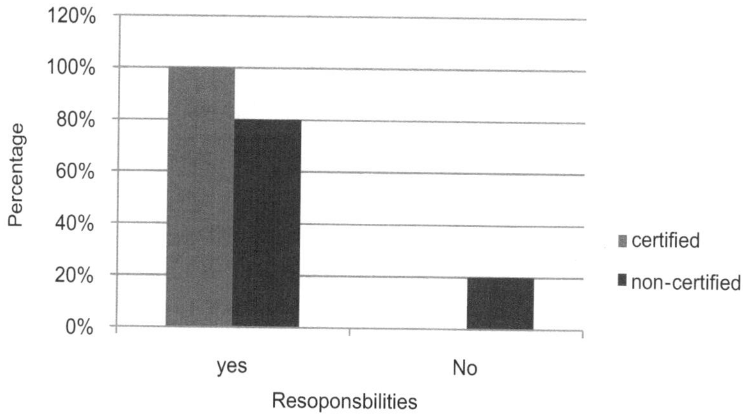

Graph 5.12: Responsibilities allocated in writing

The ISO14001 certified companies assigned the responsibilities to the supervisors in written form. 80% of the non-certified industries have allocated their supervisors responsibility in writing, and 20% of the non-certified industries have not allocated their supervisors responsibility in writing.

Question 14. The environmental monitoring tools they use on-site:

All the ISO-14001 certified industries use PPE (proposal protective equipments), SPM, PB meter; effluent is monitored on ETP which is computerized. Whereas the non-certified industries monitors with the STP, does not use PPE, rather they did not have more monitoring tools as compare to the certified industries.

Question 14 (i) Does their organization has requisite in-house testing facilities:

Table 5.14: Organization has Requisite In-house Testing Facilities

Organisation has requisite in-house testing facilities?	Certified	Non certified
Yes	100%	40%
No	0%	60%

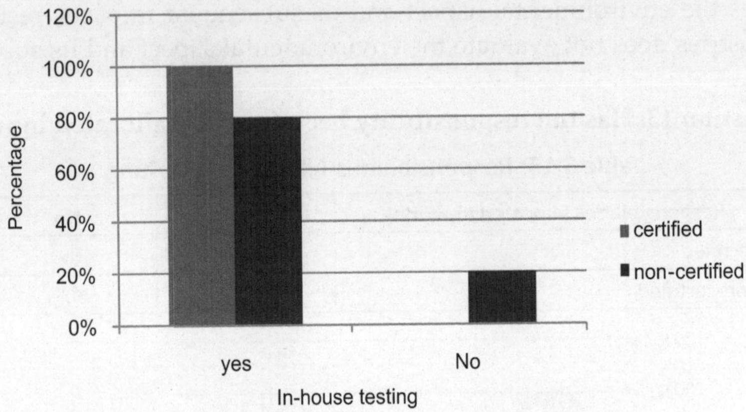

Graph 5.13: Organization has requisite in-house testing facilities

All the companies are having in-house testing facilities which are authorized. 40% of the non-certified industries have requisite in-house testing facilities, and 60% of the non-certified industries have not in-house testing facilities.

Question 14(ii) Do they seek assistance from outside testing facilities?

Table 5.15: Assistance from Outside Testing Facilities

Assistance from outside testing facilities?	Certified	Non certified
Yes	50%	100%
No	50%	0%

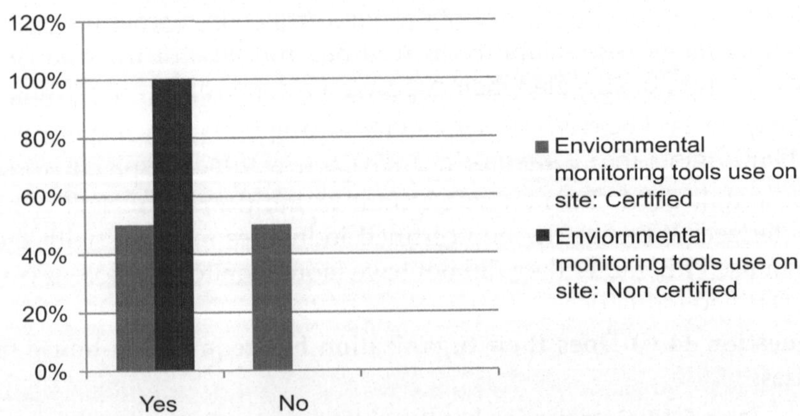

Graph 5.14: Assistance from outside testing facilities

All the ISO14001 certified industries goes for both in-house and outside testing facilities. Whereas all the non-certified industries seek their assistance from outside testing facilities.

Question 14(iii) Specify the organization from where they seek for testing:

Table 5.16: Specify the Organization from where they Seek Assistance

Specify the organisation from where they seek for assistance	Certified	Non-certified
Government Sector	60%	50%
Private Sector	40%	50%

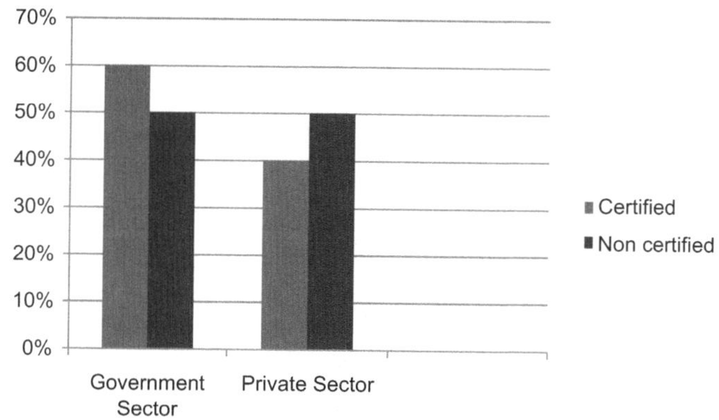

Graph 5.15: Specify the organization from where they seek assistance

Certified companies seek 60% assistance from government sector and 40% from private sector whereas non-certified industries take help from both government and private sector equally.

Question 15. Documents requirements:

Table 5.17: Document Requirement

Document requirement	Availability of ISO14001	Other documents related to the ISO14001
Certified	100%	0%
Non-certified	0%	100%

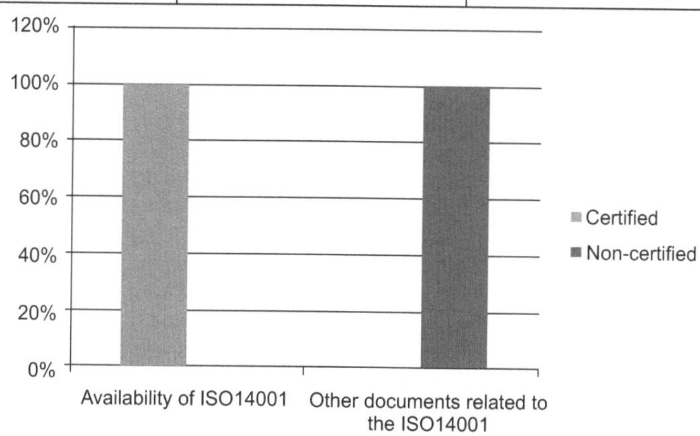

Graph 5.16: Document requirement

All the companies have both the EMS international standard ISO 14001; those are for the government specifications and their requirements. All the non-certified industries follows the other documents related to EMS requirements guidelines.

Question 16. Measure benefits they intend to derive by the implementation of EMS in their company:

Their energy is conserved, reuse of natural resources, employee safety, optimum production, environmental friendly campus, safety and health improvement. Where as in case of non-ISO14001 industries they use the latest technology which are fuel efficient and comply their equipments to meet all the stabilizing standards.

Question 17. What steps have they taken by implementing the EMS in their company?

Table 5.18: Steps they Take for Implementing EMS in their Company

Steps they take for implementing EMS in their company	Certified	Non-certified
in term effluent	100%	100%
noise control	100%	90%
land usage	100%	60%
recycling of waste water	100%	50%
oil spillage	100%	60%
proper calibration of measuring instruments	100%	70%
EMS training of all concerned	100%	0.00%
saving in material	100%	20%
E-Waste minimization	100%	0%

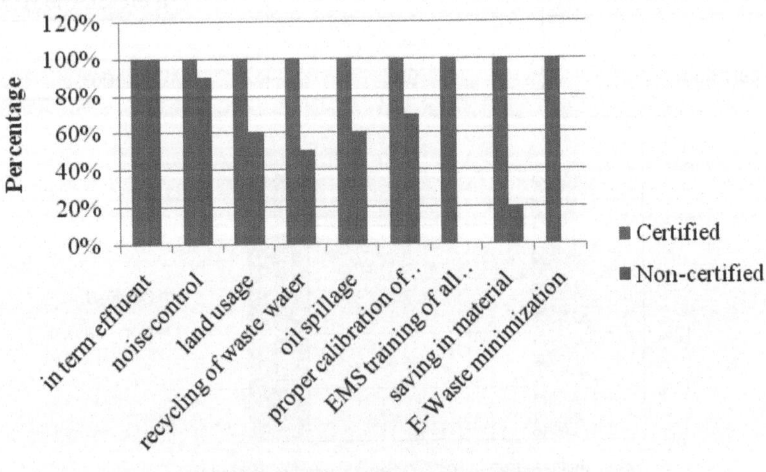

Graph 5.17: Steps they take for implementing EMS in their company

In term of effluent, noise control, land usage, recycling of waste water, oil spillage, proper calibration of measuring instruments, EMS training of all concerned supervisors, saving in material and E-waste minimization are being implemented by the ISO-14001 certified industries. Whereas in case of non-ISO14001 industries, steps implementing the non-ISO14001 industries are more in term effluent, noise control, land usage, oil spillage and proper calibration of measuring instruments as compare to the certified industries, and same in term case of recycling of wastewater. Non-certified lacks behind in case of saving in material and e-waste minimization.

CONCLUSION AND FUTURE SCOPE

1. ISO14001 certified companies have more than 500 numbers of supervisors as compare to non-ISO14001 certified companies which mostly have less than 100 numbers of supervisors but Non-ISO14001 companies have more number of technical supervisors as compare to the ISO14001 certified industries.
2. In ISO14001 certified industries, supervisors responsibilities are more as compare to the non-ISO14001 companies but only 50% of the ISO14001 units are having more than 30% of the supervisors involved in Environmental management system.
3. In the ISO 14001 certified industries, 100% of supervisor's office location is at the workplace, whereas in case of non-ISO14001 industries, only 60% of supervisor's office location is at the workplace.
4. Among the rest of the management commitments, the non-certified companies only lack in green technology for production purpose and Concern of staff members related to the environmental management system.
5. Both ISO14001 certified and non-certified, they have supervisors with engineering and diploma background, but non-ISO14001 certified industries have more practical experienced supervisors, but their experience is not profitably utilized in environmental management systems, as compare to certified industries.
6. Apart from being non-certified from ISO14001, 80% of non-certified companies are monitoring the aspects as well as impact of air, water and noise.
7. ISO14001 certified industries have in-house testing facilities, but for some tests they seek assistance from outside testing facilities. Therefore in non-ISO14001 industries, 40% have in-house testing facilities and 60% take assistance from outside testing facilities, either from government or private sectors.
8. In terms of effluent disposal, noise control, land usage, oil spillage and proper calibration of measuring instrument the non-certified industries are doing well. They lack behind in saving of material and EMS training to the employees.

REFERENCES

Lawson, V. An Evaluation of the Role of Employee Involvement in EMS Implementation and Its Influence on Implementation Success.

M., G., R., G., & K. The Role of Environmental Management Systems in Hungary: Theoretical and Empirical Insight. *12*, 180-204.

Gonzalez, C. E. (2004). Motivation and Barriers of Implementing an EMS in Spanish Organizations.

Djekic, I., & Smigic, N. (2012). Environmental Issues Revealed in Certified Bottling Companies in the Republic of Serbia.

Joshi, M. (2011). Environmental Management Systems for the Textile Industry: A Case Study. 33-38.

Ahmad, S. S., Saha, P. K., & Abhasi, A. (2009). Environmental Management System and Sustainability: Integrating Sustainability in Environmental Management System.

Nee, G. Y. (2011). Determining Factors for ISO14001 EMS Implementation Among SMEs in Malaysia: A Resource Based View. *5*.

Rodriguez, G., & Alegre, F. J. (2011). Evaluation of Environmental Management Resources (ISO14001) at Civil Engineering Construction Workplace: A Case Study of the Community of Madrid.

Christini, G., Fetsko, M., & Hendrickson, C. (2004). Environmental Management System and ISO 14001 Certification for Construction Firms. International Journal of Construction Engineering and Management, 130.

Basu, S., Mukhopadhyay, S. K., Adhyay, A., & Dastidar, S. G. (2013). Study on the Development of Environmental Management System in an Indian Pharmaceutical Industry Through Implementation of ISO14001:2004 Guidelines. *2(3)*, 12-16.

Nozawa, H. Environmental Management System (ISO14001) in Railway.

TSE, R. Y. (2001). The Implementation of EMS in Construction Firms: Case Study in Hong Kong. *3*, 177-194.

Campos, L. M. Barriers for Implementation of EMS: A Study in the Construction Industry of Brazil and Slovenia.

Tiwari, J. K., & Rawani, A. M. (2014). Motivators for Implementing Environmental Management in Thermal Power Plants: An Empirical Study in India. *3*.

Mariman, F., & Llach, J. (2011). ISO 9001 and ISO 14000 Diffusion Analysis According to Activity Sectors. International Conference on Industrial Engineering and Industrial Management.

Famiyeh, S. (2014). Factors Influencing the Implementation of Environmental Management System in Ghanaian Firms. *3*.

Shola, I. O., & Shola, O. S. (2015). Profiling the Environmental Management Practices on Construction Sites in Lagos State, Nigeria. *7*.

Ahmed, M. M., & Muhamad, N. S. (2011). Electronic Environmental Management System for Malaysian Universities Needs and Procedures for Its Development. *IJCEE*.

Sakr, D. A., & Sherif, A. (2009). Environmental Management System Awareness: An Investigation of Top 50 Contractors in Egypt.

Marjanovic, L., & Malennan, P. An Investigation of the Value Proposition for Environmental Management System Implementation in Facility Management Operations in Singapore.

Saizarbitoria, I. H., & Azorin, J. F. (2010). ISO 14001 Certification and Financial Performance: Selection-Effect versus Treatment Effect.

Foli, G., & Agyei, P. A. (2010). Effectiveness of Planning and Implementation Stages of the ISO14001 Standards EMS at the Obuasi Gold Mine Ghana.

M. I. (2005). Assessment of the ISO 14001 Implementation Process in Estonian Certified Construction Companies.

AENOR, 2004. UNE-EN ISO 14001:2004, Sistemas de gestión Ambiental. Requisitos con orientación para su uso. (ISO 14001:2004). AENOR, Madrid.

"Assessment of Environmental Management System for Agro Industries and Bottling Companies in Wami-RUVU and Pangani Water Basins" Assessed on 12 February, 2016.

Plant Biotechnology and Industrial Applications
Edited by: Alka Chauhan and Pawan Kumar 'Bharti'
ISBN: 978-93-5056-884-2
Edition: 2017
Published by: Discovery Publishing House Pvt. Ltd., New Delhi (India)

7

Environmental Impact of Leather Industries
A Review

[1]N. Jagathjothi and [1]M. Mohamed Amanullah

ABSTRACT

The leather industry plays an important role in Indian exports with an earning of about 8000 crore rupees annually. It is estimated that about 70% of the total exports of leather and leather products are from Tamil Nadu. Leather industry is not only promising sector for export but also employs more than 2.5 million persons and occupies an important role in Indian economy. On the other hand, tannery wastes are ranked as the highest pollutants among all the industrial wastes. The growth of tanning industries on par with the threatening population increase has led to high discharge of industrial wastewater spoiling ground water quality, soil and vegetation in that area. By the way of effluent treatment practices through Common Effluent Treatment Plant, the pollution level could be reduced in some amount to safeguard the environment. Also recycling of treated tannery effluent for the irrigation purpose has advantage as using a resource that would or else be leftover and ruined. Using recycled water for irrigation diminishes the pressures on the environment by reducing the use of environmental waters. There are features that could be considered, including the presence of chemical contaminants, toxic metals and pathogenic microbes in addition to salinity and effect on soil and ground water. Hence, it is environmental concern if not taken care of and becomes a threat to biosphere. A suitable control measures is needed to eradicate or trim down the pollution occurring from leather industrial discharge.

Key word: Industry, leather, tanning, effluent, pollutant, ecosystem.

INTRODUCTION

The industry is considered as a primary polluter of the environment and has a strong potential to cause soil and water pollution due to the discharge of untreated effluent. The Indian leather industry has earned a special status in the

1 Department of Agronomy, Tamil Nadu Agricultural University, Coimbatore-641003, Tamil Nadu, India

national economy but in another way its impact on the environment is ongoing and increasing problem (Belay, 2010) due to these diverse operations with an array of chemicals for leather processing.

A large amount of fresh water is used to treat leather. But availability of fresh water is already limited (Begum *et al.*, 2008) and depletion of this resource could very well create the resource crisis of the 21st century and bring up agriculture, industry, domestic as well as international conflicts (Kumar and Bhagavanulu, 2003). So, unsystematic disposal of untreated effluent from the industries were destroy suitability of fresh water for different purposes and degrade cultivable soil.

Leather Industry

In India, leather industry contributes 15% of the world's total leather production (Alam *et al.*, 2009) and it is the fourth largest foreign exchange earner with a share of around 7% in the country's total exports. It also provides employment opportunity to about 3 million people of economically weaker populations and thus leather industry by which occupies an important role in Indian economy. In our country, the main leather production centres are located in Chennai, Ambur, Ranipet, Vaniyambadi, Trichy and Dindigul (Tamil Nadu), Hyderabad (Andhra Pradesh), Bangalore (Karnataka), Jallandhar (Punjab), Delhi, Calcutta (West Bengal), Kanpur, Agra (Uttar Pradesh) and Mumbai (Maharashtra). Major tannery clusters of India are in Tamil Nadu, West Bengal, Uttar Pradesh and Punjab. Nearly 90% of the tanning capacity is concentrated in these four states only. In Tamil Nadu, 53% of the total Indian tanneries are functioning and contributing more than 50% of the export of finished leather and leather goods from India (Amarnath and Krishnamoorthy, 2001). The Indian tanning industry occupies an important position in world leather market and is competing for foreign exchange.

Though the international and local communities appreciate the potential of tanning industry in terms of economy and employment, there has been an increased awareness among the public about the adverse impacts of tannery wastes on agro-ecosystem. That means tannery wastes are ranked as the highest pollutants among all the industrial wastes (Soyalsan and Karaguzel, 2007) and global environmental regulation is challenging the leather processing industry.

Leathering Process

At present most raw hides and skins are preserved through a salting process, using between 30 to 50% of common salt on the weight of raw hide or skin. The process of converting raw hides or skins into leather is called leather tanning. Hides and skins have the ability to absorb tannic acid and other chemical substances that prevent them from decaying, make them resistant to wetting and keep them supple and durable (Verma *et al.*, 2008).

Tanning is essentially the reaction of collagen fibers in the hide with tannins, chromium, alum or other chemical agents. About 130 various chemicals are used in leather processing based on the type of raw material and finished products. The largest polluting material in the tanning industry which was very difficult to rid off is common salt. For every 10 tons of salted hides and skins processed 2-3 tons of salt is removed and in addition another one ton of salt is removed while pickling (Altaf *et al.*, 2008).

The manufacture of leather can be divided in to three separate phases. The first phase is taking place in beam-house where the hides and skins of animals are prepared for tanning through a number of stages viz., curing, soaking, de-hairing, liming, deliming, bating and pickling. The second phase is the tanning process in which the hides and skins, after removal of flesh and fat are treated with chemicals to form a stable and durable material. In the last phase, the finishing phase, hides are further processed according to their intended end use. This phase comprises retanning, dying and fat-liquoring processes (Panigrahi, 2007 and De Nicola *et al.*, 2007).

Tanning

Tannins occur usually in the wastewaters from drug, paper and leather industries. The treatment of this kind of wastewaters, including settling and biodegradation, is generally difficult because tannins are highly soluble in water and would inhibit the growth of microorganisms in activated sludge. In leather industry, tanning is the foremost process that defends leather against some environmental effects such as microbial degradation, heat, sweat or moisture (Erdem, 2006) and by which animal hides and skins are converted into stable, non-biodegradable and non-putrescible leather. The tanning involves vegetable tanning, chrome tanning, zirconium tanning, aluminium tanning and iron tanning (Bailey *et al.*, 1981). Of which, vegetable and chrome tanning have greater commercial importance in India are briefly described hereunder.

Chrome Tanning

About 90% of tanneries in the world use chromium salts as tannage materials because of the excellent properties of the chromium compounds in the tanning (Ortega *et al.*, 2005). Chrome tanning is generally used for light leather and about 85 per cent of the world's leather is being tanned using this process.

After pickling when the pH is low (2.8), chromium salts are added and tanning begins. Since the solution is strongly acidic the chromium can penetrate in to the hide without excessive surface fixation. The tanning solution has been allowed to fully penetrate for fixation of the chromium through slow increase of pH (3.4-3.6) with addition of a base ($NaHCO_3$).

The process of chromium tanning is based on the cross linkage of chromium ions with free carboxyl groups in the collagen. It makes the hide resistant to bacteria and high temperature. The chromium tanned hide contains about 2-3 dry weight percent chromium. Chrome tanned leather tends to be softer and more pliable than vegetable tanned leather and also has higher thermal and water stability with less time to produce than vegetable-tanned leather. Almost all the leather made from lighter weight cattle hides and from the skin of sheep, lamb, goat and pig is chrome tanned. General leather processing flow chart (www. iisc.ernet.in.) is given below.

Flow chart of leather processing

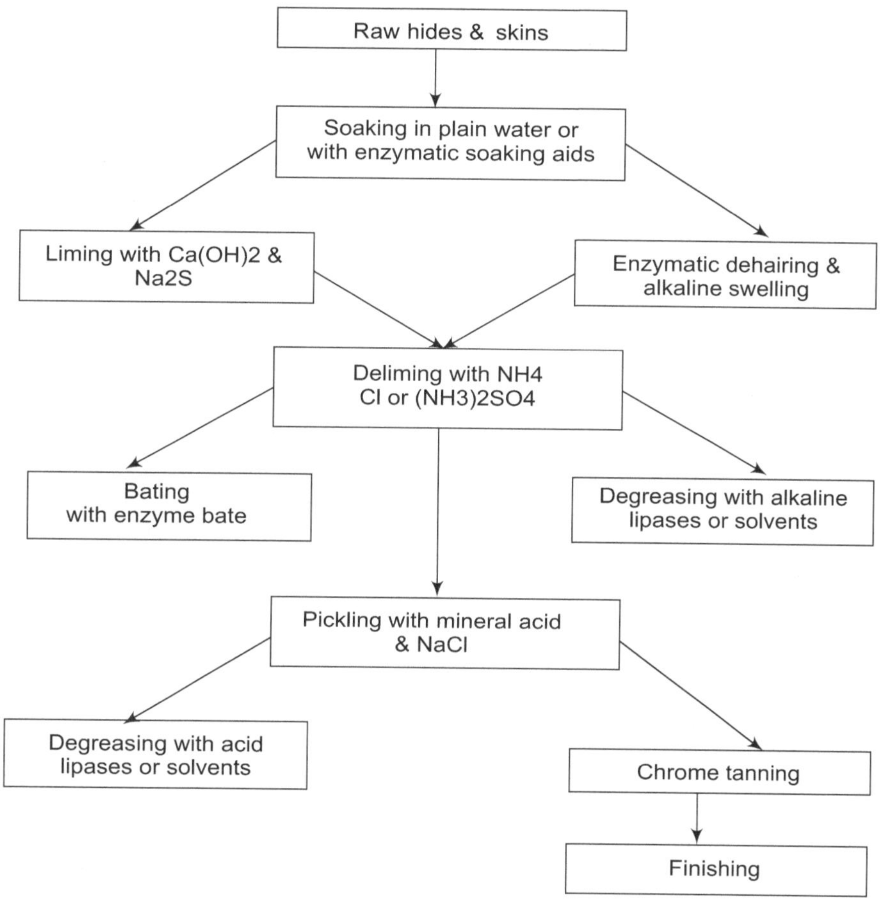

Vegetable Tanning

Vegetable tanning was the traditional tanning method until the development of commercial chrome tanning at the beginning of the twentieth century. Heavy leathers and sole leathers are produced by the vegetable tanning process. It is the oldest of any process in use in the leather tanning industry and usually accomplishes a series of vats with increasing concentrations of tanning liquor. Vegetable tannins are polyphenolic compounds with two types namely hydrolysable tannins which are derivatives of pyrogallols and condensed tannins which are derivatives from catechol (Bailey *et al.*, 1981).

The most important organic tanning agents are the vegetable tannins present in the tanning liquors. They are presented from certain parts by queous extraction including the wood (Oak, Chesnut, Eucalypts, Burma cutch, Urunday), bark (Wattle, Oak, Chestnut, Mangrove, Eucalypts, Spruce, Hemlock, Babul, Konnam, Avaram and Arjun), leaves Sumac, Dhawa, Gambier, Palmetto), fruit (Myrobalans, Valonia, Divi-divi, Algarobilla, Tara, Teri, Pomegranate pods) and roots (Canaigre, Badan, Tara) are extracted by various chemical extraction methods. But commonly used are *Acacia nilotica var. adansonni, Parkia clapperloniana, Eucalyptus citriodora* and *Mimosa tara* (Dashe et al., 1999).

Currently vegetable tanning has limited application and widely replaced by chrome tanning due to the scarce material availability and the higher cost of labour for harvesting the vegetable tanning materials. The resulting leathers also have low filling effect, hydrothermal stability and hydrophilicity. But, this process is still in practice in some tanneries of Dindigul district, Tamil Nadu.

Tannery Effluent

Leather processing result in large quantities of liquid (effluent) of about 680 million litres per day and solid waste (sludge) of about 1,24,400 tonnes per year from 1008 small and 75 large tanneries in India (Ramasamy *et al.*, 2007). The indiscriminate discharge of toxic chemical rich tannery effluent and sludge poses serious threats to the environment. About 20-30 litres of effluent is discharged per kilogram of skin/hide processed and in the case of finishing units, this quantity is about 40 liter per kilogram of skin/hide (Verma *et al.*, 2007).

Various chemicals used in tanning are sodium carbonate, sodium bi-carbonate, common salt, chrome sulphate, fat liquors, vegetable oils and dyes. Besides these, chemicals such as zinc chloride, mercuric chloride and formaldehyde are used as disinfectants, sodium chloride in curing and as bleaching powder and sodium fluoride to prevent putrefaction, lime in liming, sodium sulphate, ammonium chloride, borax and hydrochloric acid in deliming (Amita *et al.*, 2005). Tannery effluent contains inorganic cations such as Fe^{2+}, Zn^{2+}, Cu^{2+}, Ca^{+}, Na^{+}, etc., anions such as SO_4^{2-}, NO^{3-}, PO_4^{3-} and organic parameters such as dissolved oxygen and total dissolved solid.

The chrome tanning process results in toxic metals, especially chromium III passing to wastewater and are not easily eliminated by ordinary treatment process. The wastewater discharged for 100 kg of skins and hides processed varies from 3000 litres to 3200 litres. The wastewater after processing raw hide/skin into finishing leather is highly alkaline in nature with organic matter, sulphide and high amount of other toxic chemicals (Tadesse *et al.*, 2007). Eventually the effluents and sludge from leather processing operations are discharged into land and into water bodies. The high sulphide content of tannery sludge, apart from being toxic, poses serious odour problems in the environment. The dissolved and suspended solids of the effluent would affect the quality of nearby streams and ground water.

Physico-chemical Characteristics of Raw Tannery Effluent

The characteristics of tannery effluent vary considerably from tannery to tannery depending upon the size of the tannery, chemicals used for specific process and amount of water used by a tannery.

Tannery wastewater is mainly characterized by high salinity, high organic loading and specific pollutants such as chromium. The tannery effluent was highly coloured with foul smelling (Mondal *et al.,* 2005). It also contains large amounts of Chromium, pathogen and toxic organic components. The EC of the effluent was around 6.3 to 12.1 dS m^{-1}. Tannery wastewater was found to contain higher concentrations of total dissolved solids (TDS), chemical oxygen demand (COD), biological oxygen demand (BOD), chromium, chloride, ammonia, nitrate and sulphates when the samples were collected from the outlets of the industry (Calheiros *et al.,* 2008). Hence, the tannery wastewater is always characterized by its strong colour (reddish dull brown), high BOD, high pH and high dissolved solids.

Govindasamy *et al.,* (2006) stated that pH, BOD, COD, TDS and total suspended solid (TSS) of raw effluents were recorded as 6.1 mg l^{-1}, 1100 mg l^{-1}, 4117 mg l^{-1}, 7668 mg l^{-1} and 1410 mg l^{-1} respectively in tannery industries of Pallavaram region. Panigrahi (2007) reported that the chrome tanning effluent pH was vary from 7.0-8.5 and other parameters (mg l^{-1}) were TSS (2000-3000), TDS (10000-21000), BOD (1200-2700), COD (3000-6000), sulphides (25-60) and total chromium (104-250).

Jeyaseelan *et al.,* (2008) found that pH of tannery effluent varied from 8.0-8.6 and other parameters (mg l^{-1}) like BOD (1874-2262), COD (6902-7440), TSS (8000-9000), TDS (12000-13000), TSS (20000-24000) and tannin (900-1150) content was high from the tannery effluent collected from Vellore area. Munz *et al.,* (2009) found that the TDS concentration in some cases was more than 15,000 mg l^{-1}. Use of less water for leather production increased the TDS concentration.

Nutrient Content of Raw Tannery Effluent

The tannery effluent contained large amount of valuable nutrients like Nitrogen, Phosphorus and Potassium (Nava, 1997). Leta *et al.,* (2004) reported that tannery effluent contain averaged total kjeldahl nitrogen (TKN) of 273 mg l^{-1}, N-NH_3 of 153 mg l^{-1} and PO_4^{3-} of 21 mg l^{-1}.

The raw tannery effluent contains the nutrients *viz.,* nitrate, nitrite, potassium, sulphate, magnesium and calcium with the values of 440, 0.07, 600, 1080, 432 and 1440 mg l^{-1} (Usha and Kalaiselvi, 2009).

Biological Properties of Raw Tannery Effluent

More number of coliforms were detected in the tannery effluent. Presumably eggs of *helminthes* and *Ascaris lumbricoides* were detected (Contreras Ramos *et al.*, 2004). Sukumaran *et al.*, (2008) found 8 species of bacteria, 10 species of fungi and 18 species of cyanobacteria in tannery effluent. *Pseudomonas* was the dominant genera under bacteria. Among fungal genera, *Aspergillus* and *Penicillium* were donminant. *Oscillatoria* and *Phormidium* were dominant genera in cyanobacteria. *O. animalis* was observed in all the months and all seasons and hence it could be treated as indicator species of tannery effluent.

Influence of Raw Tannery Effluent on Water Source

The universal water pollution due to the raise in number of industries is a serious crisis faced by the modern world. Release of the effluents in the receiving water is the major reason for water pollution. These pollutants find their way to aquatic ecosystem such as rivers and ponds and lakes which pose a risk to the ecosystem (Rehman and Anjum, 2010). Indiscriminate discharge of industrial effluents on the surface causes severe groundwater pollution in the industrial belt of the country (Parvaze *et al.*, 2009).

Ground water is the prime source of water for different sectors in urban and rural areas of our country. The untreated effluents from the tanneries considerably affected the quality of groundwater due to extensive use of salt in the leather industries.

The major chemical constituents of the wastewater from the tanning industry are sulphide, chloride, sodium and chromium. The discharged tannery effluent pollutes the ground water permanently and makes it unfit for drinking, irrigation and other purposes (Waziri, 2006). Mondal *et al.*, (2005) reported that ground water quality in Dindigul area was deteriorated mainly due to extensive use of chemicals especially NaCl in the leather industries because contaminated ground water showed good correlation between EC and Cl (0.99), EC and Na (0.88) and high TDS of 17,000 mg l^{-1}. TDS concentration in ground water of Upper Palar River Basin varied from 3000 to 10000 mg l^{-1} and a single tannery can cause the pollution of ground water around the radius of 7-8 kilometers (Thangarajan, 1999).

Tannery effluents have plant nutrients like phosphates and nitrates which act as pollutants because huge quantities enter the hydrosphere in runoffs from industries, accelerating eutrophication of natural water bodies (Matsuo *et al.*, 2001).

Rivers have the inherent capacity to dilute and detoxify the substances discharged into them and to recover their original nutrient and oxygen levels. Recently, many rivers have become overloaded with pollutants and may lack the capacity to recover from increasing level of pollutants (Mwinyihija *et al.*, 2006). For example, the leakage of high amount of chromium and other salts from tanneries into the Ganga River increased the physicochemical parameters of Ganga water which was higher than the prescribed Indian standards for drinking purpose (Khwaja *et al.*, 2001). The different type of chemical and heavy metals carried from effluent are liberally let out into the nearby rivers causing contamination in them and the contaminated water spread wide range of water borne diseases. The agricultural fields around these water bodies are also affected (Tung *et al.*, 2009).

Chromium exists in different oxidation states ranging from –2 to +6. However, only +3 and +6 are normally found within the range of pH and redox potential common in environmental systems (Mertz, 1969). Chromium (III) is non toxic but essential for the maintenance of glucose, lipid and protein metabolism in living organisms. In contrast, Cr (IV) is toxic and mutagenic. Environmental chemistry of Cr(III) is more complex than Cr(VI) and found predominantly in insoluble forms in soils, such as sparingly soluble Cr_3O_3 and $Cr(OH)_3$, where as Cr(VI) exists in soils as a relatively soluble anion under most conditions (CrO_4^{2-} and $HCrO_4^-$). Chromium present in effluent is primarily in the less toxic trivalent form Cr (III).When this effluent is discharged into the soil, due to varying environmental condition, Cr (III) is oxidized to toxic hexavalent form which seldom remains as Cr (VI). Mahimairaja *et al.*, (2000) reported that the concentration of Cr in ground waters of Vellore district ranged from 50-990 μg l^{-1} which exceeds the maximum permissible limit (50 μg l^{-1}) and major concern is 89-96% of the Cr in most of the borewell waters was toxic form of Cr (VI).

S.No.	Parameters	Unit	Control water	Target area water
1	pH		7.21	8.14
2	EC	(mho/cm)	0.65	2.88
3	Turbidity	mg l^{-1}	0.05	1.28
4	Total alkalinity	mg l^{-1}	600	914
5	TSS	mg l^{-1}	15	418
6	TDS	mg l^{-1}	500	2467
7	Total hardness	mg l^{-1}	200	830
8	Ca hardness	mg l^{-1}	75	454
9	Mg hardness	mg l^{-1}	50	405
10	Fluoride	mg l^{-1}	1.5	0.70
11	Chloride	mg l^{-1}	600	1178
12	Chromium	mg l^{-1}	0.05	10.40
13	Nickel	mg l^{-1}	0.6	3.90
14	Z n	mg l^{-1}	4.5	7.00
15	Cadmium	mg l^{-1}	1.9	3.40

(Babyshakila, 2010)

Therefore, there is an urgent need to determine the pollution levels in the wastewater from these industries. The below table shows the extent of ground water deterioration by carried out detailed analysis of ground water quality in Dindigul region tannery effluent released area of Tamil Nadu. Biochemical characteristics of ground water near tannery industry (*i.e*) within 1 kilometer radius of the effluent discharge site is target area water sample and water collected from area 15 km away from the effluent discharge site is control water.

Hence unsafe disposal of tannery waste water on the bare land, the organic and inorganic chemical compounds present in the effluent have leached and found their way into the ground water. Thus the potable water in the industrial area was significantly contaminated with heavy metals which were used in the wet finishing process of tannery process and released along with the effluent.

Influence of Raw Tannery Effluent on Soil

Soil pollution differs from air or water pollution by the longer persistence of chemicals and heavy metals in soil compared to other compartments of the biosphere. Soil is the vital component of the environment, but it is largely under estimated, distorted and mistreated one of the earth's resources (Shokoohi *et al.*, 2009). Soil contamination has become a severe problem in all industrialized areas of the country. Soil is evenly considered as the ultimate sink for the pollutants discharged into the environment. Most of the plants and animals were depend upon the soil for their sustained growth and development. In many of the cases the rations of life in the soil matrix is harshly affected by the presence of deleterious substances or contaminants.

The tannery effluent having high amount of sodium, TDS, chlorides and sulphates resulted in saturation of soil exchange complex with sodium and increased the exchangeable sodium percentage (ESP). George (1984) found that repeated irrigation of land by tannery effluents rendered vast stretches of land salinity and decreased the fertility of soil. However, Machado *et al.*, (1984) reported that tannery residues when applied to soil increased soil pH and available Ca, Mg and P contents. The increase in pH of the soil inhibited biological function and affected the activity of enzymes like urease and dehydrogenase (Rao and Ghai, 1985).

Application of effluent reduced the hydraulic conductivity from 7.48 to 3.35 cm/hr and porosity from 41.2 to 37.6 % due to clay dispersion caused by absorption of sodium on the clay complex and increased the bulk density from 1.40 to 1.54 g cc^{-1}. The EC of the soil increased from 0.2 to 0.6 dS m^{-1} reflecting the accumulation of salts. The pH was reduced from 7.8 to 7.6. It also resulted in slight reduction in available nitrogen (Singaram, 1996).

Leather industry is also the major cause for the high influx of Cr to the biosphere, accounting for 40% of the total industrial use (Barnhart, 1997). Ramasamy and Naidu (2000) reported that the tannery industry wastes have already degraded more than 50,000 ha of productive agricultural lands in Tamil

Nadu. As a result, the total cultivated area has fallen about 10.5% in Vellore and 41% in Dindigul. Anbalagan (1997) also reported that the agricultural land has been made unsuitable for crop production because of high saline deposits over the soils in Dindigul due to tannery effluent.

Zahir *et al.*, (2001) reported that the soil enzyme activity (amylase, catalase, urease and phosphatasae) decreased with increasing soil salinity due to change in osmotic potential, specific ion toxicities and salting out effect of soluble salts on enzyme protein. The impact of pollutants on soil health has been addressed through the measurement of enzyme activity especially dehydrogenase that is when enzyme activity attaining a peak which indicates a gradual reduction of toxicity (Hongwei *et al.*, 2002) and phosphatase enzyme influenced the release of inorganic P from organically bound.

Irrigation of tannery effluent for more than 25 years had significantly increased the EC, organic carbon and total nitrogen content (Bernal *et al.*, 2006). Application of tannery effluent increased Mn^{2+} and Pb^{2+} solubility and availability in soil solution (Surita *et al.*, 2007). Tannery effluent contaminated soils found to have high Na, Ca and metals like Cr, Fe, Zn, Cu (Babyshakila and Usha, 2009).

Tannery effluent could eliminate most of the rhizosphere fungi in soil and lead to soil fertility problem (Sivasankar and Ahmed John, 2010). Tannery effluent irrigated soil showed higher value of pH (7.94), EC (0.89 μMhos cm^{-1}), water holding capacity (0.51 ml g^{-1}), organic matter (6.73 %), total nitrogen (0.23 g kg^{-1}), phosphorus (4.28 mg g^{-1}) and potassium (28 μg g^{-1}). Also bacterial and fungal population was $10^7 \times 10^4$ and 5×10^4 cfu g^{-1} of soil with higher protease enzyme activity than the control soil (Pradeep and Narasimha, 2012). Free disposal of the sludge and effluent on the land affects the soil property and fertility of the soil in the long run. On the basis of above discussion it is concluded that the effluent discharged from tannery industry is much contaminated and exceeding the values prescribed by the Standards of Environmental Protection Act and Ministry of Environment Forest, New Delhi and thus, it should be treated appropriately prior to disposal in the environment.

Influence of Tannery Effluent Treatment

Practice of releasing untreated effluent to the environment, besides damaging human health, soil and crop productivity these effluents exert deleterious effects on water source (Misra, 1981). By the way of augment of recent industrialization, the quality of groundwater has become an escalating concern due to effluent discharge (Abskharan *et al.*, 2009). To protect the existing water resources, the reuse of wastewaters and industrial effluents had become a common practice. But the effluent treatment plants in industrial setup to reduce the toxic and hazardous levels of various wastes releasing them within permissible limits (Metcalf and Eddy, 1995).

Also operating individual effluent treatment plant by each industrial unit is not easy because of the extent of operations or need of extra space or technical manpower. There are 1008 small scale and 75 large scale tanneries in India which shows that most of the units are operated in small scale manner. The amount of pollutants discharged by small scale industry clusters may be more than compared to an equivalent large scale industry, since the specific rate of generation of pollutants is generally higher because of the inefficient production technologies adopted by small scale industries.

Keeping in view the key role played by small scale industries and the constraints in complying with pollution control norms individually by these units, The Ministry of Environment and Forests (MoEF) initiated an innovative technical and financial support scheme to ensure their growth in an environmentally compatible manner. The scheme promoted common facilities for treatment of effluents generated from small scale industries located in clusters through liberal financial assistance. The financial assistance provided under this Common Effluent Treatment Plant (CETP) scheme was as follows:

- Central Government subsidy - 25% of the project capital cost
- State Government subsidy - 25% of the project capital cost
- Loans from financial institutions - 30% of the project capital cost and
- Entrepreneurs' contribution - 20% of the project capital cost.

State-wise Distribution and Classification of the Operational CETPs on the Basis of Number of Member Units is as Below

State	No. of CETPs	No. as % of total	No. of CETPs having <100 members	No. of CETP shaving >100 to 400 members	No. of CETPs having >400 members
AP	3	3.4	2	1	0
Delhi	11	12.5	0	0	11
Gujrat	16	18.2	6	5	3
Haryana	1	1.1	0	1	0
Karnataka	2	2.3	2	0	0
Maharashtra	11	12.5	2	3	1
MP	1	1.1	1	0	0
Punjab	2	2.3	2	0	0
Rajasthan	8	9.1	4	2	2
Tamil Nadu	29	33.0	21	1	0
UP	3	3.4	2	1	0
West Bengal	1	1.1	0	0	1
Total	88		42 (57%)	14 (19%)	18 (24%)

(CPCB, 2005)

The CETP scheme was instituted initially for a period of 10 years with effect from the year 1991 but MoEF has decided to continue financial assistance under the scheme beyond this period. Most of the 88 CETPs constructed and commissioned so far were financed under the CETP scheme of Government of India.

Over view of Dindigul region (Tamil Nadu) CETP

Generally this CETP concept was implemented as a approach to attain end of pipe treatment of combined wastewater at lower unit cost than could be achieved by individual industries, and to facilitate discharge, monitoring and enforcement by environmental regulatory agencies and the investment of substantial government finances in the CETP scheme was justified on the basis of potential benefits in terms of pollution reduction and environmental improvements.

Treatment Technology of Tannery Effluent

Treatment of tannery wastewater is of great of need since it damages the normal functioning of the ecosystem. Different treatment procedures are widely followed to reduce the pollution of soil, water and atmosphere as a whole caused due to the discharge of heavy metals and contaminants from the raw effluent. The main aim of the effluent treatment is reducing the toxicity level before letting into the land.

Some of the physico-chemical treatment methods are chemical precipitation (Zhou *et al.*, 1993), electrochemical precipitation (Kongsricharoern and Polprasert, 1996), ion exchange (Tiravanti *et al.*, 1997), reduction or oxidation (Seaman *et al.*, 1999), adsorption (Gupta *et al.*, 1999), membrane (Kozlowski and Walkowiak, 2002) and photocatalytic reduction (Testa *et al.*, 2004). Nanotechnology, cycloning, electro flotation and filtration processes are some of the chemical methods for removing the toxicity in the effluent. Continuous flow and fixed film bioreactors were used for the reduction of chromium compounds (Dermou *et al.*, 2005). Biosorption is another effective and versatile method (Arvindhan *et al.*, 2004) and could be easily adopted in low cost to remove heavy metals from large amount of industrial wastewater.

The processes used most frequently for biological treatment of tannery effluent in CETP's in India are the activated sludge process (ASP) and the upflow anerobic sludge blanket (UASB) process (Jawahar *et al.*, 1988). ASP treatment is energy intensive and expensive from an operation and maintenance point of view compared to UASB (Rajamani *et al.*, 1997). Removal efficiency was above 90 and 80% for BOD and COD when the ASP is operated at mixed liquor volatile suspended solid (MLVSS) concentration of 3500 mg l^{-1} keeping an aeration time of 12 hrs (Haydar *et al.*, 2007).

Combination of the UASB with an aerobic treatment enhanced the performance of the overall effluent treatment process and COD removal efficiency from 78% to 96%. Some of the organisms used for biological treatment are *Trichoderma, Pseudomonas, Escherichia, Aspergillus* (Sharma and Goyal, 2010; Durai and Rajasimman, 2011) and salt tolerant bacterial strains (*P. aeruginosa, B. flexus, E. homiense and S. aureus*) addition in tannery wastewater reduced 80% COD (Sivaprakasam *et al.*, 2008).

Vermiculite clay mineral barrier (VCMB) treatment system was found very effective in achieving a complete Cr removal from the tannery effluent. This system reduced the Cr in the out let end soil layer by 66.1% than the inlet end soil layer (Jayabalakrishnan and Mahimairaja, 2007). Technology like electro coagulation could give very high removal of chromium (98%) and reproducibility to developing countries due to its low cost (Belay, 2010).

Generally conventional methods for removal of metal caused secondary pollution and adverse effect on biological activities, soil structure and fertility (Ghani *et al.*, 2009). Recent studies have shown that heavy metals can be removed using biomaterials (Farooq *et al.*, 2010). The use of plants (*Thypa latifolia* and *Eichhornia crassipes)* for extraction of contaminants from the environment or for lowering their toxicity defined as phytoremediation is yet another method for toxicity removal (Rai, 2010).

Wastewater treatment eliminates most of the suspended solids, large quantities of dissolved organic chemicals and ammonical nitrogen but it has hardly effect on TDS.

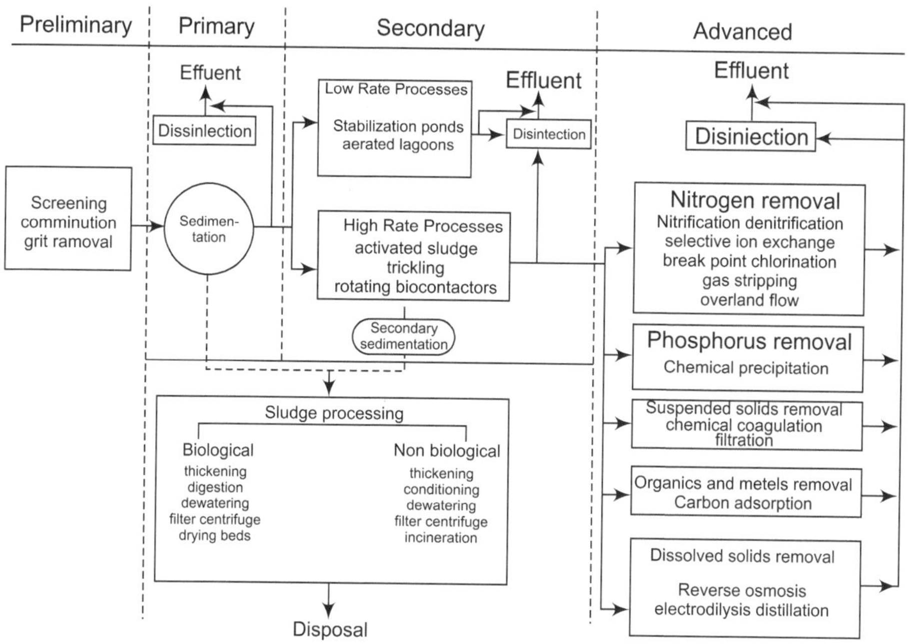

General flows chat for wastewater treatment (Asano and Pettygrove, 1987)

The technologies like evaporation and reverse osmosis (RO) are under investigation for reduction of TDS. But natural evaporation requires large area, taking into account typical average evaporation rates of not more than 5 mm per day in sunny condition. In case of reverse osmosis, it requires relatively high investment and running costs. In either case, the TDS content is not actually treated or disposed off. It is merely separated from the rest of the effluent (IUE, 2008). The choice of the treatment process is strictly related to the presence of significant fractions of slowly hydrolysable and inhibiting compounds (Munz *et al.,*, 2008).

Influence of Treated Tannery Effluent on Soil

Tannery effluent might help to improve the organic and nitrogen content of the soil by providing some amount of nutrients (Chadha and Pandey, 1993). The treated tannery effluent application found to increase the soil pH, EC and nutrient content *viz.,* N, P, K, Ca and Mg for higher range in black soil than red soil. Enzymes (phosphatase, dehydrogenase and urease) and microbial (actinomycetes, bacteria and fungi) activities were higher with lower concentration of tannery effluent (Indra, 2003).

Abhijeet (2010) also stated that soil nutrients *viz.,* N, P, K, Ca and Mg increased with tannery effluent application. Increased available N, P, K, organic carbon and exchangeable cations of the soil was noticed by Sumithabharathi (2011) with the application of treated tannery effluent.

Use of Tannery Effluent for Irrigation Purpose

The foundation of water reuse is built upon three principles:

(*i*) Providing reliable treatment of wastewater to meet strict water quality requirements for the intended reuse application,

(*ii*) Protecting public health, and

(*iii*) Gaining public acceptance.

A treated effluent suitable for an intended water reuse application is known as 'Reclaimed water'. 'Water reuse' is the use of treated wastewater for beneficial purposes such as agricultural irrigation and industrial cooling (Asano, 2001). The tannery effluent may be utilized for irrigation purpose through proper dilution depending upon the soil type, climatic conditions, nature of the plant and its adaptability to increased nutrient status (Chadha and Pandey, 1993). Dilution helps in reducing the concentration of pollutants present in the effluent. The level of dilution depends on many things such as water availability, level of effluent at which it stimulates plant growth and puts forth no harm or the accumulation of toxic constituents in the plant parts. Karunayal *et al.*, (1994) reported that 100 per cent concentrated effluent killed the plants. The dilution of effluents brings down the toxic effects there by used for irrigation successfully (Jamal *et al.*, 2002).

CONCLUSION

The strict environmental protection guidelines and cost of environmental protection made a drastic decline in leather tanning in developed countries, but resulted substantial growth of leather industries, in developing countries like India. However the progress of tanning industry is a great benefit to the economy, it poses severe threat to environment. The last twenty years of waste disposal on to productive land and river systems had resulted extensive contamination of water resource, soil and plant ecosystems.

This has led to concern over the reuse of tannery effluent after the treatment processing would help to reducing the pollution load on the environment and bring out the usefulness of this wastewater. However, the toxic components present in this effluent restrict the use of them. Hence, an appropriate management technique also needed for the effective utilization in a safer manner.

REFERENCES

Abhijeet, K.S. (2010): Impact of Mixed Treated Tannery Effluent Along with Domestic Wastewater Irrigation and Soil Amendments on Crops. *M.Sc., (Ag.) Thesis,* Department of Environmental Science, Tamil Nadu Agric. Univ., Coimbatore.

Abskharan, R.N.N., Rab, S.M.F.G.E., Hassan, S.H.A. and Shoreit, A.A.M. (2009): Reduction of Toxic Hexavalent Chromium by *E. coli. Global J. Biotech. Biochem.,* 4(2): 98-103.

Alam, M. Z., Malik, A. and Ahmad, S. (2009): Genotoxic and Mutagenic Potential of Agricultural Soil Irrigated with Tannery Effluents at Jajmau (Kanpur), India. *Arch. Environ. Contam. Toxicol,* 57: 463–476.

Altaf, M.M., Masood, F. and Malik, A. (2008): Impact of Long Term Application of Treated Tannery Effluent on the Emergence of Resistance Traits in *Rhizobium sp.* Isolated from *Trifolium alexandrium,* Turkey. *J. Biol.,* 32: 1-8.

Amarnath, J.S. and Krishnamoorthy, S. (2001): Study on Relationship between Productivity, Inputs and Environmental Quality in Tannery Effluent Affected Farms of Tamil Nadu. *Water Resources Mgt.,* 15: 1–15.

Amita, D.A., Verma, S., Tare, V. and Bose, D. (2005): *In:* Proc. Oxidation of Chromium (III) in Tannery Sludge for Chromium (IV): Field Observations and Theoretical Assessment. *J. Hazard. Matter,* 121: 215-222.

Anbalagan, K. G., Karthikeyan, I. and Narayanasamy, N. (1997): Assessing Pollution from Tannery Effluents in a South Indian Village. PLA Notes (1997), Issue 30, IIED, London. pp. 3–6.

Arvindhan, R., Madhan, B., Rao, J.R., Nair, B.U. and Sami, R. (2004): Bioaccumulation of Chromium from Tannery Wastewater: An Approach for Chrome Recovery and Reuse. *Environ. Sci. Techol.,* 38: 300-306.

Asano, T and Pettygrove, G. S. (1987): Using Reclaimed Municipal Wastewater for Irrigation. *California Agriculture,* March-April, 15-18.

Asano, T. (2001): Water from (Waste) Water—The Dependable Water Resource. 11th Stockholm Water Symposium, August 12-18, 2001, Stockholm, Sweden.

Babyshakila, P. and Usha, K. (2009): Effect of Diluted Effluent on Soil Properties and Plant Growth. *Adv. Studies in Biol.,* 1(8): 391-398.

Babyshakila, P. (2010): Effect of Tannery Effluent on Water and Soil Profile, Plant Growth and Human Health. *Ph.D., Thesis,* Department of Biochemistry, Avinashilingam Deemed University for Women, Coimbatore.

Bailey, D.G., Bulcher, P.R., Evereh, A.L. and Feairheller, S.H. (1981): Leather. *In:* Proc. Encyclopedia of Chemical Technology. M. F. Mark, D. F. Othmer and C.G. Oveperger (Eds.). John Wiley and Sons, Inc., New York, pp. 200-231.

Barnhart, J. (1997): Occurrences, Uses and Properties of Chromium. *Regul. Toxicol. Pharm.,* 26: 3-7.

Belay, A.A. (2010): Impacts of Chromium from Tannery Effluent and Evaluation of Alternative Treatment Options. *J. Environ. Protec.,* 1: 53-58.

Bernal, D.A., Ramos, S.M.C., Tapia, N.T., Portugal, V.O., Hernandez, J.T.F. and Dendooven, L. (2006): Effects of Tanneries Wastewater on Chemical and Biological Soil Characteristics. *Applied Soil Ecol.,* 33: 269-277.

Calheiros, C.S.C., Rangel, A.O.S.S. and Castro, P.M.L. (2008): The Effects of Tannery Wastewater on the Development of Different Plant Species and Chromium Accumulation in *Phragmites australis. Arch. Environ. Contam. Toxicol.,* 55: 404-414.

CBCB (Central Pollution Control Board). (2005): Performance Status of Common Effluent Treatment Plants in India. *cpcb.nic.in.*

Chadha, A. and Pandey, S.N. (1993): Industrial Poll. Plants. Vol. II. Ashish Publishing House, New Delhi, p. 33.

Contreras Ramos, S. M., Alvarez-Bernal, D., Trujillo Tapia, N. and Dendooven, L. (2004): Composting of Tannery Effluent with Cow Manure and Wheat Straw. *Biores. Technol.,* 94: 223-228.

Dashe, B.B., Ukoha, P.O., Shok, M. and Amu-Pitan, J. (1999): Characterisation and Application of Tannins of the Exudute of E. citriodora (*Eucalyptus coolibah*). *In:* Proc. XXV IULTCS

Congress. (Eds.). January 27-30. Central Leather Research Institute, Chennai. Tata McGraw-Hill Publishing Company Limited. New Delhi, pp. 160-165.

De Nicola, E., Meric, S., Della Rocca, C., Gallo, M., Iaccarino, M., Manini, P., Petruzzelli, D., Belgiorno, V., Cheggour, M., Di Gennaro, A., Moukrim, A., Tunay, O. and Pagano, G. (2007): Wastewater Toxicity of Tannin-versus Chromium-based Leather Tanneries in Marrakesh, Morocco. *Arch. Environ. Contam. Toxicol,* 53: 321-328.

Dermou, E., Velissariou, A., Xenos, D. and Vayenas, D.V. (2005): Biological Chromiumreduction Using a Trickling Filter. *J. Hazard. Matter,* 126(1-3): 78-85.

Durai, G., and Rajasimman, M. (2011): Biological Treatment of Tannery Wastewater—A Review. *J. Environ. Sci. Technol.,* 4(1): 1-17.

Erdem, M. (2006): Chromium Recovery from Chrome Shaving Generated in Tanning Process, *J. Hazard. Mater.,* 129:143–146.

Farooq, U., Kozinski, J.A., Khan, M.A. and Ather, M. (2010): Biosorption of Heavy Metal Ions Using Wheat Based Biosorbents a Review of the Recent Literature. *Biores. Technol.,* 101(14): 5043-5053.

George, J.F. (1984): CoC 771: Eminently Suited for Saline Areas of Ambur Cooperative Sugar Mills. Seminar on "Advanced Sugarcane Technology" at Tiruchirapalli on 12th and 13th, June, pp. 13.

Ghani, N.T.A., Hegazy, A.K. and Chaghaby, G.A. (2009): Typha Domingensis Leaf Powder for Decontamination of Aluminium, Iron, Zinc and Lead: Biosorption Kinetics and Equilibrium Modelling. *Int. J. Environ. Sci. and Technol.,* 6(2): 243-248.

Govindasamy, P., Madhavan, S.D., Revathi, S. and Shanmugam, P. (2006): Performance Evaluation of Common Effluent Treatment Plant for Tanneries at Pallavaram CETP. *J. Environ. Sci. and Engg.,* 48 (3): 213-220.

Gupta, V.K., Mohan, D., Sharma, S. and Park, K.T. (1999): Removal of Chromium (VI) from Electroplating Industry Waste using Bagasse Fly Ash a Sugar Industry Waste Material. *Environmentalist.* 19: 129-136.

Haydar, S., Aziz, J.A. and Ahmad, M.S. (2007): Biological Treatment of Tannery Wastewater using Activated Sludge Process. *Pak. J. Eng. Applied Sci.,* 1: 61-66.

Hongwei, Y., Zhanpeng, J., Shaoqi, S. and Tang, W.Z. (2002): INT-dehydrogenaseactivity Test for Assessing Anaerobic Biodegradability of Organic Compounds. *Ecotox. Environ. Safe.,* 53: 416-421.

Indra, K. (2003). Studies on the Effect of Tannery Effluent on Soil and Crop System.

M.Sc., (Ag.) Thesis, Department of Environmental Science, Tamil Nadu Agricultural University, Coimbatore.

IUE (International Union of Environment). (2008). IUE-3: Document on Total Dissolved Solids in Tannery Effluents. International Union of Environment (IUE) Commission of International Union of Leather Technologists and Chemists Societies (IULTCS), October, pp. 1-2.

Jamal, A., Ayub, N.M., Usman and Khan, A.G. (2002): Arbuscular Mycorrhizal Fungi Enhance Zinc and Nickel Uptake from Contaminated Soil by Soybean and Lentil. *Int. J. Phytoremediation.* 4(3): 205-221.

Jawahar, A.J., Chinnadurai, M., Ponselvan, J.K.S. and Annadurai, G. (1988): Pollution from Tanneries and Options for Treatment of Effluent. *Ind. J. Environ. Protec.,* 18: 672-672.

Jayabalakrishnan, R.M. and Mahimairaja, S. (2007): Vermiculite Clay Mineral Barrier Treatment System for Chrome Tannery Effluent. *J. Applied Sci.,* 7(11): 1547-1550.

Jeyaseelan, A., Sivashamugam, K. and Jayaraman, K. (2008): Comparative Application of Bioreactor and Shake Flask System for the Biodegradation of Tannin and Bio Treatment of Composite Tannery Effluents. *Poll. Res.*, 27(3): 371-375.

Karunyal, S., Renuga, G. and Paliwal, K. (1994): Effects of Tannery Effluent on Seed Germination Leaf Area, Biomass and Mineral Content of Some Plants, *Biores. Technol.*, 47(3): 215-218.

Khwaja, A.R., Singh, R. and Tandon, S.N. (2001): Monitoring of Gangawater and Sediments vis-a-vis Tannery Pollution at Kanpur (India): A Case Study. *Environ. Monit. Assess.*, 68: 19-35.

Kongsricharoern, N. and Polprasert, C. (1996): Chromium Removal by a Bipolar Electrochemical Precipitation Process. *Water Sci. Technol.*, 34: 109-116.

Kozlowski, C.A. and Walkowiak, W. (2002): Removal of Chromium (VI) from Aqueous Solutions by Polymer Inclusion Membranes. *Water Res.*, 36: 4870-4876.

Kumar, K.V. and Bhagavanulu, D.V.S. (2003): Adsorption of Basic Dye from Its Aqueous Solution onto Bio-organic Waste (Part 4). *J. Industrial Poll. Cont.*, 19: 165-172.

Leta, S., Assefa, F., Gumaelius, L. and Dalhammar, G. (2004): Biological Nitrogen and Organic Matter Removal from Tannery Waste Water in Pilot Plant Operations in Ethiopia. *Applied Microbiol. Biotechnol.*, 66: 333-339.

Machado, M., Diaz, A. D. and Zonta, E. P. (1984): Effect of Tannery Residue on Irrigatied Rice and Chemical Properties of Soil. *Agropecuaria*, pp. 211-218.

Mahimairaja, S., Divakaran, J., Sakthival, S., Ramasamy, K. and Naidu, R. (2000): Chromium Contamination of Groundwater in Vellore, India: Evidence of Chromium Mobility at Contaminated sites. *In:* Proc. PR088: Towards Better Management of Soils Contaminated with Tannery Waste. Australian Centre for International Agricultural Research, Canberra, Australia, pp. 83-88.

Matsuo, T., Hanaki, K., Takizawa, S. and Satoh, H. (2001): Advances in Water and Wastewater Treatment Technology: Molecular Technology, Nutrient Removal, Sludge Reduction and Environmental Health. Elsevier, Amsterdam, London, New York Oxford, Paris, Shanon, Tokyo, pp. 129-139.

Mertz, W. (1969): Chromium Occurrence and Functions in Biological Systems. *Physiol. Rev.*, 25: 163-239.

Metcalf and Eddy (1995): Waste Water Engineering, Treatment, Disposal and Reuse. 3rd Tata McGraw Hill Publication Limited, New Delhi, pp. 633-704.

Misra, R. (1981): Effect of Urbanization and Industrialization on the Natural Vegetation of India. A.K. Sharma and A. Sharma (Eds) Impact of the Development of Science and Technology on Environment. Indian Science Congress Association Publication, Calcutta. pp. 5-38.

Mondal, N.C., Saxena, V.K. and Singh, V.S. (2005): Impact of Pollution Due to Tanneries on Groundwater Regime. *Curr. Sci.*, 88 (12): 1988-1994.

Munz, G., Gori, R., Cammilli, L. and Lubello, C. (2008): Characterization of Tannery Wastewater and Biomass in a Membrane Bioreactor using Respirometric Analysis. *Biores. Technol.*, 99: 8612-8618.

Munz, G., De Angelis, D., Gori, R., Mori, G., Casarci, M. and Lubello, C. (2009): The Role of Tannins in Conventional and Memberane Treatment of Tannery Wastewater. *J. Hazard. Matter.* 164: 733-739.

Mwinyihija, M., Meharg, A., Dawson, J., Strachan, N.J.C. and Killham, K. (2006): An Ecotoxicological Approach to Assessing the Impact of Tanning Industry Effluent on River Health. *Arch. Environ. Contam. Toxicol.*, 50: 316-324.

Nava, H. (1997): Agricultural Reuse of Wastewater: Nation-wide Cost Benefit Analysis. *Agric. Ecosyst. Environ.*, 66: 113-119.

Ortega, L.M., Lebrun, R., Noel, I.M. and Hausler, R. (2005): Application of Nanofiltration in the Recovery of Chromium (III) from Tannery Effluents, Sep. *Purif. Technol.*, 44: 45–52.

Panigrahi, S.K. (2007): Environment Management Practices-in Indian Tanneries. *Environ. Sci. Engg.*, 13-33.

Parvaze, A.W., Mohammad, S.K. and Zaidi, A. (2009): Chromium Reduction, Plant Growth Promoting Potentials and Metal Solubilization by Bacillus. Sp. Isolated from Alluvial Soil, *Curr. Microbiol.*, 54: 237-243.

Pradeep, M.R. and Narasimha, G. (2012): Effect of Leather Industry Effluents on Soil Microbial and Protease Activity. *J. Environ. Biol.*, 33: 39-42.

Rai, K.P. (2010): Phytoremediation of Heavy Metals in a Tropical Impoundment of Industrial Region. *Environ. Monit. Assess.*, 148: 75-84.

Rajamani, S., Suthathrarajan, R., Ravindranath, E., Mulder, A., Groenestijn, J.W.V. and Langerwerf, J.S.A. (1997): Treatment of Tannery Wastewater using Upflow Anaerobic Sludge Blanket (USAB) System. Proceedings of the 31st Leather Research Industry get-together (LRIGT'97), Central Leather Research Institute. Adyar. India, p. 57.

Ramasamy, C., Natarajan, S., Mahimairaja, S. and Udayasoorian, C. (2007): Environmental Impact of Industrial Wastes and Eco-friendly Technologies for Sustaining Environmental Health. *J. Sci. Trans. Environ. Technol.*, 1(1): 1-14.

Ramasamy, K. and Naidu, R. (2000): Status of Tanning Industries in India. *In:* Towards Better Management of Soils Contaminated with Tannery Waste. (Eds.) Naidu, R., I. R. Willet, S. Mahimairajah, R. Kookana and K. Ramasamy. ACIAR Proceedings No. 88. Australian Centre for International Agricultural Research, Australia, pp. 13-21.

Rao, D. L. N. and Ghai, S. K. (1985): Urease and Dehydrogenase Activity of Alkali and Reclaimed Soils. *Aust. J. Soil Res.*, 23: 661-665.

Rehman, A. and Anjum, M.S. (2010): Cadmium Uptake by Yeast from Industrial Effluents and Its Potential Use in Wastewater Cleanup Operations. *Water, Air and Soil Pollution,* 205:149-159.

Seaman, J.C., Bertsch, P.M. and Schwallie, L. (1999). In situ Cr(VI) Reduction within Coarse-Textured, Oxide-coated Soil and Aquifer Systems Using Fe(II) Solutions. *Environ. Sci. Technol.*, 33: 938-944.

Sharma, I. and Goyal, D. (2010): Adsorption Kinetics: Bioremoval of Trivalent Chromium from Tannery Effluent by Aspergillus sp. Biomass. *Res. J. Environ. Sci.*, 4(1): 1-12.

Shokoohi, R., Saghi, M.H., Ghafari, H.R. and Hadi, M. (2009): Biosorption of Iron from Aqueous Solution by Dried Biomass of Activated Sludge. *Iran J. Environ. Health Sci. Engg.*, 6(2): 107-114.

Singaram, P. (1996): Characterisation of Tannery Effluent and K Effect on Soil Physicochemical Properties. *Madras Agric. J.*, 819(10): 549-551.

Sivaprakasam, S., Mahadevan, S., Sekar, S. and Rajakumar, S. (2008): Biological Treatment of Tannery Wastewater by Using Salt-tolerant Bacterial Strains. *Microbial Cell Factories*. 7-15.

Sivasankar, P. and Ahmed John, S. (2010): Effect of Sugarcane Press-mud on Tannery Effluents. *J. Ecotoxicol. Environ. Monit.*, 20(5): 463-466.

Soyaslan, I. and Karaguzel, R. (2007): Investigation of Water Pollution in the Yalvac Basin into Egirdir Lake, Turkey. *Environ. Geol.*, 55: 1263-1268.

Sukumaran, M., Ramamurthy, V., Raveendran, S., Sriharan, G., Nethaji, S. and Boominathan, M. (2008): Biodiversity of Microbes in Tannery effluent. *J. Ecotoxicol. Environ. Monit.,* 18(4): 313-318.

Sumithabharathi, V. (2011): Impact of Treated Tannery Effluent Mixed with Domestic Wastewater Irrigation on Flower Crops. *M.Sc., (Ag.) Thesis,* Department of Environmental Science, Tamil Nadu Agric. Univ., Coimbatore.

Surita, C.A., Gloaguen, T., Montes, C.R. and Dias, C.T.S. (2007): Assessment of Soil Solution Chemicals after Tannery Effluents Disposal. *American J. Applied Sci.,* 4 (12): 1063-1070.

Tadesse, I., S.A. Isoaho, F.B. Green and J.A. Puhakka. 2007. Lime Enhanced Chromium Removal in Advanced Integrated Wastewater Pond System. Biores. Technol., 97(4): 529-534.

Testa, J.J., Grela, M.A. and Litter, M.I. (2004). Hetrogenous Photocatalytic Reduction of Chromium (III) over TiO_2 Particles in the Presence of Oxalate: Involvement of Cr (VI) Species. *Environ. Sci. Techol.,* 38: 1589-1594.

Thangarajan, M. (1999): Modeling Pollutant Migration in the Upper Palar River Basin, Tamil Nadu, India. *Environ. Geol.,* 38(3): 209-222.

Tiravanti, G., Petruzzelli, D. and Passino, R. (1997): Pretreatment of Tannery Wastewater by an Ion Exchange Process for Cr (III) Removal and Recovery. *Water Sci. Technol.,* 36: 197-20.

Tung, P.G.A., Yusoff, M.K., Majid, N.M., Joo, G.K. and Huang, G.H. (2009): Effect of Nitrogen and Potassium Fertilizers on Nutrient Leaching and Groundwater Quality under Mature Oil Palm in Sabah during the Monsoon Period, *American J. Applied Sci.,* 6(10): 1788-1799.

Usha, K. and Kalaiselvi, K. (2009): Physico-chemical Analysis and Microbial Characterization of Tannery Effluent. *J. Ecobiol.,* 25(2): 163-166.

Verma, T., Ramteke, P.W. and Garg, R. (2007): Quality Assessment of Treated Tannery Waste Water with Special Emphasis on Pathogenic E.coli Detection through Serotyping. *Environ. Monit. Assess.,* 145(1-3): 243-249.

Verma, T., Pramod, W., Ramteke, S. and Kumar, G.S. (2008): Quality Assessment of Treated Tannery Waste Water with Special Emphasis on Pathogenic E.Coli Detection through Serotyping. *Environ. Monit. Assess.,* 145: 243-249.

Waziri, M. (2006): Physicochemical and Bacteriological Investigation of Surface and Ground Water of Kumadugu-Yobe Basin, *Ph.D., Thesis,* University of Maiduguri, Nigeria, 88-96.

Zahir, A.Z., Rehman Malik, M.A. and Muhammad Arshad. (2001). Soil Enzymes Research: A Review. *J. Biol. Sci., 1(5): 299-307.*

Zhou, X., Korenaga, T., Takahashi, T., Moriwake, T. and Shinoda, S. (1993): A Process Monitoring/controlling System for the Treatment of Wastewater Containing Chromium (VI). Water Res., 27: 1049-1054.

www. iisc.ernet.in.

Index